IMAGES
of America

HOPEWELL AND CITY POINT

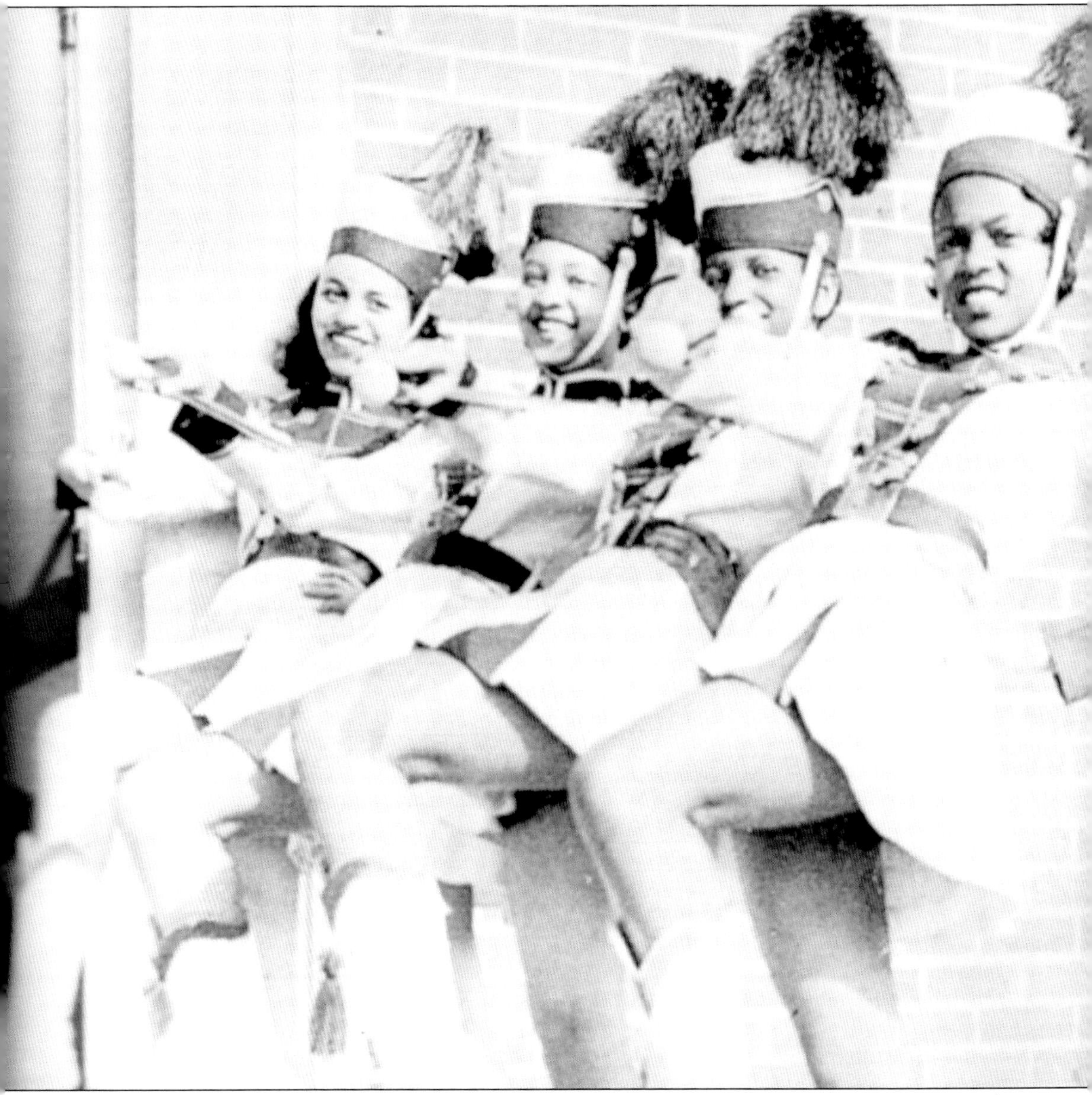

This majorette foursome, from about 1960, represents the drum corps of the Carter G. Woodson School, originally an African American school during the time of educational segregation. They signify the exuberance of an energetic and resourceful city. (Photograph by Modern Arts Studio of Norfolk, courtesy of Juanita Chambers.)

On the Cover: Companies have played significant roles in Hopewell and City Point. Industries such as DuPont and Tubize Artificial Silk Company sponsored civic and cultural clubs. Pictured is a ballet club photographed in 1925. Just like the spirit of these ballerinas, Hopewell was the city that would not die. The August 19, 1934, *Richmond-Times Dispatch* said, "Hopewell rose Phoenix-like from the ashes of a conflagration that destroyed half the buildings in the main business district." Here, Hopewell ballerinas, likely formed from one of the clubs sponsored by DuPont, reiterate the rebirth-from-ashes theme in a grace that only the human form can make. (Photograph courtesy of the Appomattox Regional Library System and Jack Daniel.)

IMAGES
of America

HOPEWELL AND CITY POINT

Ronald K. Bullis, PhD, JD

ARCADIA
PUBLISHING

ISBN 978-0-7385-8773-8

Published by Arcadia Publishing
Charleston, South Carolina

Printed in the United States of America

Library of Congress Control Number: 2011922072

For all general information, please contact Arcadia Publishing:
Telephone 843-853-2070
Fax 843-853-0044
E-mail sales@arcadiapublishing.com
For customer service and orders:
Toll-Free 1-888-313-2665

Visit us on the Internet at www.arcadiapublishing.com

This book is dedicated to those who have contributed so much to Hopewell's spirit, grit, and promise, as well as to all who continue that tradition. The staff and leadership of the Appomattox Regional Library System have been a thorough, helpful, and resourceful avenue of photographs, artifacts, and historical information. Their public work of preservation and education provided inspiration and indispensable research for me. Additionally, I wish to thank the First Presbyterian Church of Hopewell, in existence since 1916; it has become much more than my employer, serving also as a place of colleagues and friends.

Contents

Acknowledgments

By far, the single most frequent local source of photographs for this volume has been the Appomattox Regional Public Library. Any photograph or document without a specific courtesy line of attribution is from the Appomattox Regional Library System. Please see the About the Organizations page for further attribution.

The second main source for photographs is the Library of Congress. Additionally, many other persons and organizations have contributed to either the information or photographs or, in most cases, both. I am in their debt and cite them individually in alphabetical order:

Johnny Altman Sr. is a lifelong resident of Hopewell, who enjoys history thanks to teacher Ms. Basile. Altman has a wealth of personal and survey data on the area, especially related to the Civil War.

Millie Basile's family (her husband was Tony) appears in the People section. A history teacher for more than 40 years, she was one of the first to teach Virginia history in the Hopewell Public Schools system.

Juanita Chambers is a longtime educational leader in Hopewell. She was a principal at Carter Woodson and the Hopewell Occupational Work Center, and she served on the Hopewell School Board from 1989 to the writing of this book.

Jack Daniel, proprietor of the Daniel and Daniel Realty agency, is a local historian and the only Hopewell High graduate to serve as a principal there. Many of the photographs in his collection were given to him by the *Hopewell News*, to which I am also grateful.

The Reverend Rudolph Dunbar is pastor of City Point Baptist Church.

The Robert Gill family has been in what is now the Hopewell area for at least 200 years and is related by marriage to Pocahontas and her husband, John Rolfe. Their family started with a land grant of 1,600 acres from King George II.

Historic Hopewell Foundation, Inc., has done so much to preserve historic sites and educate the public.

The *Hopewell News*, with publisher Mike Davis, was an invaluable resource for this book's photographs.

Linda Hyslop is a longtime educator and administrator at Hopewell Public Schools.

The Honorable Paul Karnes is a former Hopewell mayor and longtime local historian.

The Honorable Brenda Pelham is a longtime educator and former mayor.

Patty Ramey and Ray Watson of Hopewell Public Schools were also invaluable contributors.

Introduction

The principal question asked by this book is, "What makes Hopewell special?" The chapters of Place and Promise, People and Invention, and Products and Imagination drive the attempt at an answer. But these are not historic answers, and this book is not history. While this book presents historic or vintage photographs, history is a systematic undertaking. This book, in contrast, offers vignettes of reasonably available photographs and a limited amount of text. This is a selection of photographs intended to vividly bring historical moments to mind. These images claim to be representative of neither history nor its people. Additionally, history is chronologically and evidentially precise. The photographs included are intended to present more of a feel of Hopewell than its facts.

This book represents a taste of a different time for Hopewell City Point. Because using the phrase "Hopewell–City Point" too constantly in the text is awkward, the author often uses the term "Hopewell" as a generic indicator for the general location of where City Point was and where Hopewell now exists. However, where City Point (which was settled first) should be specifically noted, such as during the Civil War, that term is used.

The following defines the limitations of this work. First, photographs tell vivid stories but never the whole story. Second, this volume's size only accommodates around 185 images from early etchings to around the mid-1960s. Indeed, this book series specializes in vintage photographs, so the author limited recent images to about the 1960s. Third, this book is more like a family picture album or the artifacts of a cultural excavation. Family albums rarely contain a family history consistently or comprehensively. They rarely capture all the family's births, graduations, funerals, and weddings. Certain family members or events are recorded more than others, and sometimes, the family photographer was not present to capture a family event. There are gaps in the coverage of times and places. Similarly, an archaeological excavation reveals only the physical things that have been preserved by time: other humans and the natural elements. The photographs here are those that have been preserved and are in the largely free public domain to which the author had access.

The current availability of photographs for this book depends upon the presence or absence of photographers, the technology available, the safekeeping and storage of photographs, and the availability of those images for a project such as this. Like an archaeological dig or a family album, this work uses images, not text, as its principal means of expression. The images largely speak for themselves.

However, images are also incomplete. If no images are readily available, such people, events, or places are not included in this book. Omission does not make that part of history unimportant. It only means the author had no reasonable access to the image, or it was impossible to include in this brief survey of Hopewell's images. There were other limitations, such as the time to gather and produce the book, the quality of old images, copyright restrictions, the cost of permissions and reproduction, and knowledge that an image is available. Some events, personalities, places, and people are unrepresented or underrepresented. These omissions resulted from constraints on the author's time, funds, information, or energy—not from indifference or disrespect.

A gap, for example, exists in photographs of Hopewell and City Point from around 1880 to about 1910. Near the end of the Civil War, General Grant built up the City Point depot and docks into one of the largest ports in the world. He was providing for his 100,000 soldiers during the Siege of Petersburg and nearby battles. In the aftermath of the Civil War, however, the amount of existing photographs of Hopewell and City Point almost disappeared. Then, in the years just before World War I, large-scale industry began to move into the area, accompanied by large-scale immigration. As the population and national and international importance of the Hopewell–City Point area increased, so did photographs of the area. And so this "family album" has gaps.

Several people should be included in this book but are not because the author had no reasonable access to images of them. Solomon Lightfoot Michaux (1884–1968) was an early evangelist, founder of the Church of God, and businessman, who was one of the first to use radio as an evangelistic tool. He lived in Hopewell, where he had business interests, around 1917. Others who would have appeared include Sam Jackson, the folksinger, and Richard Bauer, who, according to a 1934 issue of the *Richmond Times-Dispatch*, was the first mayor of Hopewell; apparently, he elected himself to the post. Bauer called Hopewell "the Wonder City" and wrote an unpublished book titled *When I Was King of Hopewell*.

Popular photography on a large scale came into practice just before World War I. Since then, photographs are a perfect expression of democracy. Everyone can take photographs if they have the equipment and can chose for themselves their photographic subjects. But even this potential diversity creates an uneven plane of coverage. Not everyone takes photographs of everything. Even if they did, not every photograph is reasonably available.

This book's first purpose is to help others appreciate Hopewell's family and cultural history. It is to encourage those with vintage photographs to cherish and preserve them; they are nonrenewable resources. Once they are gone, that person, time, place, and occasion may be lost forever. The second purpose is to encourage those individuals who have vintage or historic photographs to share or otherwise donate them to a place that will make them easily and readily available to the public. Many individuals hold historically significant photographs, maybe without even realizing it. Such personal treasures may also hold enormous public value. History unknown is no history at all.

So what makes Hopewell special? This book's response is, its place, its people, and its products.

Authors have both the most intimacy and the most ignorance of the works they create. Through the course of preparing this book, the author's appreciation of the work of others and his own limitations has only grown. The author is not a lifelong resident of Hopewell–City Point. Therefore, he very much recognizes and appreciates the works of those listed in the Acknowledgments. This book is, at best, a continuation of their profound and previous work. The author hopes that a future lover of images will discover, preserve, and publish even more of them.

One

Place and Promise

In one sense, the most fundamental event in Hopewell occurred about 600 million years ago. According to the James Madison University document "The Geological Evolution of Virginia and the Mid-Atlantic Region" (www.csmres.jmu.edu/geollab/vageol/vahist/index.html), the Earth's tectonic plates collided like giant, prehistoric fighting beasts. This conflict of earth eventually led to channels and contours in the land, which led to the confluence of the Appomattox and James Rivers. The second greatest event that shaped Hopewell hurtled from outer space around 35 million years ago. The *National Geographic News* says that a meteor smashed into what is now Eastern Virginia at around 70,000 miles per hour. It jammed through thousands of feet of earth and sent a plume of water 30 miles high. The hole it left became the Chesapeake Bay and serves as a huge natural harbor 80 miles downriver from Hopewell. Geology yields its own gifts.

Places sometimes transcend geography. A place is more than a location on a map. Place is a spiritual and emotional orientation as well as a physical location. The word "place" encompasses the feelings, memories, reflections, and inspirations about a place. It is likely that Hopewell-City Point started out as a place of necessity and adventure. Native Americans could find food, clothing, and shelter within its abundant resources of water and forest. English explorers and settlers came for new wealth and a new life. In the Civil War, General Grant found its rail and water routes strategically suited for his Siege of Petersburg. DuPont found Hopewell's location both convenient to transport its goods and safe from enemy attack because the port was so far inland.

Hopewell has adapted its location with imagination and grit. Its land helped make legends. Perhaps it was the incident of geography that made the location, the rivers, and harbor, but it was the people and their imagination that made the difference in the place. The people's imagination found expression here. Hopewell is also a place of intuition and premonition, including President Lincoln's dream of his own death.

Hopewell and City Point were not always synonymous. They shared space and history on the confluence of the James and Appomattox Rivers, but City Point was incorporated in 1826, and Hopewell was incorporated in 1916. It was only in 1923 that they began to be politically joined. They show how a physical location can have impacts upon the motivations, drives, and outlook of those who live in Hopewell.

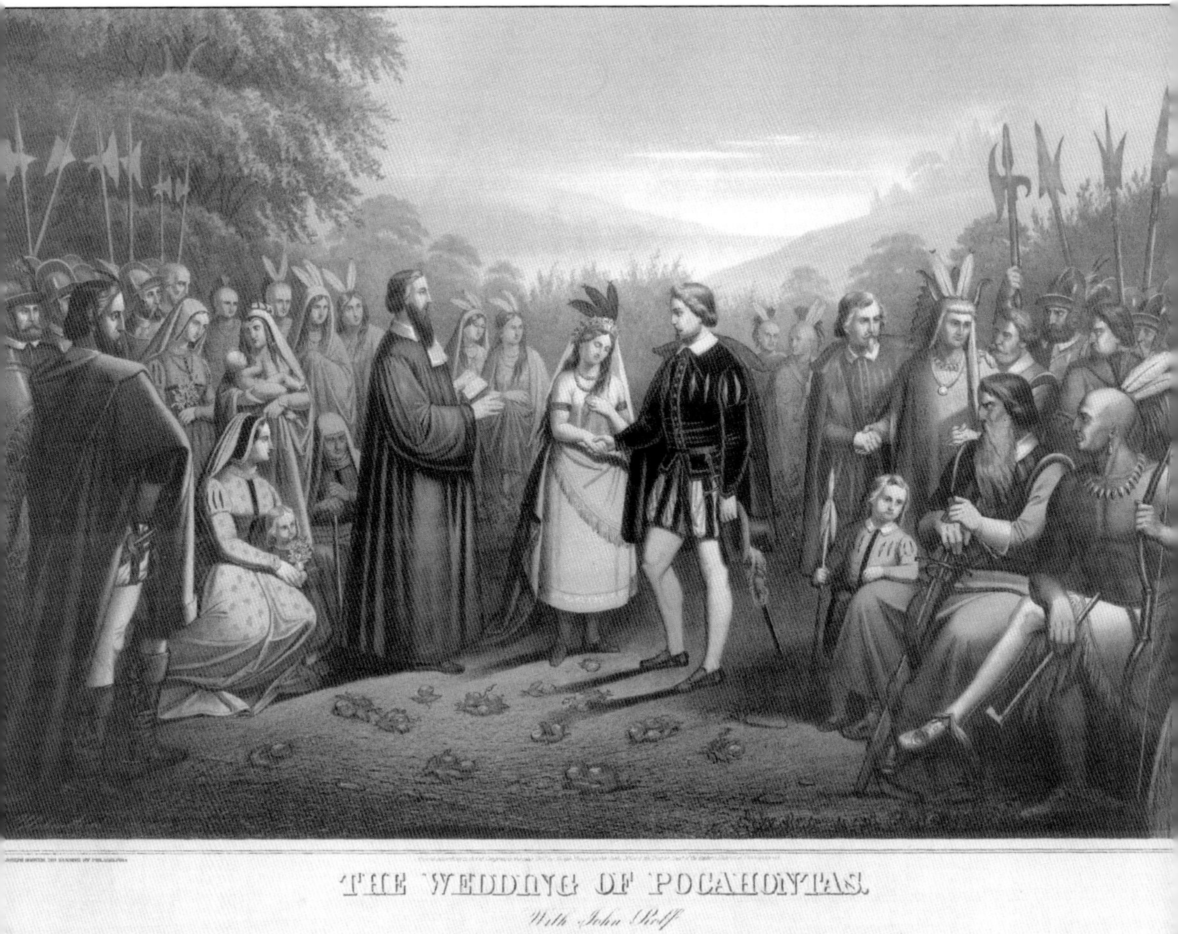

Sometimes people follow places. Sometimes people follow people. Hopewell's confluence of rivers is an almost prophetic invitation of the confluence of cultures. Here, Paramount Chief Powhatan's famous daughter Pocahontas weds John Rolfe. When Christopher Newport and other explorers arrived in 1607, they landed among three indigenous language groups: the Algonquin, Siouan, and Iroquoian. The Algonquin group called this land Tsenacomoco. Paramount Chief Powhatan forged together a confederacy of 32 tribes, which had included the Hopewell-City Point area and was a power to be reckoned with when the English arrived. This drawing may depict Powhatan second to the right of Rolfe, perhaps receiving congratulations from an English explorer. The following photographs illustrate again how Hopewell–City Point lies at the vortex of history. (Engraving by Theodor DeBry, after artist John White; photograph courtesy of the Library of Congress.)

This cover of DuPont's *Splinters* magazine, creatively named for the linters of cotton that helped make smokeless gunpowder during World War I, illustrates Hopewell's significant contribution to the war effort. However, the cover makes clear that the price of war is very dear. This cover of the June 1917 issue came only two months after President Wilson asked Congress for a declaration of war against Germany. (Magazine courtesy of the Appomattox Regional Library.)

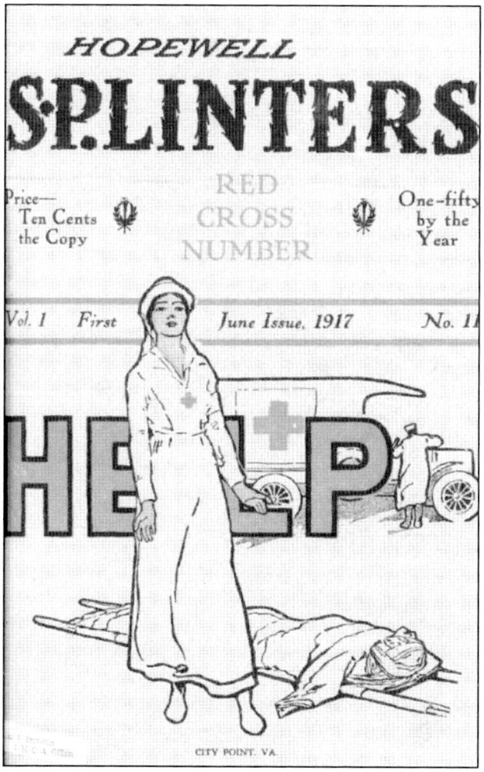

HOPEWELL
SPLINTERS
Price— Ten Cents the Copy
RED CROSS NUMBER
One-fift by the Year
Vol. 1 First June Issue, 1917 No. 1
HELP
CITY POINT, VA.

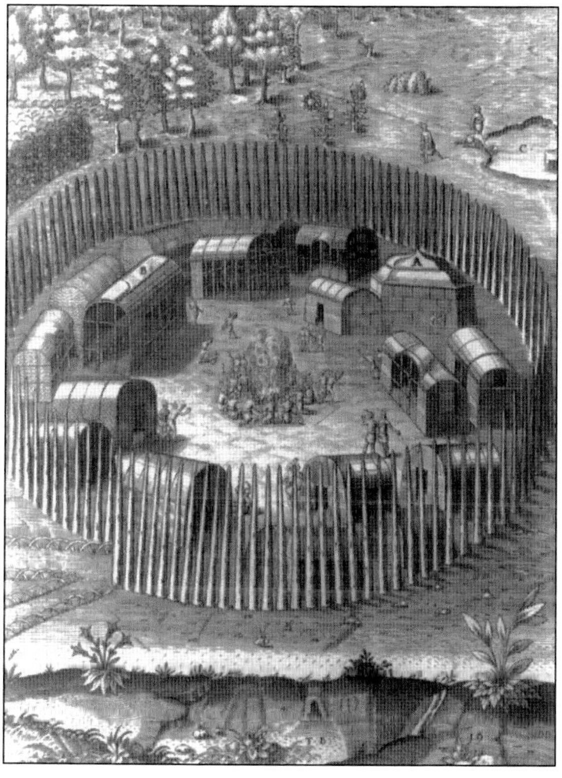

This graphic renders Pomejocj, a Native American village in Virginia. The village is laid out with order and organization. Text accompanies the etching: "The towne of Pomejocj and true forme of their houses, covered and enclosed w[i]th matts, and w[i]th barcks of trees All compressed about w[i]th smale poles stock thick together in stedd of a wall." (Photograph courtesy of the Library of Congress.)

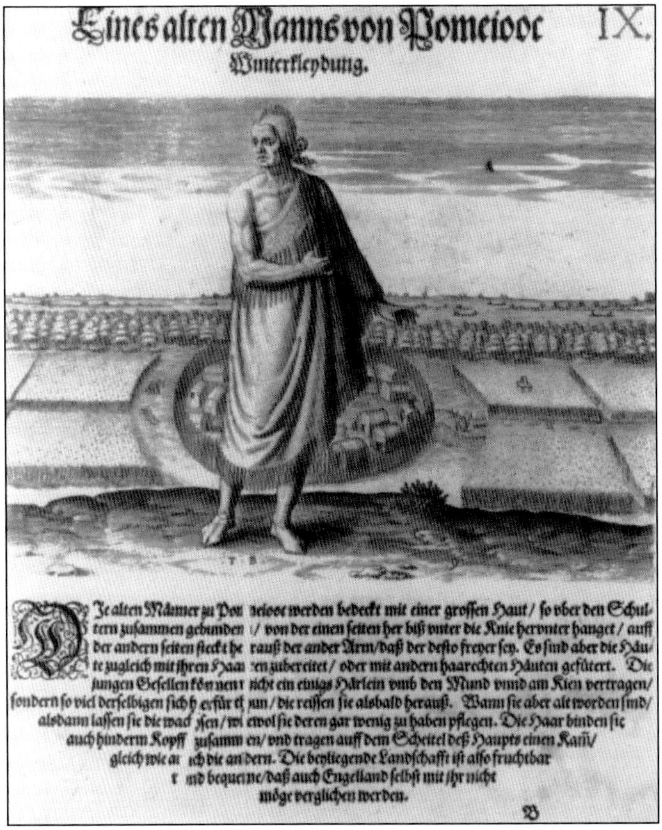

This lithograph depicts a "senior" in winter clothes in front of Pomejocj. Even though the original caption translates to say the man is a senior citizen, this picture shows a well-muscled gentleman with cloak standing in front of town. The background land is laid out in a circular fashion in the manner indicated in the previous caption and image. Note the orderly garden plots, indicating a sophisticated appreciation for horticulture. (Photograph courtesy of the Library of Congress.)

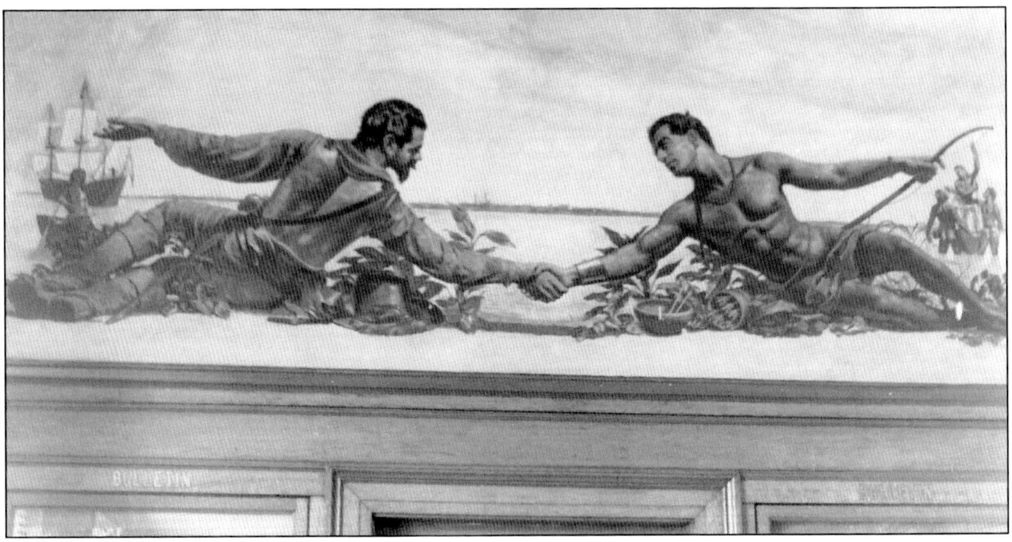

Capt. Francis Eppes, sailing on the *Hopewell*, received a land grant in 1635. He called the land Hopewell Farms. Construction of the Appomattox plantation began there in 1763. Once taken by Union troops during the Civil War, the property became a focal point for command of the Army of the Potomac under General Grant, whose headquarters were a stone's throw from the manor itself. Today, it houses the offices and museum operated by the US National Park Service. (Photograph courtesy of the National Park Service and the Library of Congress.)

African Americans were an integral part of the plantation economy and, later, the war economy at City Point. Here, teamsters are dressed in Union uniforms and helped work the docks and the transportation between ship and shore and the front lines. This photograph was taken at Bermuda Hundred, just upriver from City Point, a hotly contested area during the Civil War. (Photograph courtesy of the Library of Congress.)

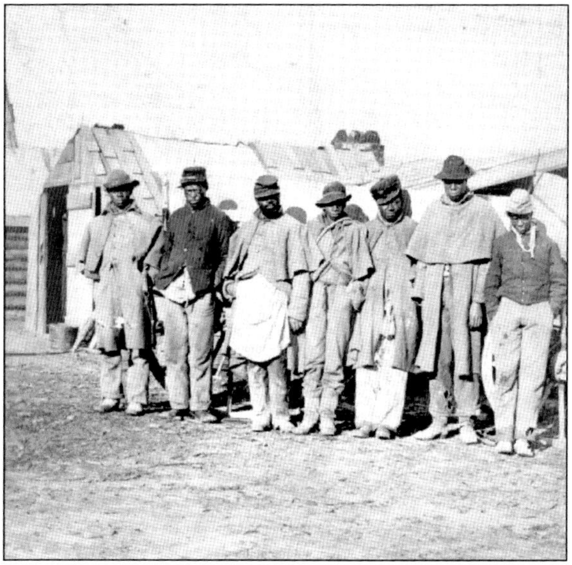

1861. **1865.**

THE WAR FOR THE UNION.

Photographic History.

This series of pictures are *original* photographs taken during the war. Nearly a quarter of a century has passed since these photographs were made, and during this time the "negatives" have undergone chemical changes which makes it very slow and difficult work to get "prints" from them. The value of these pictures is apparent: Of course no more "negatives" can be made, as the scenes represented have passed away forever. These photographs can be obtained only from the undersigned.

JOHN C. TAYLOR,

17 Allen Place, Hartford, Conn.

This is the photographer's label of the preceding photograph. It identifies the name of the photographer and tells the audience where it might get a copy of the photograph. City Point was heavily photographed during the Civil War. City Point combined the beauty of location with the brawn of a military campaign. Not only was it a crucial strategic point at the close of the war, but it was also a photogenic place. The high bluffs overlooking the confluence of the James and Appomattox Rivers provides dramatic backdrops for photography and paintings. (Photograph courtesy of the Library of Congress.)

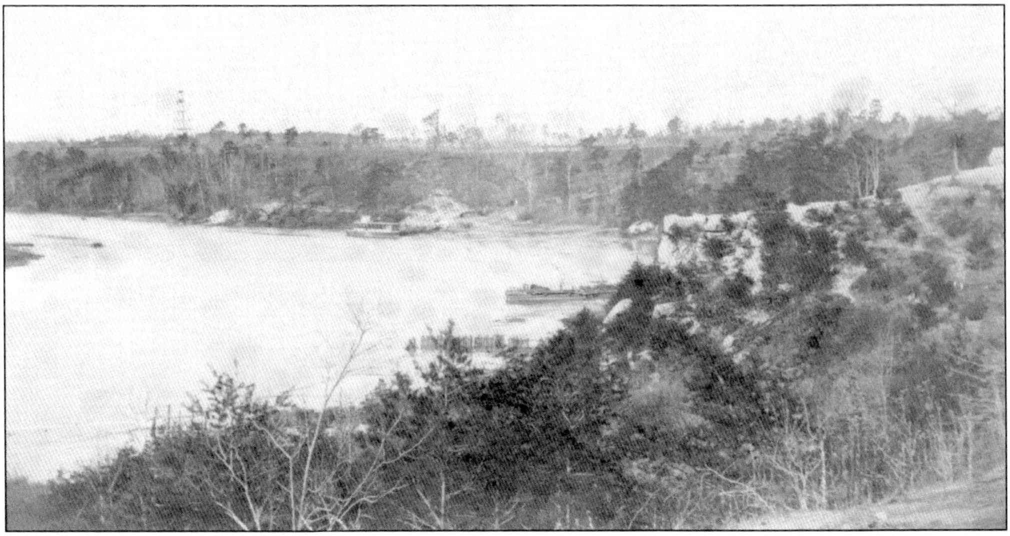

This photograph shows the bank opposite City Point and evidence of its use in the form of transports, pilings, and a signal tower (upper left). The picture also illustrates the broad, smooth sweep of the James River as the viewer looks north. Richmond, the capital of the Confederacy, seemed so close but so far. (Photograph courtesy of the Library of Congress.)

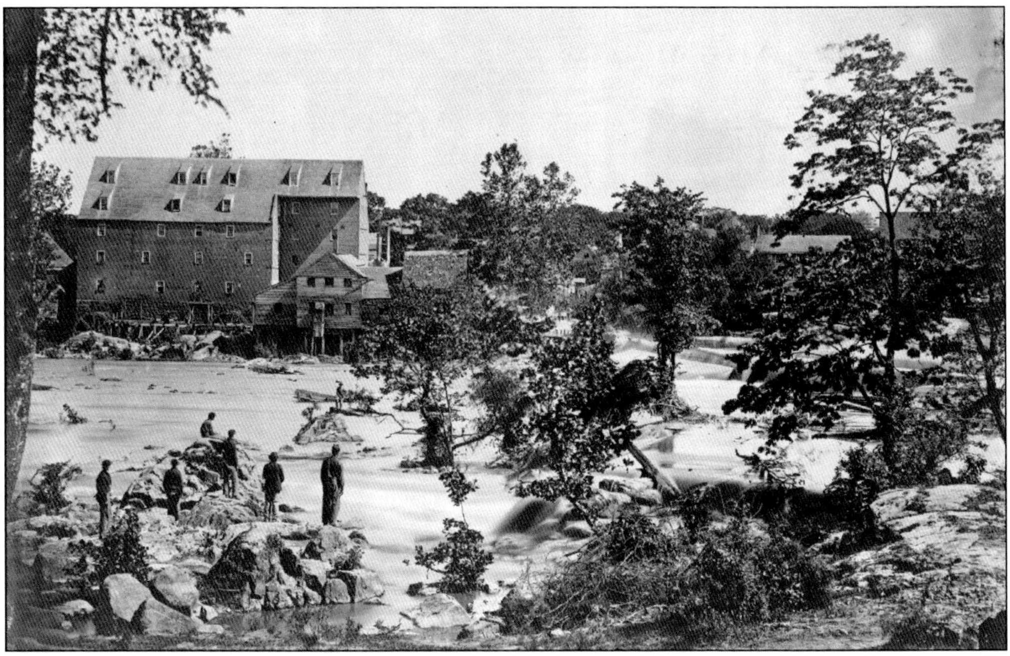

This mill on Appomattox River was part of a system providing sources of food, ways to transport that food, and the means to make it edible. Mills provided power for many things, including refining grains. Control of a resource as valuable as a river was essential in warfare. Prior to the so-called third dimension of warfare—control of the air—rivers were used for strategic transportation and for defensive perimeters. (Photograph courtesy of the Library of Congress.)

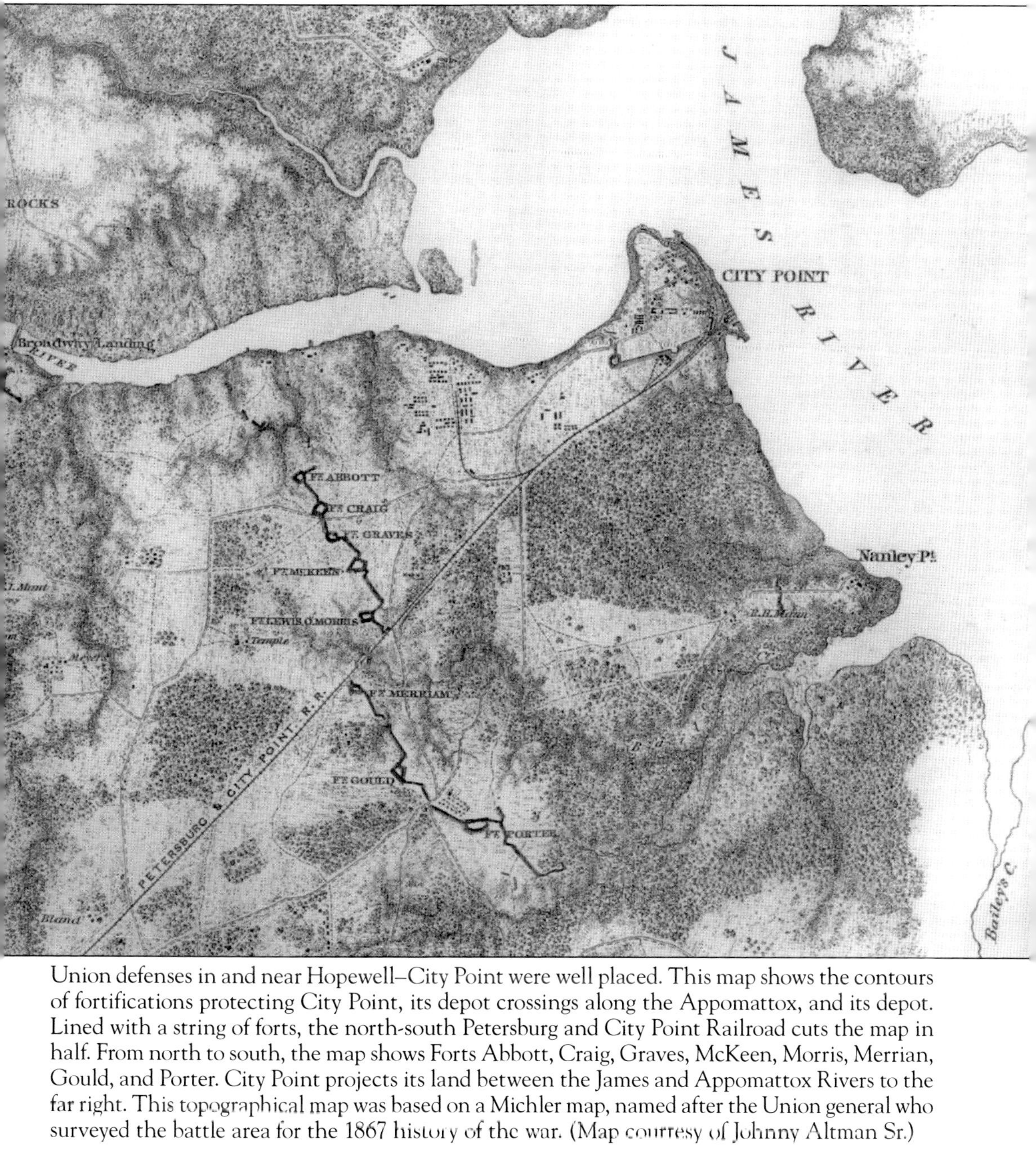

Union defenses in and near Hopewell–City Point were well placed. This map shows the contours of fortifications protecting City Point, its depot crossings along the Appomattox, and its depot. Lined with a string of forts, the north-south Petersburg and City Point Railroad cuts the map in half. From north to south, the map shows Forts Abbott, Craig, Graves, McKeen, Morris, Merrian, Gould, and Porter. City Point projects its land between the James and Appomattox Rivers to the far right. This topographical map was based on a Michler map, named after the Union general who surveyed the battle area for the 1867 history of the war. (Map courtesy of Johnny Altman Sr.)

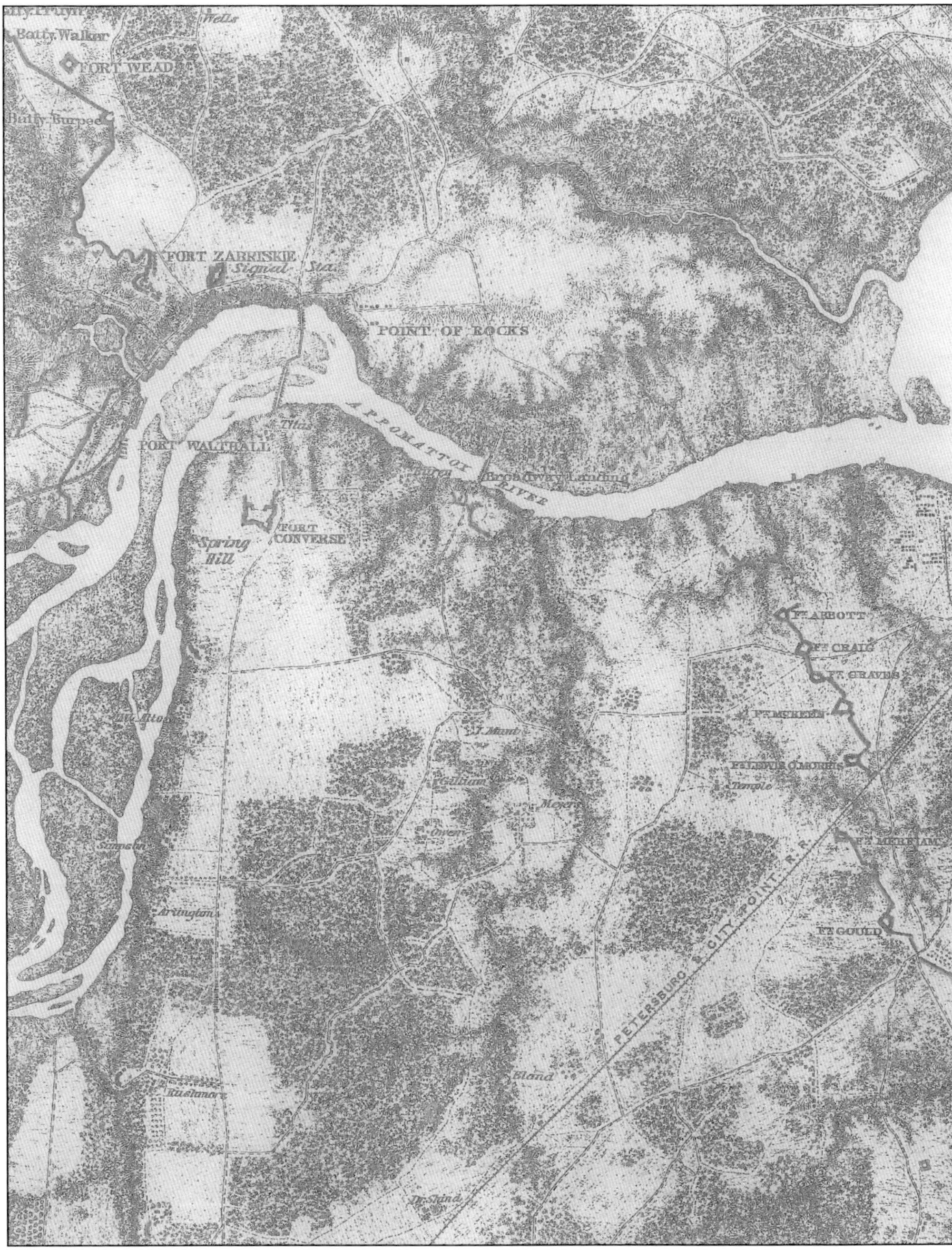

The previous photograph is only half of the story of the strategic position of the Union forts around City Point. The other half of the story is to the left of the previous photograph—toward the major railhead of Petersburg. Petersburg will be located off the map to the lower left. The Confederate army, as will be seen in subsequent photographs, was dug in deep to defend that city under the command of Gen. P.G.T. Beauregard (who appears later). This photograph shows the Petersburg and City Point Railroad (lower right) and the Appomattox River at Broadway Landing and Fort Zabriskie and its signal station. South of the Appomattox, the map shows Fort Converse near Spring Hill. (Map courtesy of Johnny Altman, Sr.)

An elaborate system of Union army wharves was constructed to accommodate the size and purpose of the huge armada of ships entering and leaving City Point. Some of the wharves extended far into the confluence of the Appomattox and James Rivers. Caissons for cannons are neatly lined along the wharf. (Photograph courtesy of the Library of Congress.)

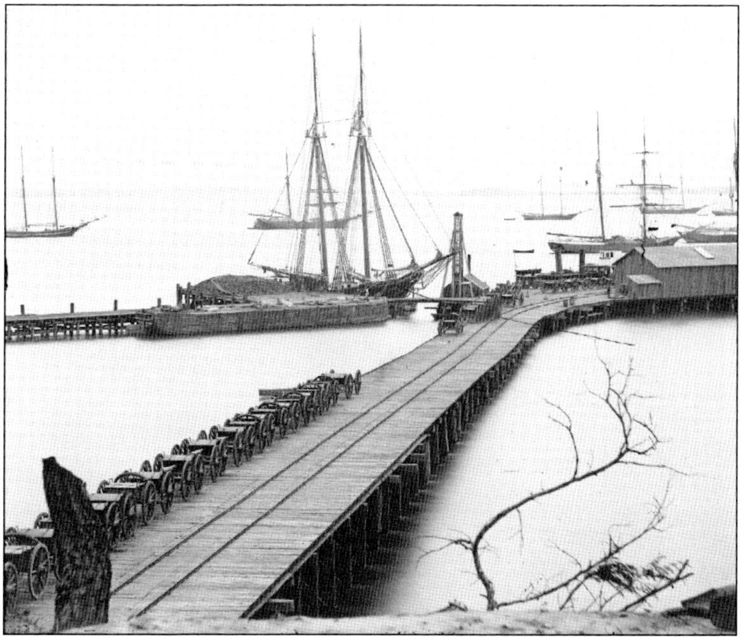

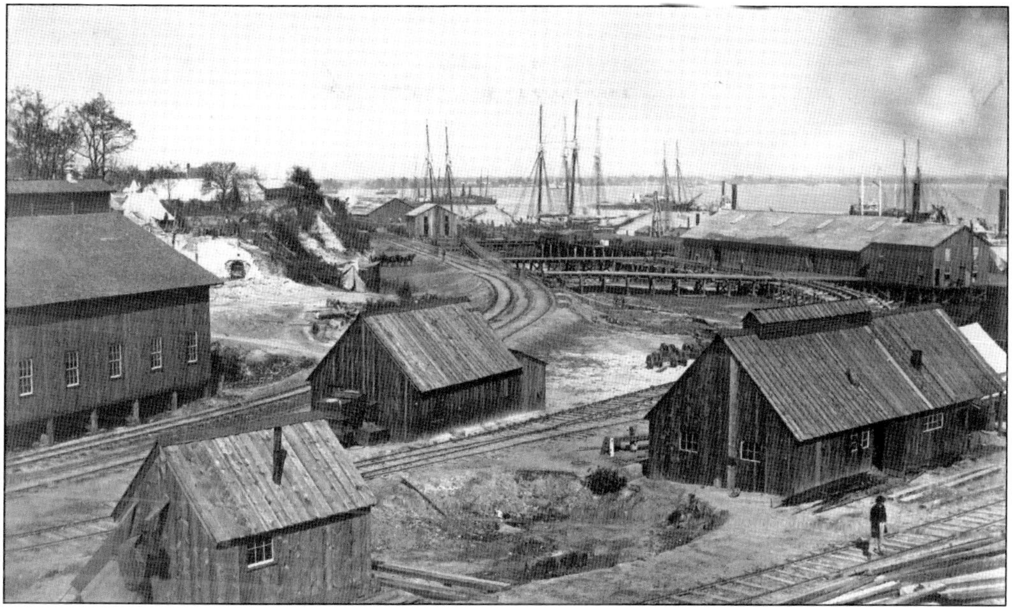

This photograph represents three ways to supply the necessities of war. Supply by water is as old as the Athens-Persian Wars 2,500 years ago. War supply by railroad was new. The Civil War was the first time rail was used in large-scale military operations. Both sides used railroads to travel inside their own lines (interior lines) and to meet the enemy. The third mode is the tried-and-true method of using carts and animals. Such a team of horses can be seen in the center of this photograph. (Photograph courtesy of the Library of Congress.)

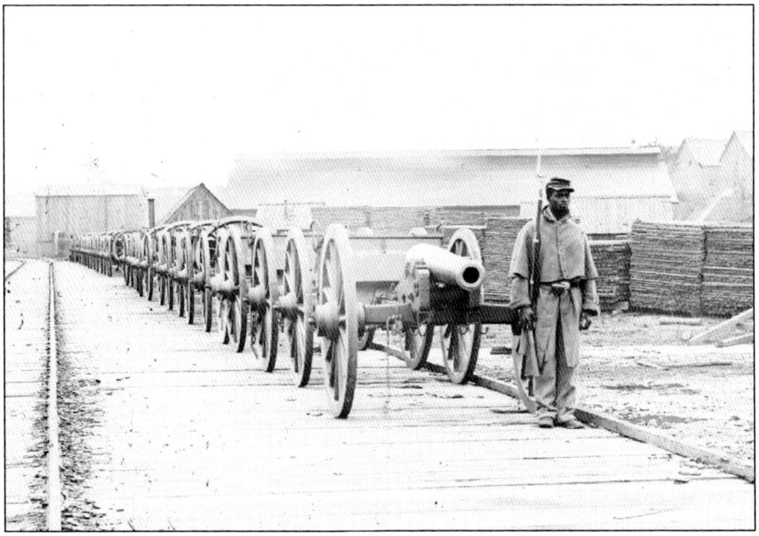

The supplies off-loaded at City Point included all provisions and arms to support Grant's combined forces. These cannons, lined up on an ordnance wharf, represented some of the firepower used to support the Siege of Petersburg. (Photograph courtesy of the Library of Congress.)

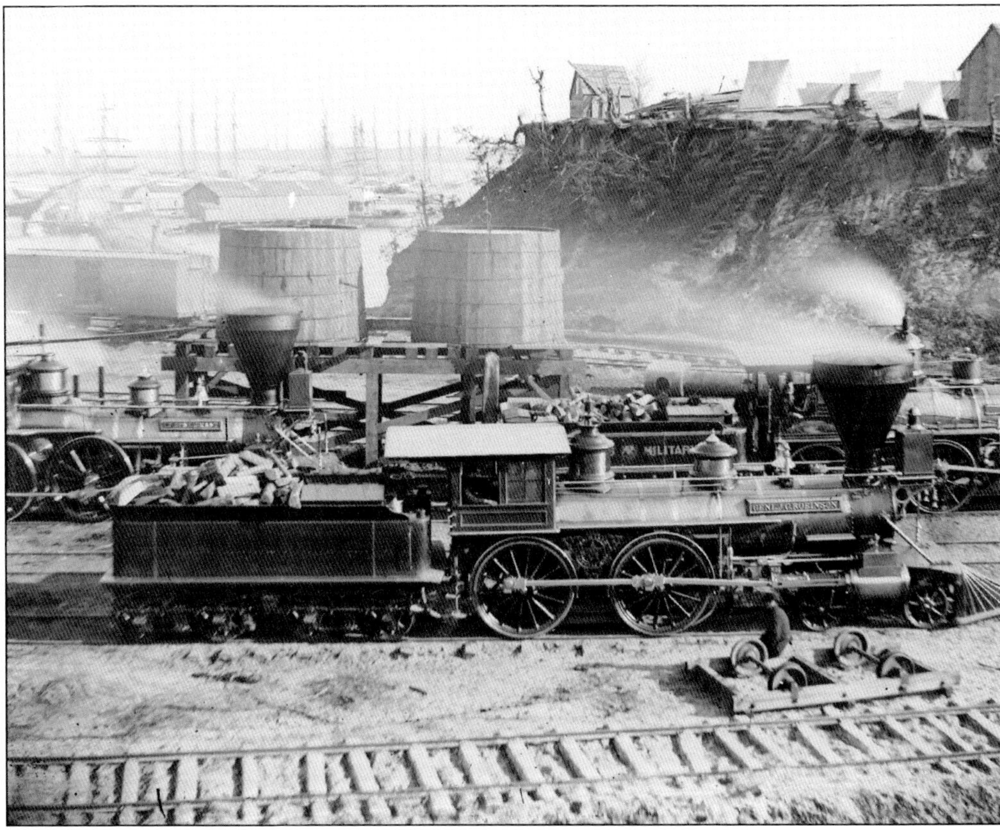

This photograph of a train engine called the General Robinson was part of a logistical system of hauling soldiers and supplies to and from the Petersburg siege lines. The engine was probably named after Gen. John Robinson, a veteran of the Manassas, Seven Days, Chancellorsville, and Gettysburg campaigns. Near the Battle of Alsop's Farm, Robinson was wounded and one of his legs had to be amputated. Congress awarded him the Medal of Honor for his bravery. (Photograph courtesy of the Library of Congress.)

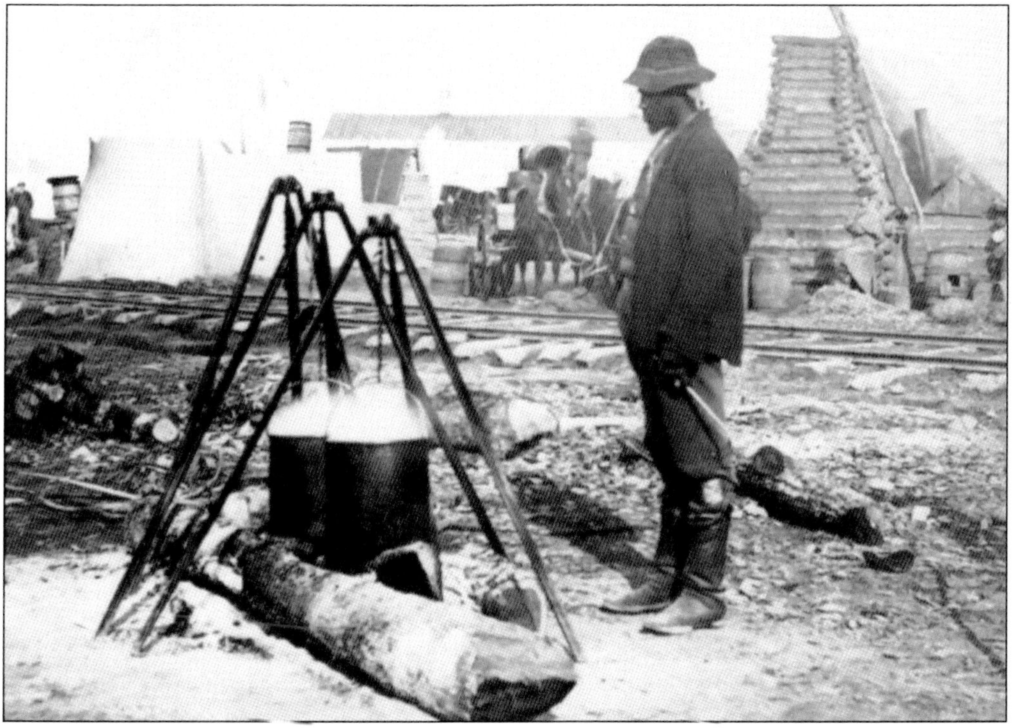

Soldiers and civilians served not only as frontline combatants but also in logistical operations that provided the means for the soldiers to fight. African Americans did much more than cook in Hopewell. They helped charge and capture City Point for the Union in the first place. Additionally, in June 1864, African American troops fought at the Battle of Baylor's Farm, now in Hopewell, in a tactical movement against Beauregard's forces that were entrenched in Petersburg. (Photograph courtesy of the Library of Congress.)

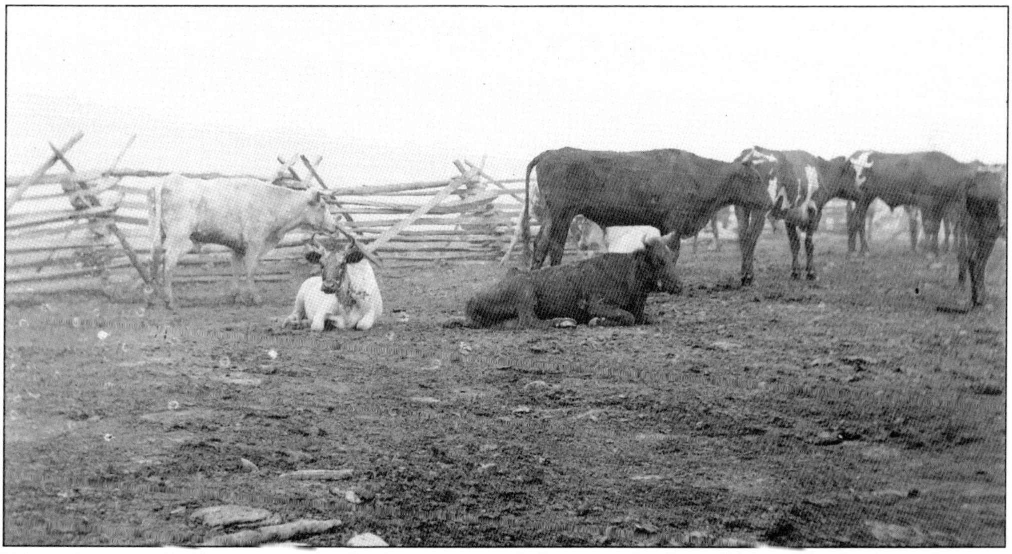

This photograph depicts some of what was needed to supply the soldiers. Herds of cattle were necessary to feed the army. The soldiers were lucky to get fresh meat. (Photograph courtesy of the Library of Congress.)

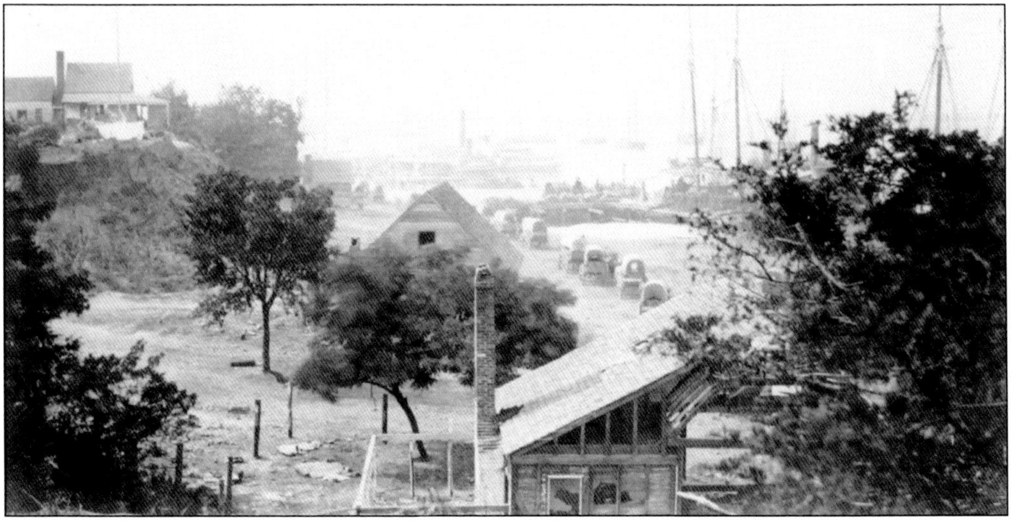

Huge armies required a constant supply to the front. Many believe the steady stream of supplies was a strong reason for the defeat of the Confederacy. Ships in City Point harbor can be seen at the top of this photograph. The other form of traditional military transport was by horse and wagon. Gen. Marsena Patrick's headquarters probably presides over the bluff to the left. (Photograph courtesy of the Library of Congress.)

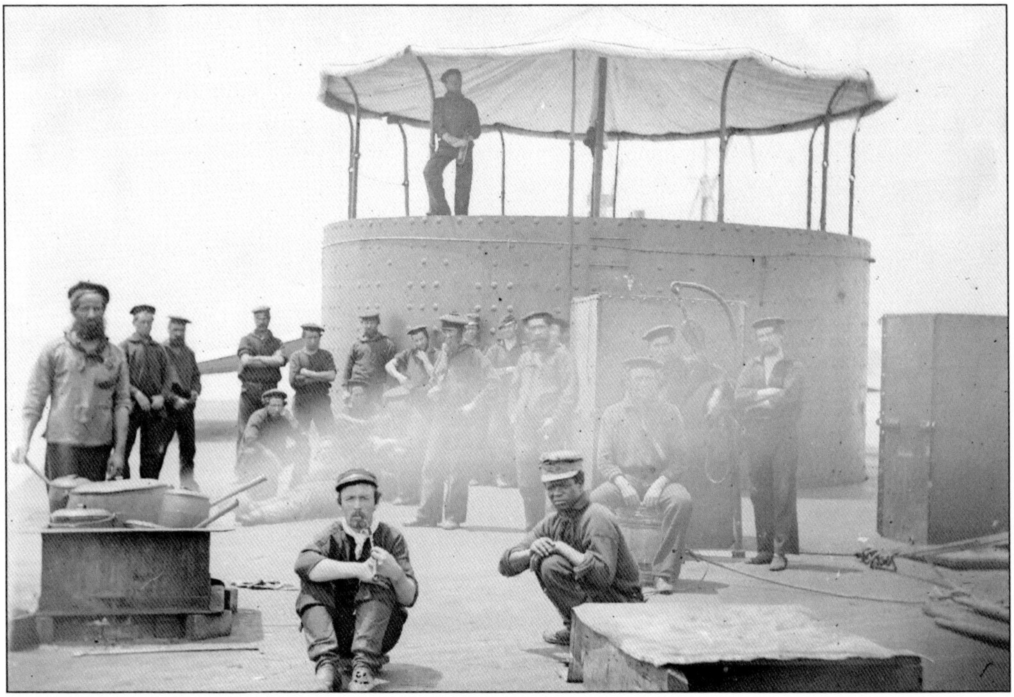

The James River was hotly contested. The famous ironclad gunboat *Monitor* continued to play an important role, even after its historic engagement with the Confederate ironclad CSS *Virginia* (Merrimack) in the first battle between ironclad vessels. Before the *Monitor* sunk in high seas off the Virginia coast, it tried to run the Confederate gauntlet up the James from City Point. This photograph shows two of the USS *Monitor*'s most important features: the revolving gun turret and a cooking pot to feed the crew. (Photograph courtesy of the Library of Congress.)

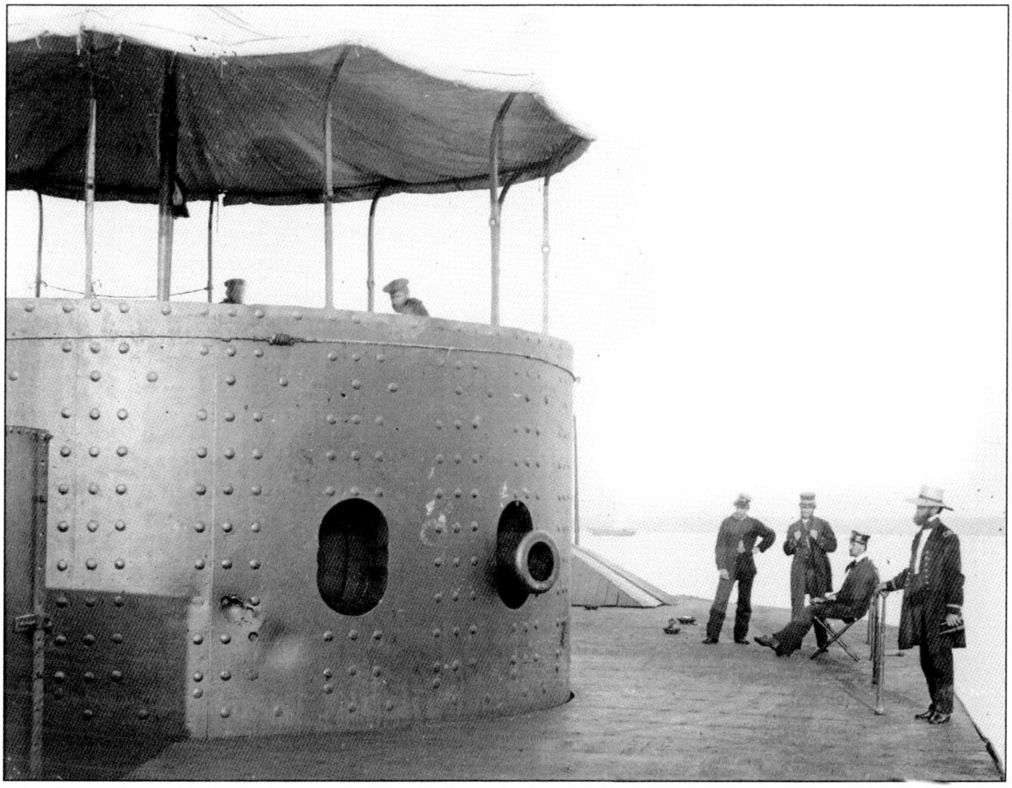

The USS *Monitor*'s gun platform is moored on the James River. On May 15, 1862, the heavy gun battery of Drewery's Bluff (a few miles from City Point toward Richmond) drove back the USS *Monitor* and four other warships. This gun battery was located just a few miles upriver toward Richmond from City Point. This engagement ended the Union's hopes for a waterborne assault on Richmond at that time. This photograph shows the USS *Monitor*'s two ports for cannons in the turret and their relative proportion to the crew. (Photograph courtesy of the Library of Congress.)

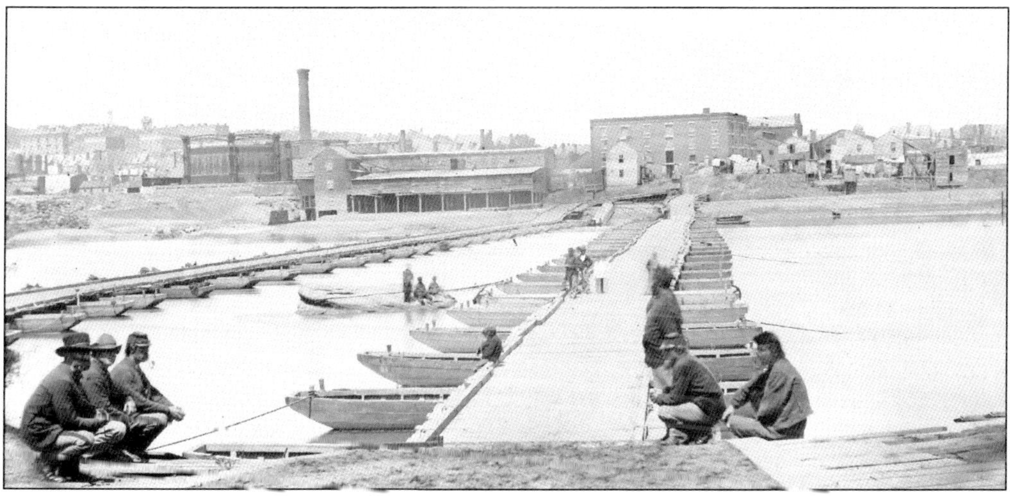

Pontoons over the Appomattox River toward Petersburg provided important linkages for troops and supplies. From the troops' depot at City Point, the Union strategy could also support a river assault of Petersburg. (Photograph courtesy of the Library of Congress.)

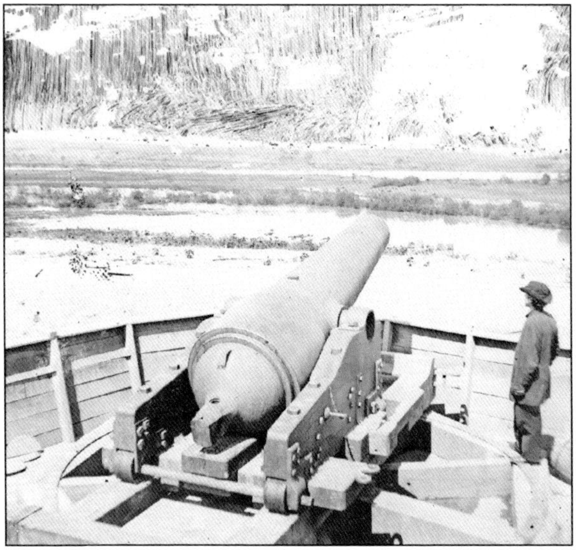

This shows the formidable Confederate defenses at Dutch Gap. Confederates vigorously defended the route to Richmond all along the James River from City Point. Near the traditional Colonial-era site of Henricus, the Confederate defenses frustrated Union attempts at a river invasion of the capital. Here, heavy cannons cover this portion of the James. (Photograph courtesy of the Library of Congress.)

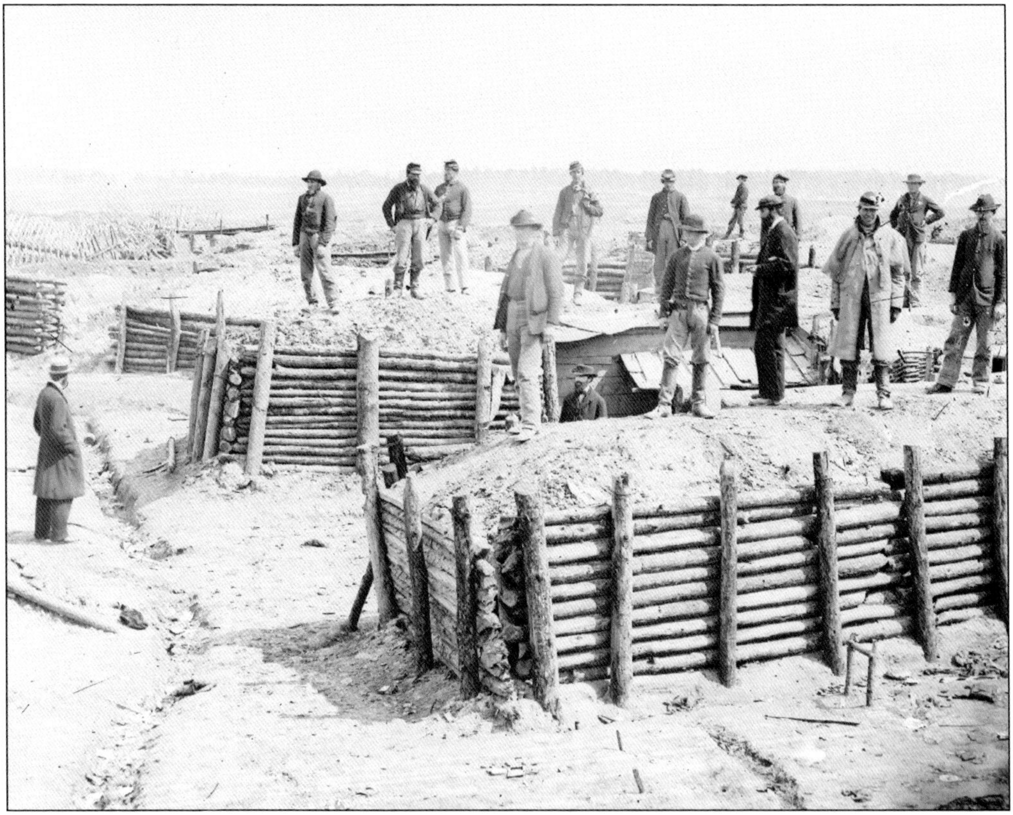

Confederate defenses at Fort Mahone, Petersburg, are shown. The Confederate defenders at Petersburg were well aware of the significance of their duty. If Petersburg fell, the defense of Richmond would be untenable. So they dug in with defensive, anti-siege works of their own. This made for hard and bitter fighting for both sides. Some commentators liken the Union and Confederate lines to the costly and woeful trench warfare of World War I. (Photograph courtesy of the Library of Congress.)

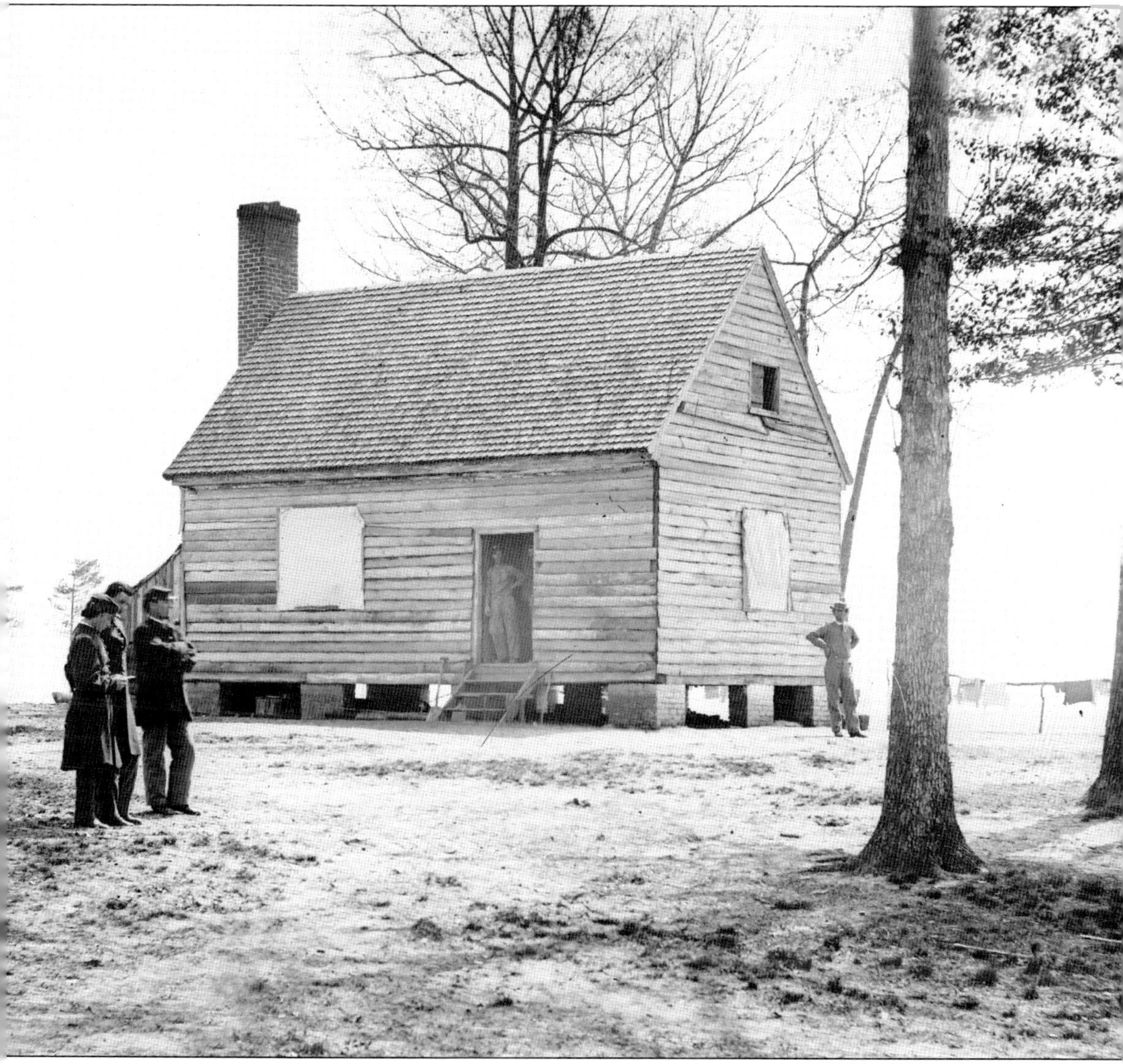

City Point was also a place of mysteries and revelations. Pictured is the Union Secret Service headquarters in City Point. Military intelligence was essential for both the Union and Confederates to gauge the strength, location, and disposition of troops and intentions of the commanders. With the capital of the Confederacy so close and the Union army—only 25 miles downriver on the James—City Point was a perfect focus for spotting and reporting military movements. (Photograph courtesy of the Library of Congress.)

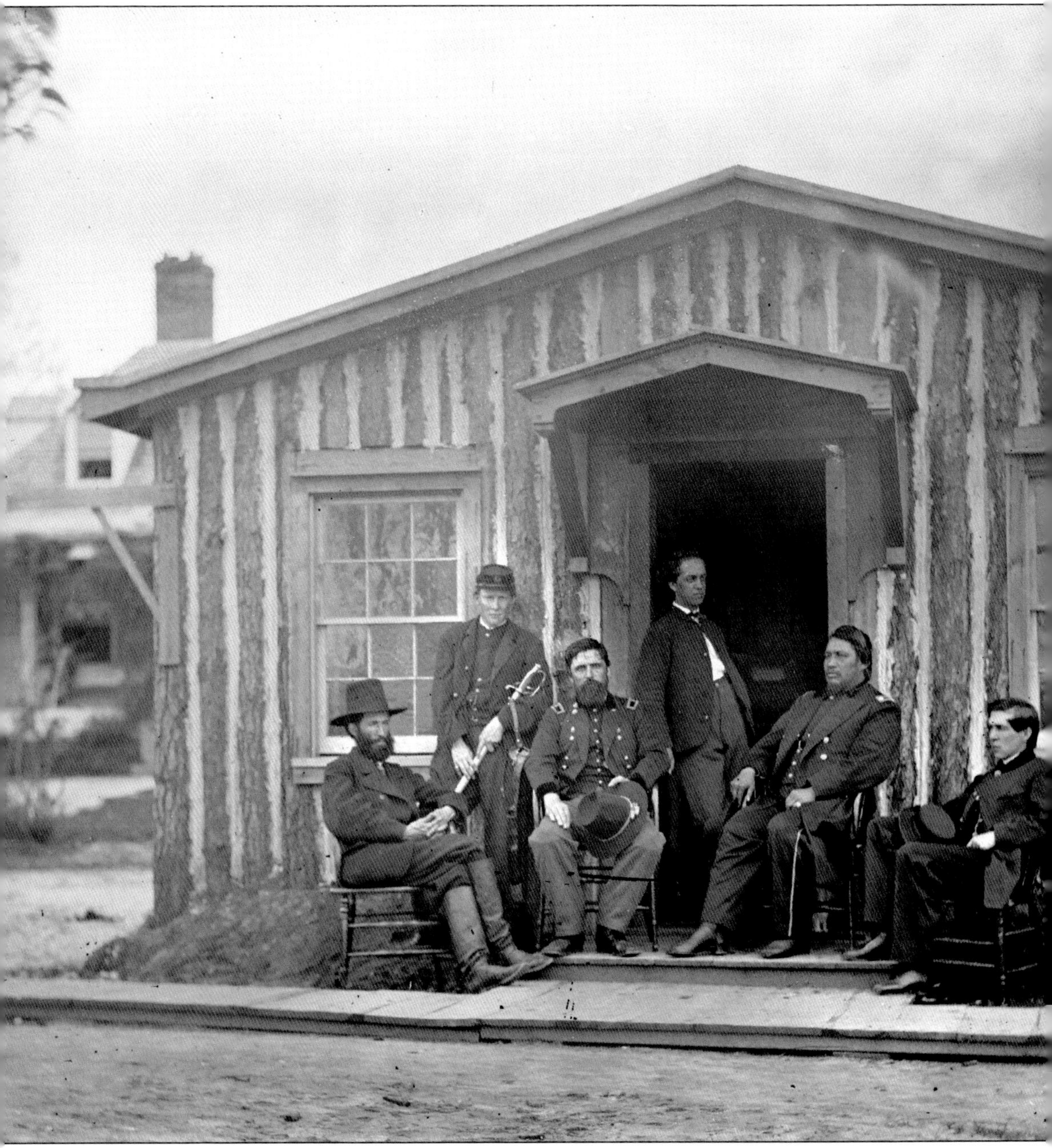

Hopewell–City Point was a place that helped form fame. Col. Ely Parker, seated second from the right, was perhaps the highest-ranking Native American in the Union army. Born in Indian Falls, New York, he was a bilingual full-blooded Seneca. He once tried to take the bar examination to become a lawyer but was refused because he was considered a noncitizen. Native Americans were not considered citizens until 1924. Parker, a friend to General Grant before the war, was a 7th Division engineer at the Siege of Petersburg and was present during the surrender at Appomattox in April 1865. After the war, President Grant appointed Parker as the Commissioner of Indian Affairs (1869–1871) (www.pbs.org/wnet/historyofus). Pictured third from the right is Brig. Gen. John Rawlins, noted later. (Photograph courtesy of the Library of Congress.)

Here, some of these workers appear to be soldiers and some civilians. The row of masts over the crated boxes of supplies suggests the seemingly limitless resource the Union could pour into the war effort. (Photograph courtesy of the Library of Congress.)

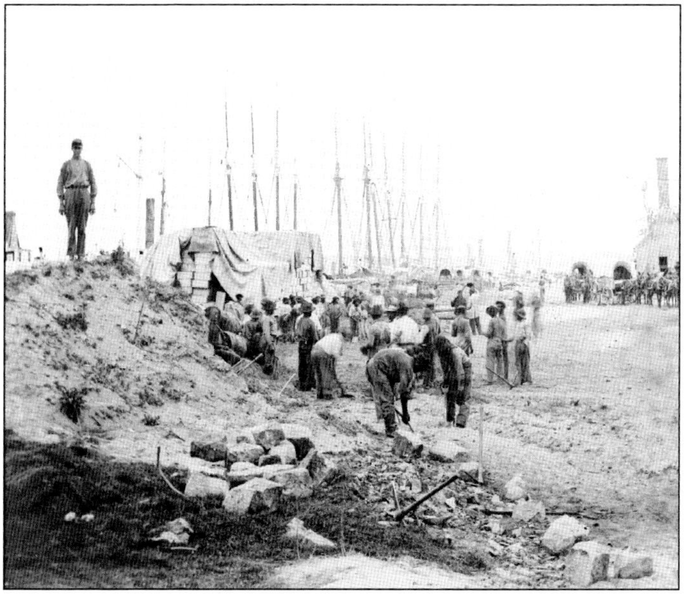

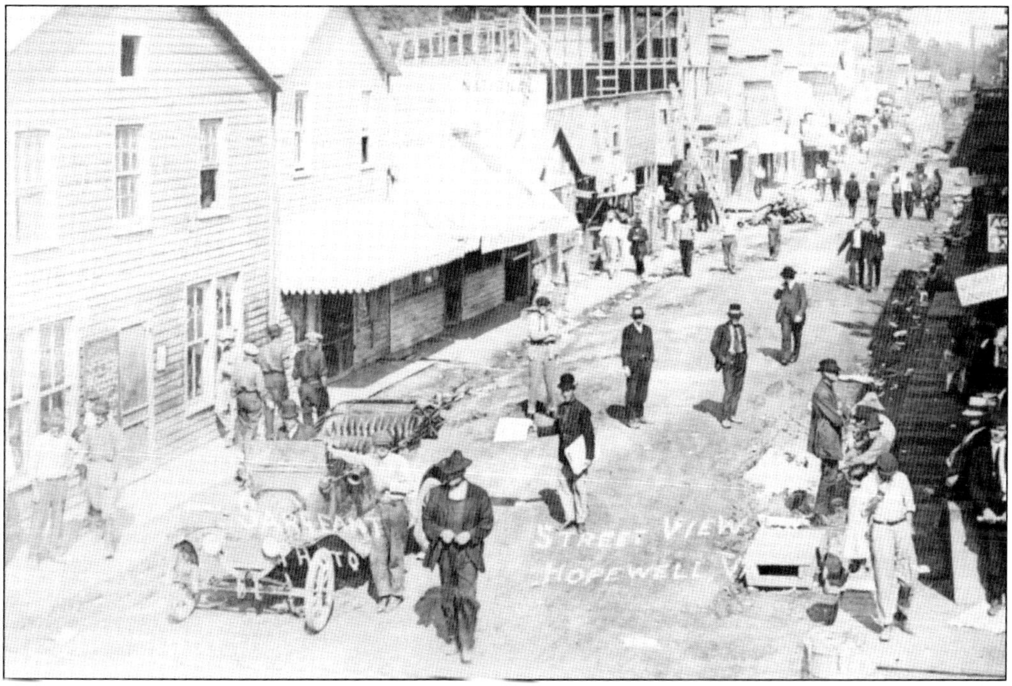

Hopewell was also a boomtown in boom times. On August 8, 1912, DuPont purchased land from the Eppes family to manufacture dynamite and guncotton for smokeless powder. World War I loomed in Europe and officially began two years later. In its peak, DuPont employed 28,000 people, and Hopewell's population swelled to more than 40,000. In 1915, the company's biweekly payroll was $775,000—in 1915 dollars. DuPont built what were to be the A-Village and B-Village (discussed later), the DuPont Hotel for executives, and a segregated Young Men's Christian Association (YMCA). Cottages rented for $6 per month. While virtues abounded, many today say that vices also thrived in the Wild West–like environment of Hopewell. (Photograph by A. Robbins Jr., courtesy of the Appomattox Regional Library.)

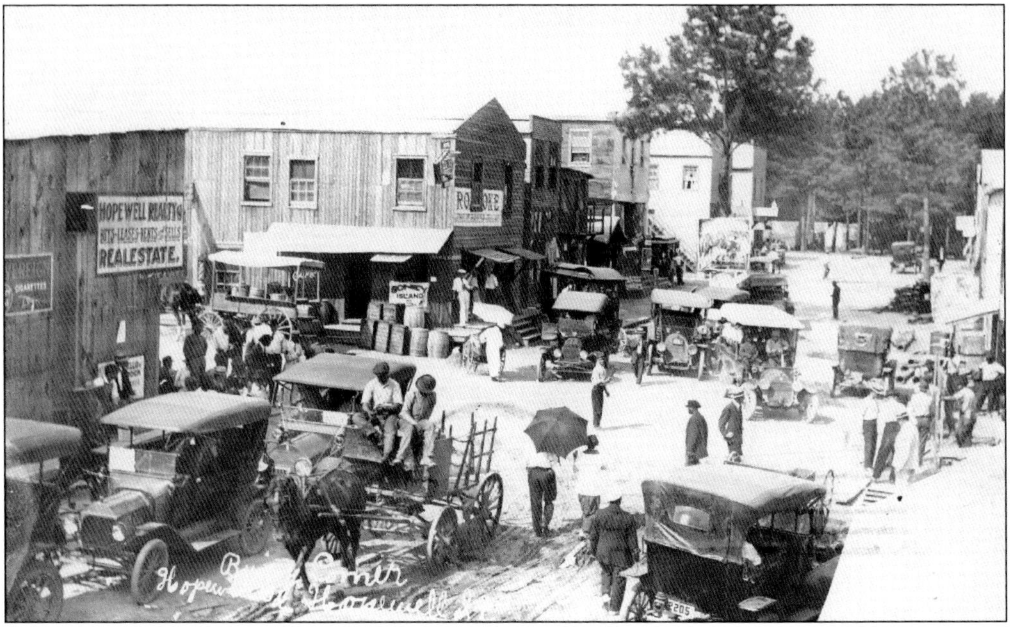

The rule of law sometimes meant the rule of the street. Immediately before and during World War I, Hopewell's industry was a boon to the state and county but was a burden on its health and law enforcement resources. According to *The City That DuPont Built*, Hopewell had 40 illegal places to buy beer and 200 saloons. It is said that places rented beds by the hour so that when one worker's shift ended, he could get a few hours sleep, and when he got up, another tenant could take his place. Law courts were held in the open. (Photograph by A. Robbins Jr., courtesy of the Appomattox Regional Library.)

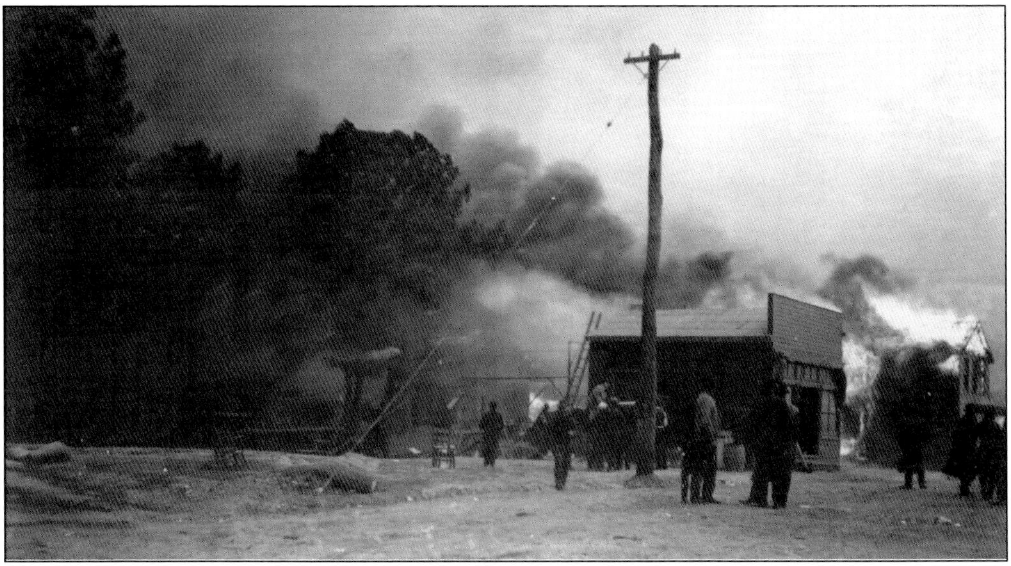

Hopewell recovered from a devastating fire. In December 1915, downtown Hopewell was destroyed by fire that had been whipped into a frenzy by the winter wind. The flames damaged downtown, and it was astounding that no one was killed. But the destruction was only half the story. The other half was the response of its people and their grit to rebuild. (Photograph by A. Robbins Jr., courtesy of the Appomattox Regional Library.)

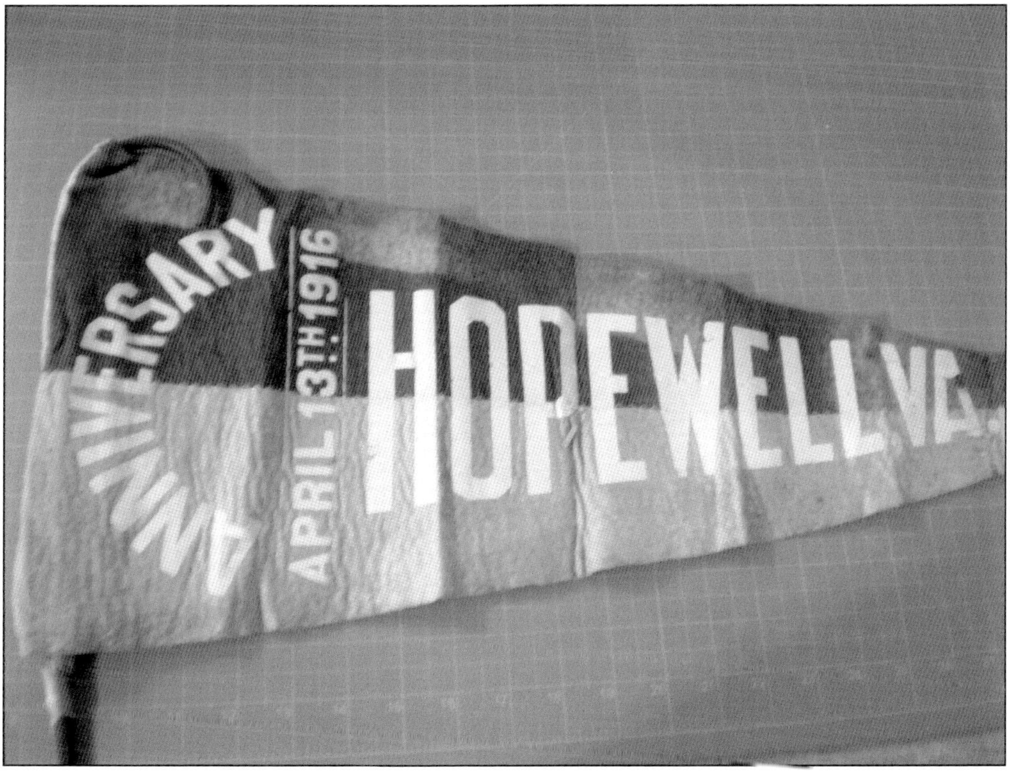

Hopewell not only recovered from the fire of 1915, it flourished. This banner, preserved at the Appomattox Region Library System, demonstrates the verve and vigor with which Hopewell celebrated its first year of incorporation. The banner notes the anniversary of the date that Hopewell was incorporated, April 13, 1916. (Photograph by author, banner courtesy of Appomattox Regional Library.)

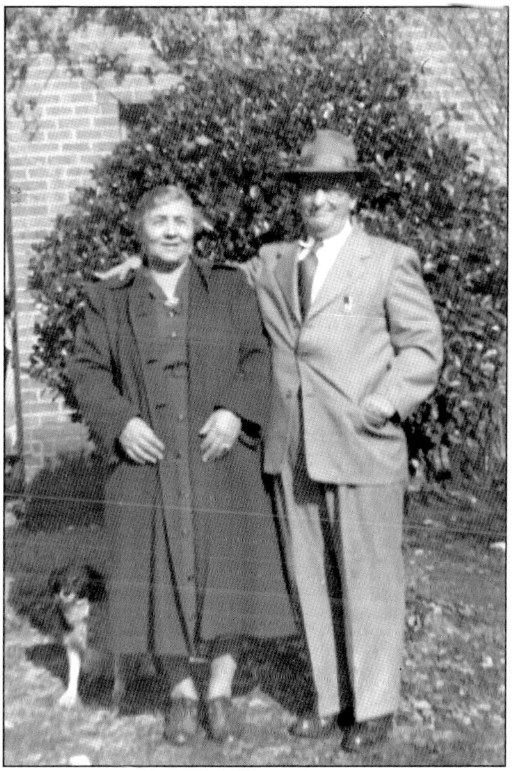

Hopewell made room for others. Pasquale Basile, emigrating from Italy to the United States, found a home in Hopewell in 1915. Pasquale, or "Pete" as he was called, was a barber. When he first arrived in Hopewell, he cut hair for customers who sat on a sack of goods in his brother's grocery store until he established the O.K. Barber Shop in downtown in December 1915. His wife, Maria Sabastiano, joined him from Italy in 1920. (Photograph courtesy of Millie Basile.)

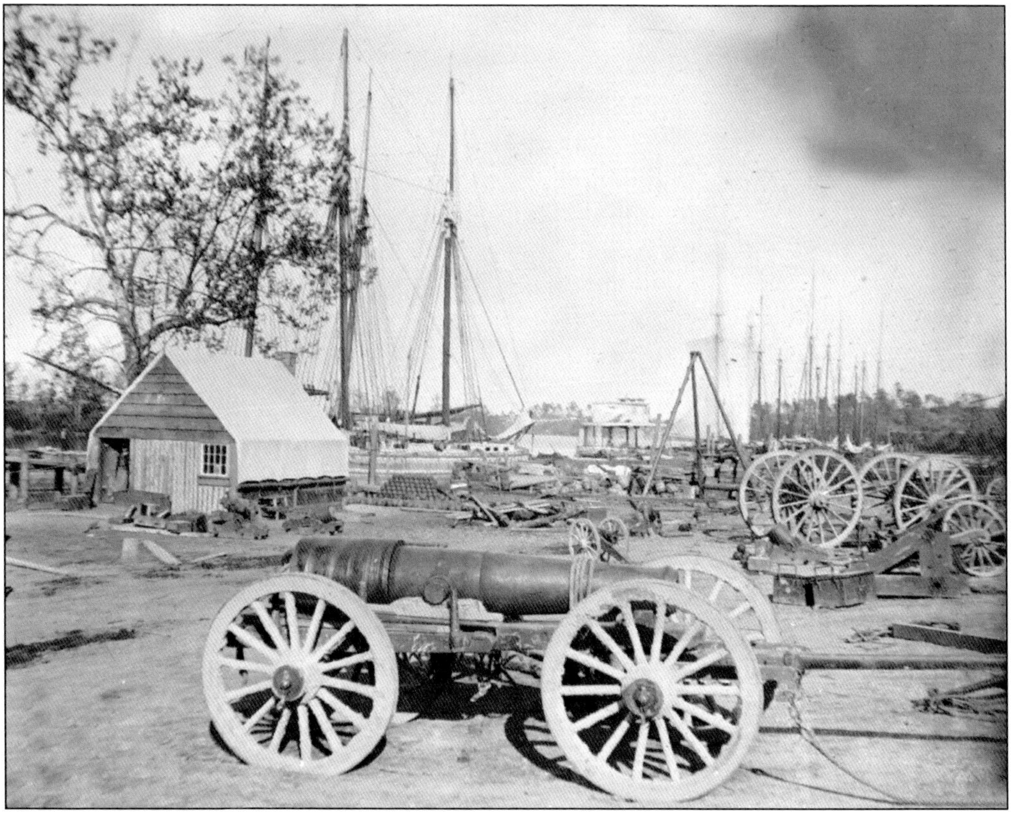

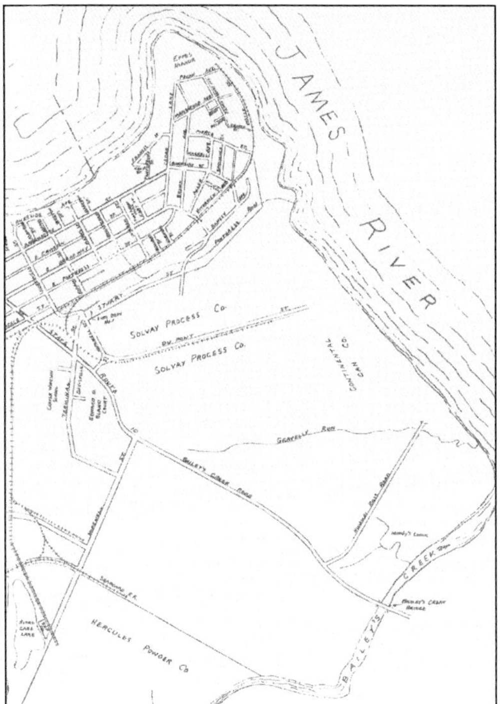

Imagination and industry had a long tradition in Hopewell, as shown in this photograph. Taken at Broadway Landing and labeled "Artillery Park," this photograph also shows a forest of ship masts in the background. The sheer weight of industry and logistics has been noted as a reason for Union success during the Civil War and in later wars as well. One wonders if City Point helped press that concept home to future military planners. (Photograph courtesy of the Library of Congress.)

This 1952 map of the area overlooks the James River (upper right), the Appomattox River (upper left), and the location of related industries, including the Solvay Processing Plant, Continental Can, and the Hercules Powder Company. (Map courtesy of Paul Karnes.)

An aerial view of the Hopewell marina area from about 1965 offers yet another view of the Hopewell waterfront and the then-new bridge across the Appomattox River. This bridge is called the Charles Hardaway Marks Memorial Bridge in honor of a local legislator. (Photograph courtesy of the Appomattox Regional Library.)

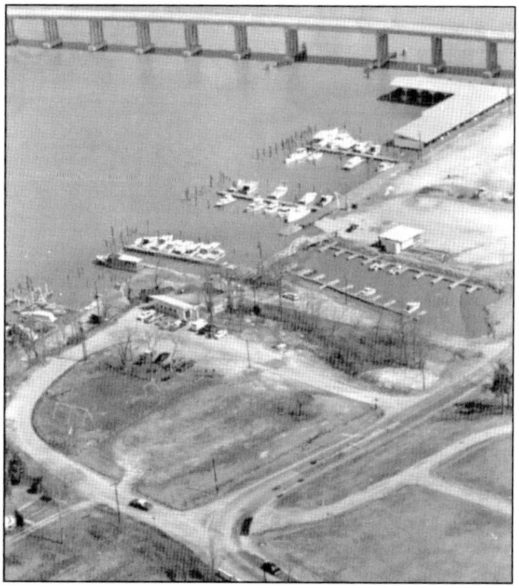

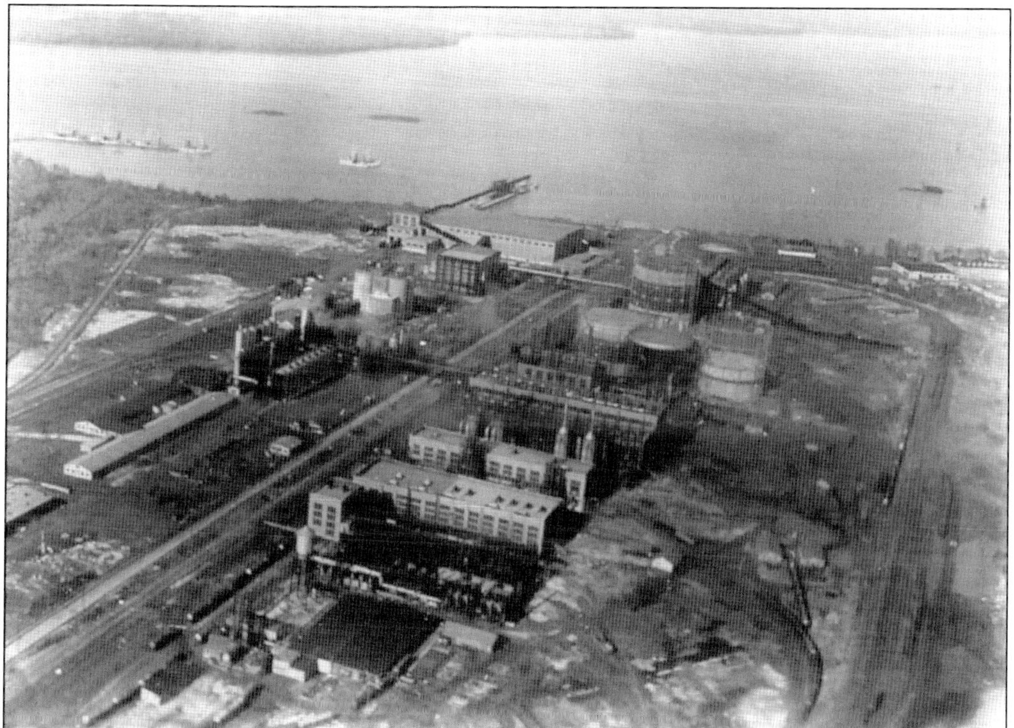

This is an aerial view of the Hopewell and City Point area from about 1930. Dominating the photograph is the National Atmospheric and Nitrogen Company, a predecessor of Allied Corporation. This company made chemicals for fertilizer and an early kind of fiber called rayon. The arrow in the photograph points to Hummel Ross (HR), a company that, during the 1920s, was the first to produce craft board, a kind of cardboard. HR enjoyed many incarnations, including Smurfitt Stone. The railroad lines to the right and bottom center of the photograph connect the harbor with the production lines. The harbor could bring goods all the way to the Atlantic Ocean through the Chesapeake Bay. (Photograph courtesy of Paul Karnes.)

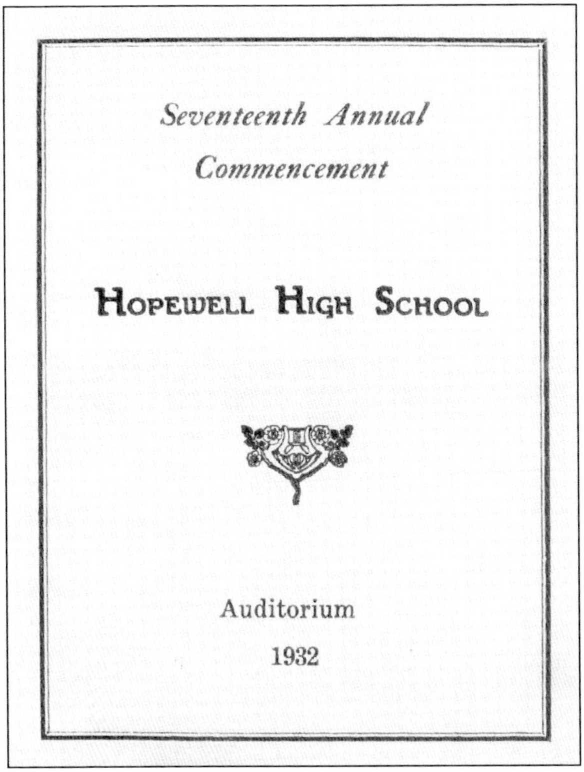

Seventeenth Annual
Commencement

HOPEWELL HIGH SCHOOL

Auditorium
1932

The Hopewell High School commencement program of 1932 is shown. The 17th annual commencement service included a junior-senior dinner in the school cafeteria. That year's sermon, given annually, was delivered by Rev. J.A. Engle, pastor of Trinity Methodist Church in City Point. J.E. Malloree, principal, awarded the diplomas. (A school was later named after him.) Interestingly, the senior class was divided into sections: academic course, scientific course, and commercial course. (Courtesy of Hopewell Public Schools and Jack Daniel.)

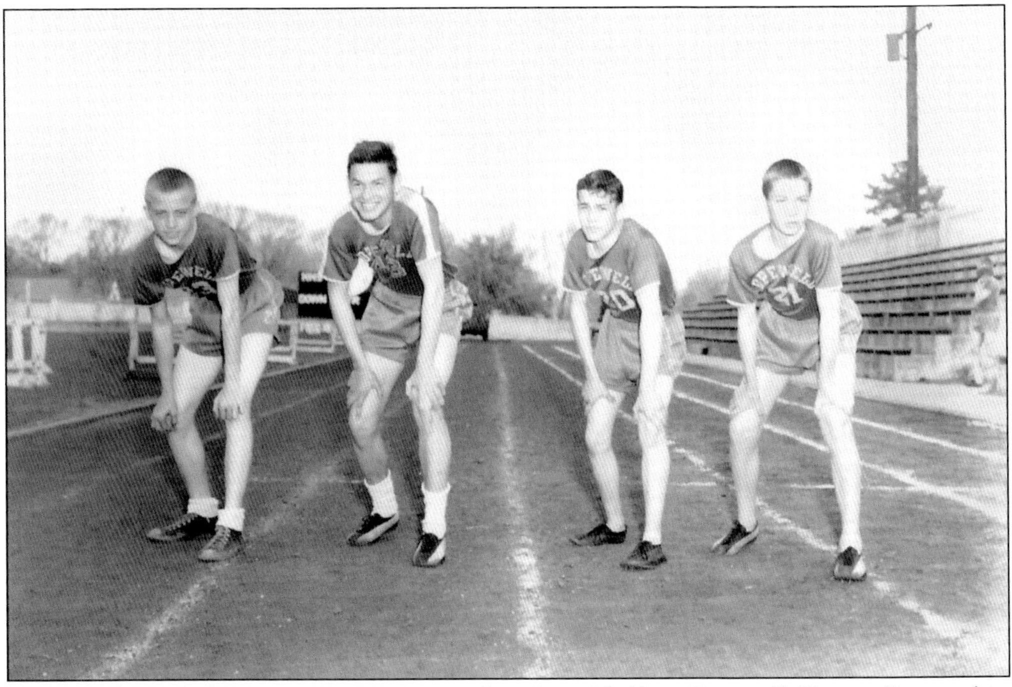

These students are heirs to a long tradition of track and field in Hopewell. Hopewell started its track and field program in 1936 and has always considered sports and other extracurricular activities part of a well-rounded education. (Photograph courtesy of Jack Daniel and the *Hopewell News*.)

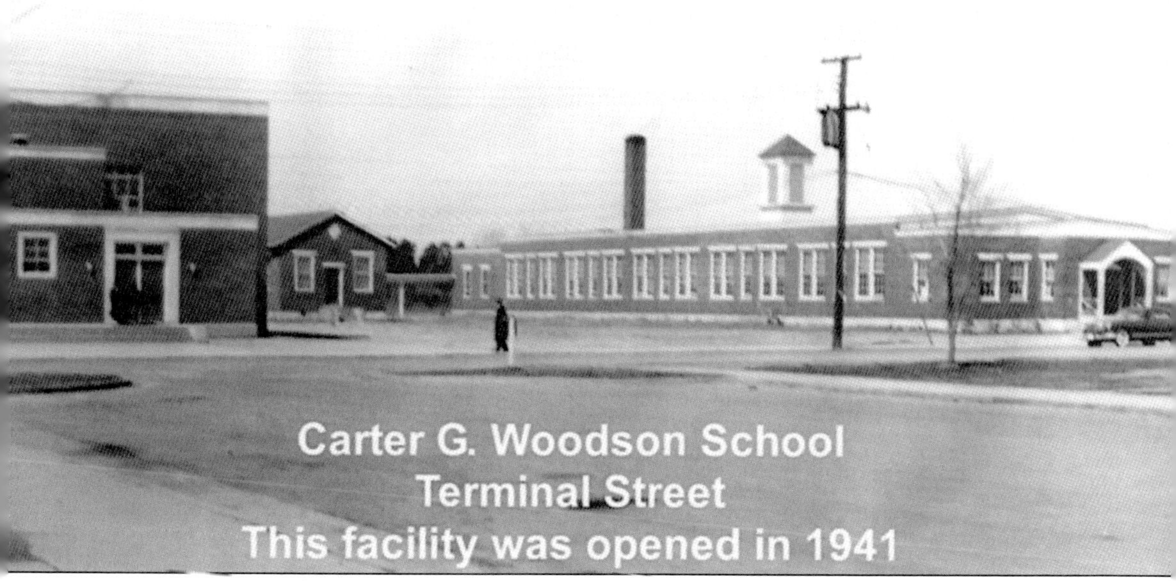

According to the 2009 *Hopewell Public Schools Alumni Directory*, formal African American education began in 1916, and an early building used was a YMCA building. In 1921, the school board purchased this building for the Hopewell Colored School, as it was then known. It was located behind the modern fire station No. 1 on Station Street, and in 1924 it enjoyed an enrollment of 249 students, including 242 elementary and seven high school students. The Carter G. Woodson School (as it was later called) was moved to a second location on Terminal Street in September 1941. In a 2009 plaque unveiling for this historic school, such notables as the Honorable Curtis Harris Sr. (the first African American mayor), the Honorable Brenda Pelham (then-mayor of Hopewell), Avon Miles (chair of public schools), Juanita Chambers (school board member), the Reverend Rudolph Dunbar (of the First Baptist Church of City Point), and Ida Allen (a former graduate) all helped lead the ceremonies. (Photograph courtesy of Juanita Chambers and Hopewell Public Schools.)

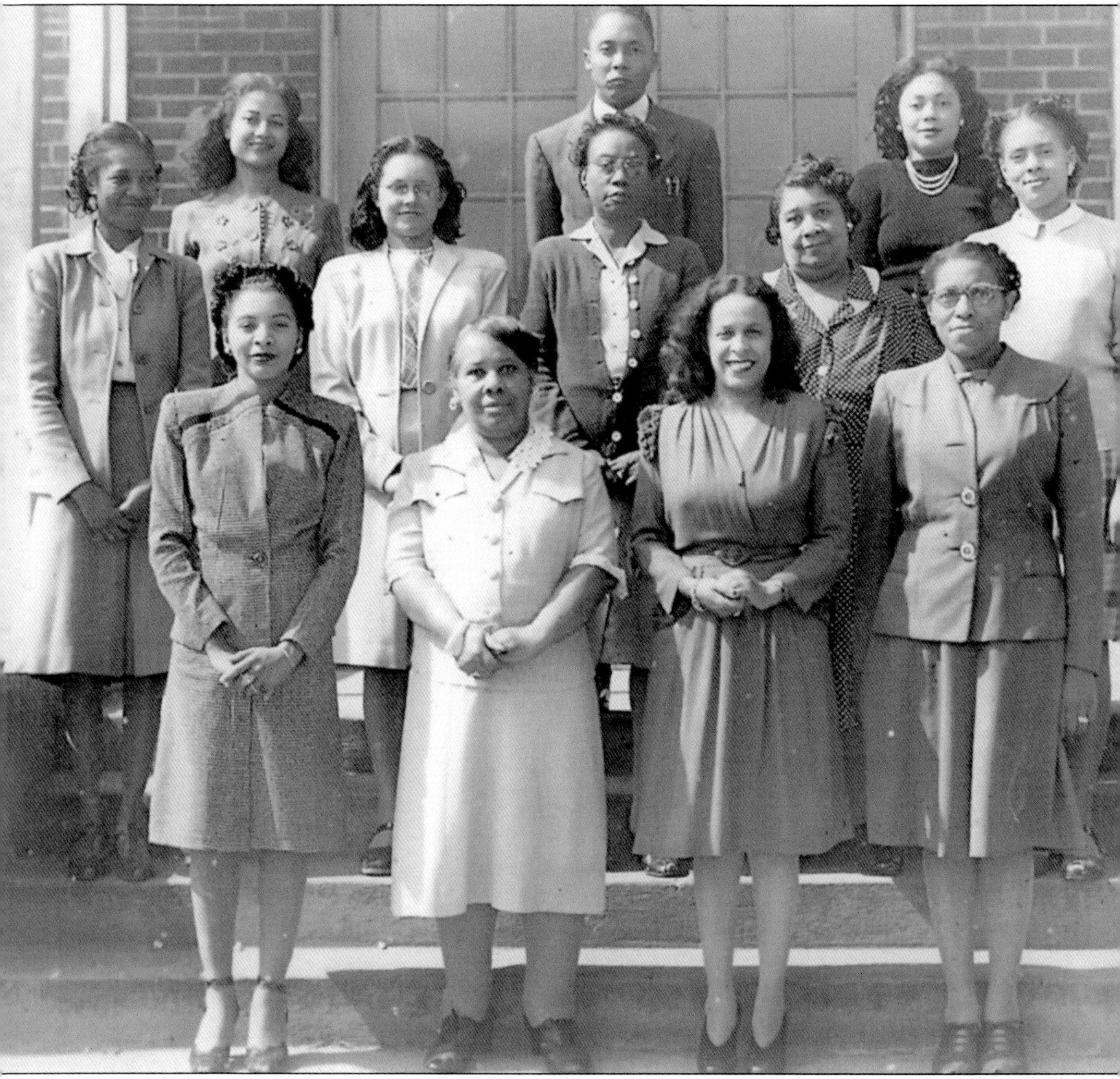

This photograph shows teachers of the Carter G. Woodson School in 1946. In 1958, the school was moved from its location on Terminal Street to its present location on Winston Churchill Drive. There, instructors taught grades one through 12, until the school became the citywide middle school in 1969. The school had an enviable record of extracurricular athletics, including a championship basketball team in the 1955–1958 seasons and again in 1963. From 1946 until 1971, Bernard Epps served as principal. (Photograph courtesy of Juanita Chambers and Modern Arts Studio of Norfolk, and the Hopewell School Board.)

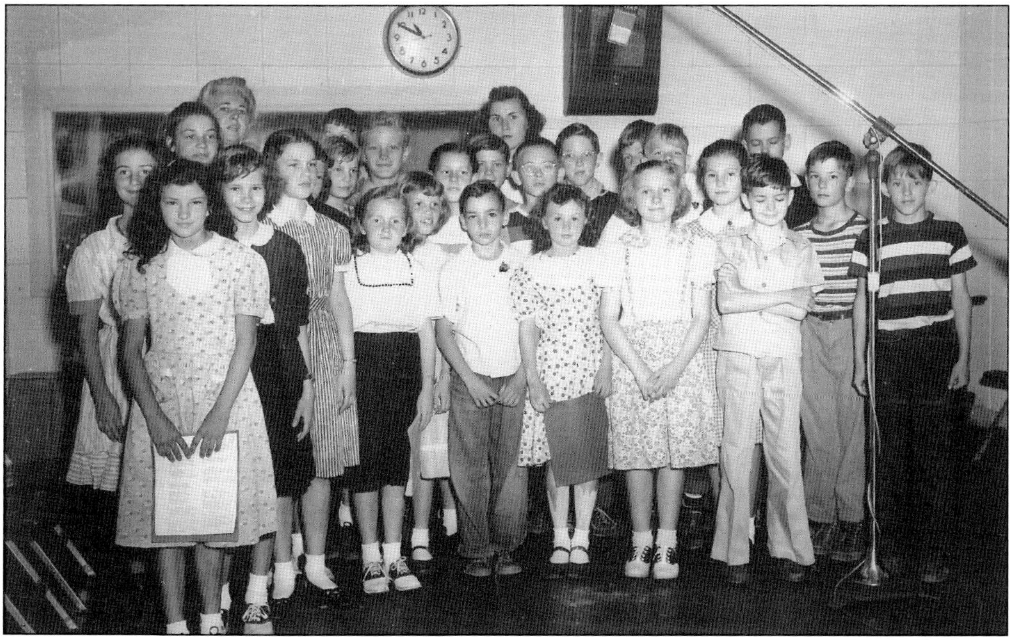

A fifth-grade class conducts a broadcast in the studio of station WHAP, located off Mesa Drive. The station's first broadcast commenced on January 16, 1949. It had broadcast a total of 18,304 hours through 1951 and is still broadcasting today. (Photograph courtesy of Paul Karnes and the *Hopewell News*.)

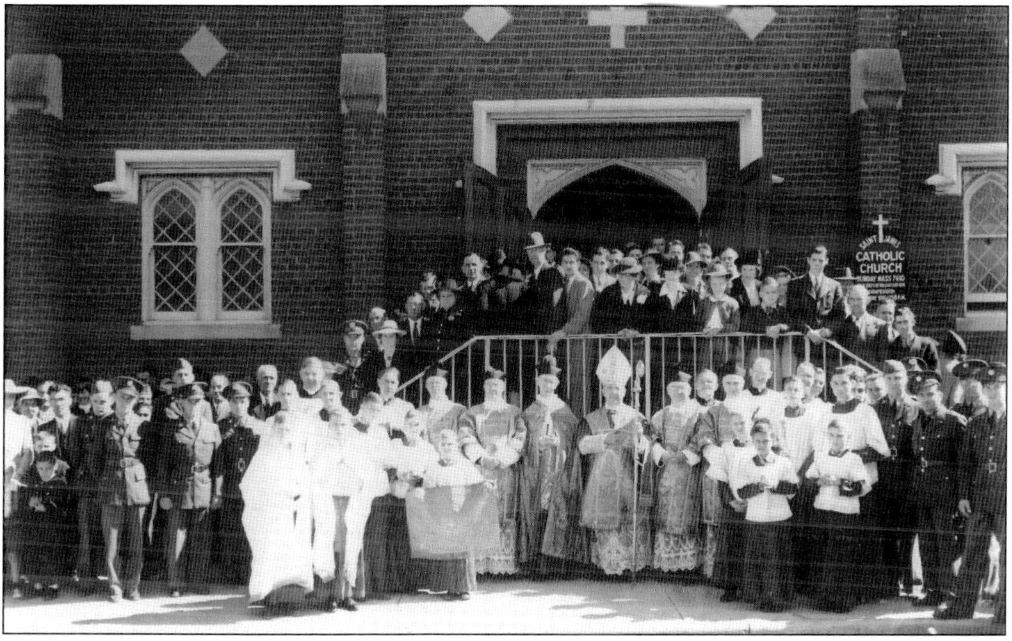

Located at Sixth Street and City Point Road, St. James Roman Catholic Church was an early church built in Hopewell. DuPont contributed $30,000 in 1915 to the church for its construction. The bishop (center) has come from Richmond for this unnamed event. Tony Basile (whose father, Pasquale Basile, was introduced earlier) stands in civilian clothes in the front row on the landing to the right of the man with the hat. (Photograph courtesy of Millie Basile.)

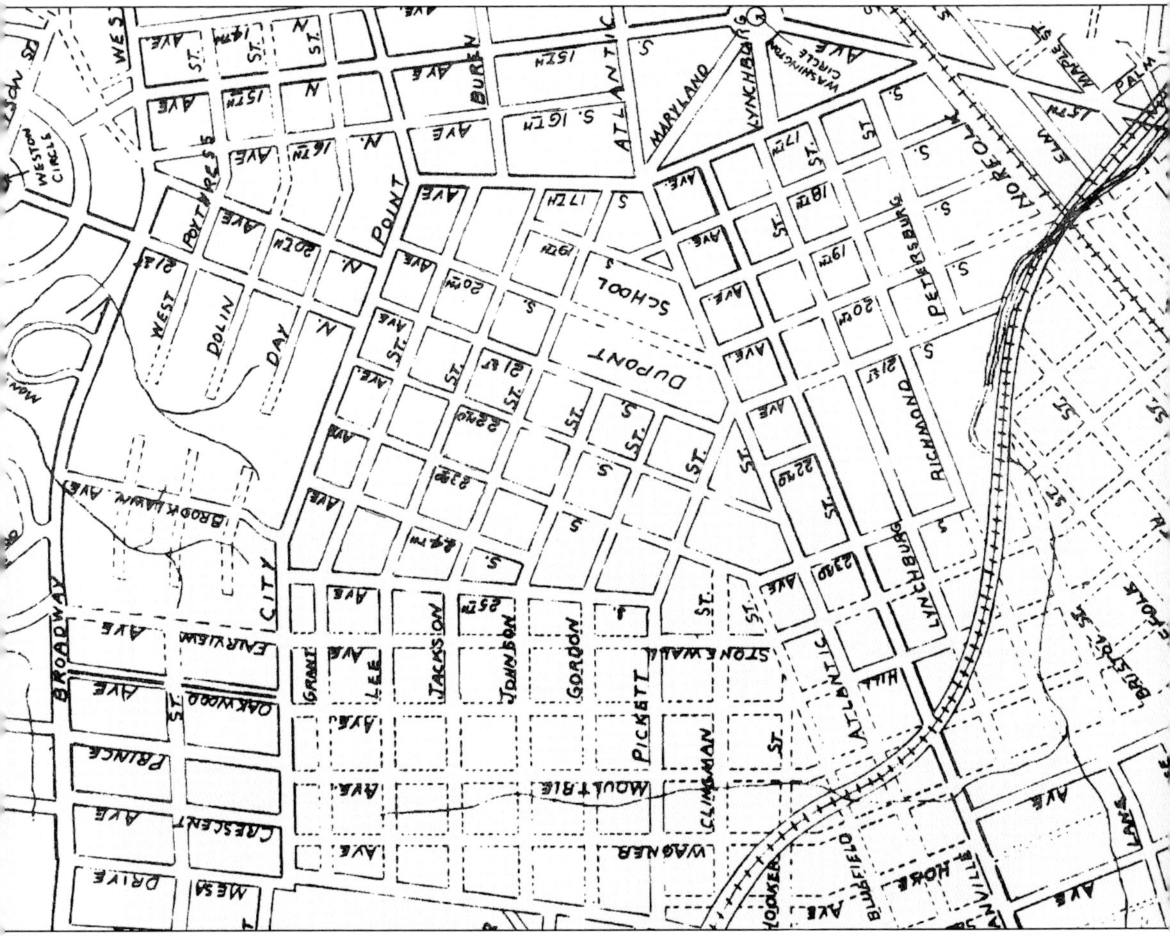

This map from 1952 shows the railroad running through some of the streets in Hopewell. These newer railroads reflect the role of industry and transportation that has always been a part of Hopewell. In a very early expression of railroads, the City Point Railroad Company began in 1936 to link up with the major rail lines in Petersburg. Two lines of track intersect each other at Norfolk Street (upper right). During the Civil War, the rail line was known as the Petersburg and City Point Railroad; it then became the Norfolk and Western, and later, the Norfolk Southern. (Map courtesy of Paul Karnes.)

Two

People and Invention

Places attract people. The harbor and railroads offered attractions for many different people over many generations. Some came to Hopewell–City Point for fame, some for adventure, some for military information, some for fortune, some for a home, and some for wartime training or embarkation.

Native Americans lived around Hopewell for as long as 17,000 years, according to Virginian archaeological studies—a finding that has challenged long-standing beliefs. In 2011, Virginia recognized eight tribes. English settlers, including Capt. Christopher Newport, sailed 50 miles west of Hopewell on May 8, 1607. Some, including Thomas Dale, continued sailing to what is now Hopewell City Point at the mouth of the Appomattox River. Sir Thomas Dale, sailing up the James a little past Hopewell, founded the Citie (sic) of Henricus in 1611. Dale offered a land grant to William Cawson near present-day Hopewell in 1613. The settlement, Bermuda Cittie, later called City Point, began with the construction of buildings by 1622. Paramount Chief Powhatan and his daughter Pocahontas became legends. Plantations such as Weston Manor, built in 1789, and Appomattox Plantation, begun in 1763, grew and exported products from the docks along the James and Appomattox Rivers. In 1826, City Point was incorporated, and by 1840, the town's population was about 300.

African American history in Hopewell was concurrent with Colonial history. The English who sailed up the James and Appomattox Rivers brought with them both indentured servants and slaves. Near Hopewell, in Bermuda Hundred, more African slaves were off-loaded than in any other part of Virginia. Yet, in the 1700s, both the numbers and the freedoms of liberated African Americans grew in this area. The US Colored Troops captured City Point and engaged Confederate forces, including an assault at Baylor's Farm in Hopewell.

After the war, City Point's population resumed its prewar levels of around 300. In 1910, the population remained the same. Then came the first rumblings of World War I. Industrial plants arrived (see the next chapter), and the population swelled to boomtown proportions. The need for 40,000 industrial employees attracted immigrants from all across Europe. As one local historian put it, "When I came to Hopewell, I didn't need to travel to Europe. Europe had come here." After World War I in 1921, the population rose to around 7,000 because of increased industry. In 2011, Hopewell's population was around 29,000.

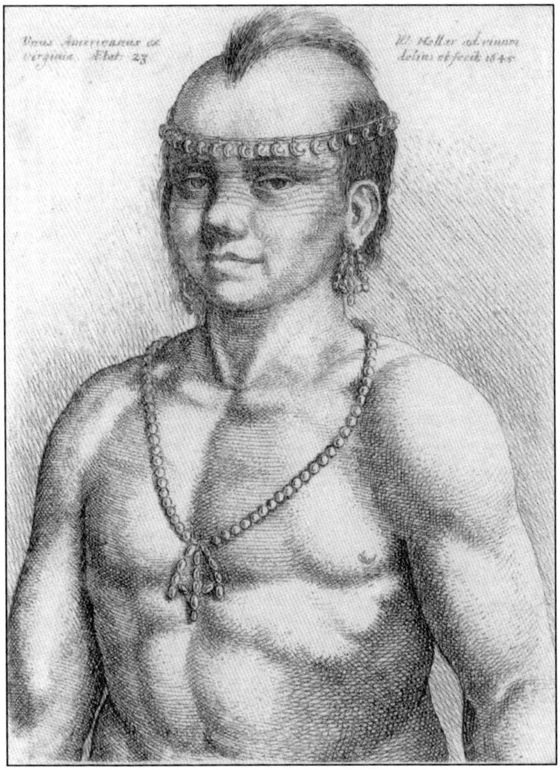

This is a rendering of a 23-year-old Algonquian man from Virginia. Dated 1645, almost two generations after the first contacts with English settlers, the drawing was done by Wenceslaus Holler (1607–1677). Note the subject's facial markings and necklace. The Algonquians were one of the three linguistic groups extant in Virginia at the time of European contact. The others were the Siouan and the Iroquoian. (Photograph courtesy of the Library of Congress.)

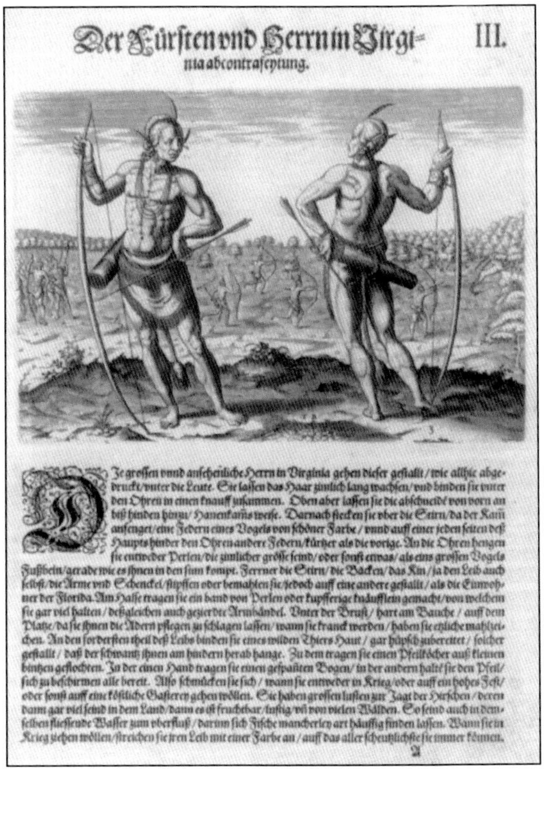

Der Fürsten vnd Herrn in Virginia abcontrafeytung. III.

Die grossen vnnd ansehnliche Herrn in Virginia gehen dieser gestallt/ wie allhie abgedruckt/ vnter die Leute. Sie lassen das Haar zimlich lang wachsen/ vnd binden sie vnter den Ohren in einen knauff zusammen. Oben aber lassen sie die abschneide von vorn an biß hinden hinzu/ Hanenkamms weise. Darnach stecken sie vber die Stirn/ da der Kamm anfenget/ eine Federn eines Vogels von schöner Farbe/ vnnd auff einer jeden seiten deß Haupts hinder den Ohren andere Federn/ kürtzer als die vorige. An die Ohren hengen sie entweder Perlen/ die zimlicher grösse seind/ oder sonst etwas/ als eins grossen Vogels Fußbein/ gerade wie es jhnen in den sinn kompt. Ferrner die Stirn/ die Backen/ das Kin/ ja den Leib auch selbst/ die Arme vnd Schenckel/ stipffen oder bemahlen sie/ jedoch auff eine andere gestallt/ als die Einwohner der Florida. Am Halse tragen sie ein band von Perlen oder kupfferige knäufflein gemacht/ von welchem sie gar viel halten/ deßgleichen auch gezierte Armbändel. Vnter der Brust/ hart am Bauche/ auff dem Platze/ da sie jhnen die Adern pflegen zu schlagen lassen/ wann sie kranck werden/ haben sie etzliche mahlzeichen. An den fordersten theil deß Leibs binden sie eines wilden Thiers Haut/ gar hüpsch zubereitet/ solcher gestallt/ daß der schwantz jhnen am hindern herab hange. Zu dem tragen sie einen Pfeilköcher auß kleinen binzen geflochten. In der einen Hand tragen sie einen gespannten Bogen/ in der andern halte sie den Pfeil/ sich zu beschirmen alle bereit. Also schmücken sie sich/ wann sie entweder in Krieg/ oder auff ein hohes Fest/ oder sonst auff eine köstliche Gasterey gehen wöllen. Sie haben grossen lusten zur Jagt der Hirschen/ deren dann gar viel seind in dem Land/ dann es ist fruchtbar/ lustig/ vñ von vielen Wälden. So seind auch in denselben fliessende Wasser zum vberfluß/ darinn sich Fische mancherley art häuffig finden lassen. Wann sie in Krieg ziehen wöllen/ streichen sie jren Leib mit einer Farbe an/ auff das aller scheutzlichste sie immer können.

A

Chieftains, known as *weroans*, are shown in about 1590. Powhatan, the paramount chief, or *mamanatowick*, of what was called the Powhatan Confederacy, was a major influence around the time of English contact. The Confederacy consisted of 32 tribes with 150 villages. The leadership council of the Chickahominy tribe was called *mungai*, meaning "great men," and consisted of both religious leaders and tribe elders. The Powhatan Confederacy included lesser chiefs, and some tribes did not join. (Photograph of engraving courtesy of the Library of Congress.)

Here, a Native American woman carries a jar, and a youngster, possibly her child, shakes a rattle and holds a doll. Records indicate an ethos of strong family ties. From a DeBry and White work, the Latin phrase above the etching can be translated as "Noble woman of Pomejocj." (Photograph courtesy of the Library of Congress.)

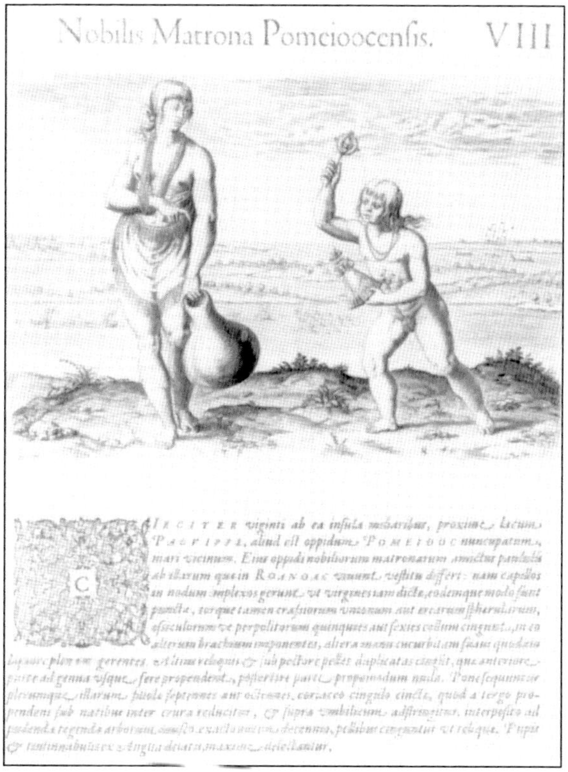

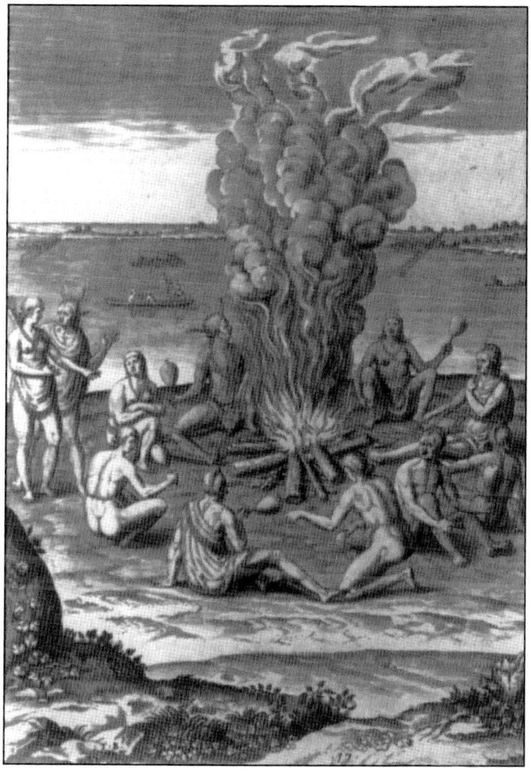

This photograph shows the social life of Virginia Native Americans along a river. Conversations, storytelling, discussions, singing, and praying were often conducted in public places. Note four of the Native Americans with rattles. Today, tribes near Hopewell hold annual ceremonials that are open to the public where singing, music, and dance play prominent roles. (Photograph courtesy of the Library of Congress.)

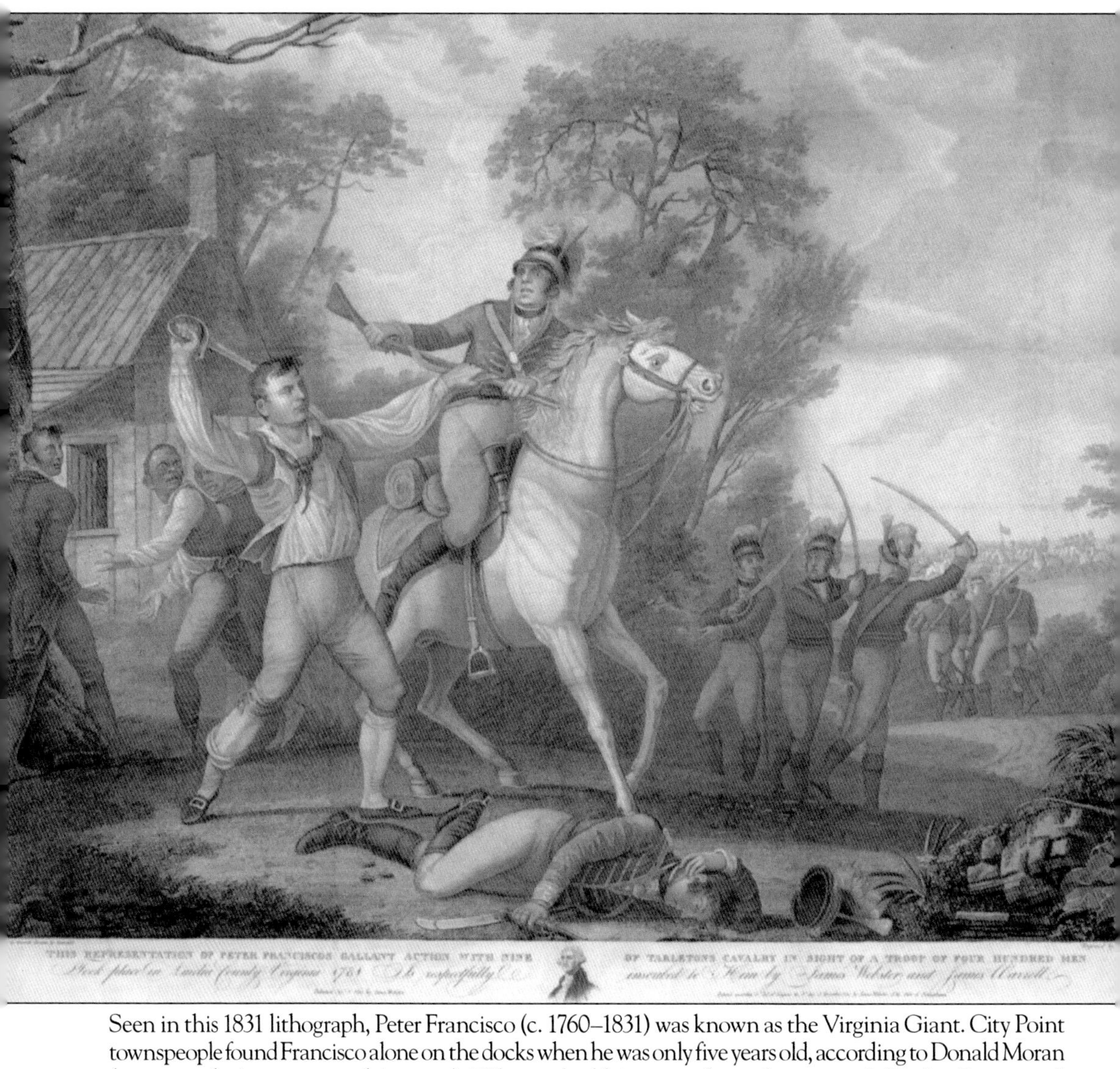

Seen in this 1831 lithograph, Peter Francisco (c. 1760–1831) was known as the Virginia Giant. City Point townspeople found Francisco alone on the docks when he was only five years old, according to Donald Moran (www.revolutionarywararchives.org). When asked his name, he only repeated, "Pedro Francisco." Consigned to a local poorhouse, he eventually grew to an unusual height for the time: over six feet, six inches. His exploits during the Revolutionary War made him renowned for both his height and his heroics. He single-handedly trounced several of British general Banastre Tarlton's cavalrymen. Tarlton was nicknamed "the Butcher" because he allegedly shot down surrendering Continental soldiers during a battle. General Washington was known to have fashioned a five-foot-long sword for Francisco to accommodate his size. The grave of Peter Francisco is in the Shockhoe Cemetery in Richmond. (Photograph courtesy of the Library of Congress.)

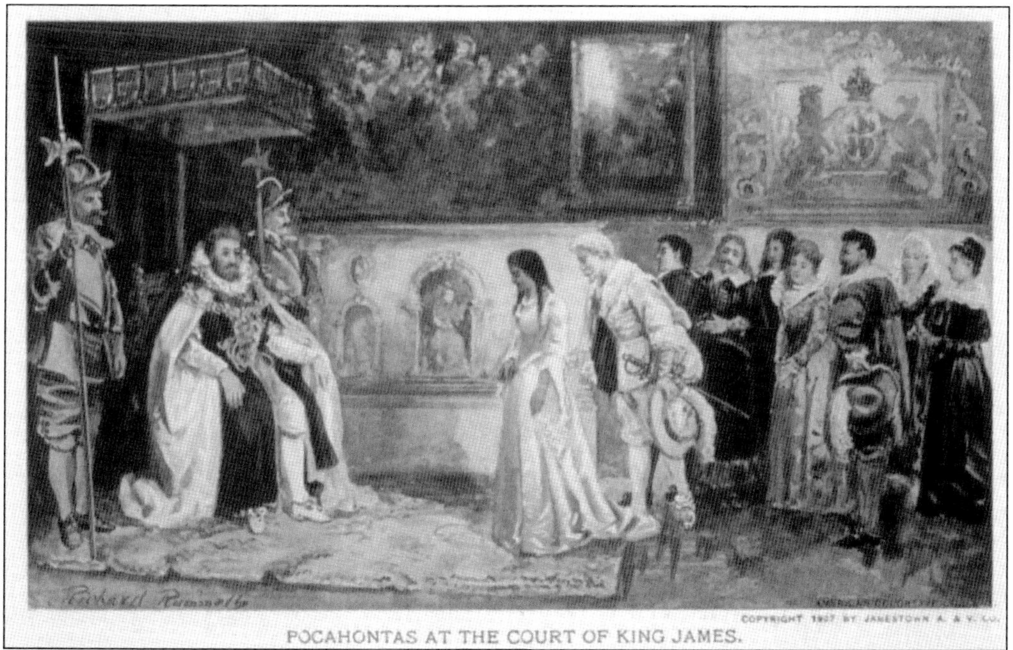

Pocahontas, Paramount Chief Powhatan's daughter, is depicted before King James of England. She married tobacco merchant John Rolfe in 1614 at the Citie of Henricus, about 80 miles up the James River from Jamestown and just a few miles from Hopewell. Later, she traveled to England with Rolfe and died there in 1616. She had taken the name Rebecca. After Pocahontas died, Rolfe continued to grow and trade tobacco in Virginia. (Photograph courtesy of the Library of Congress.)

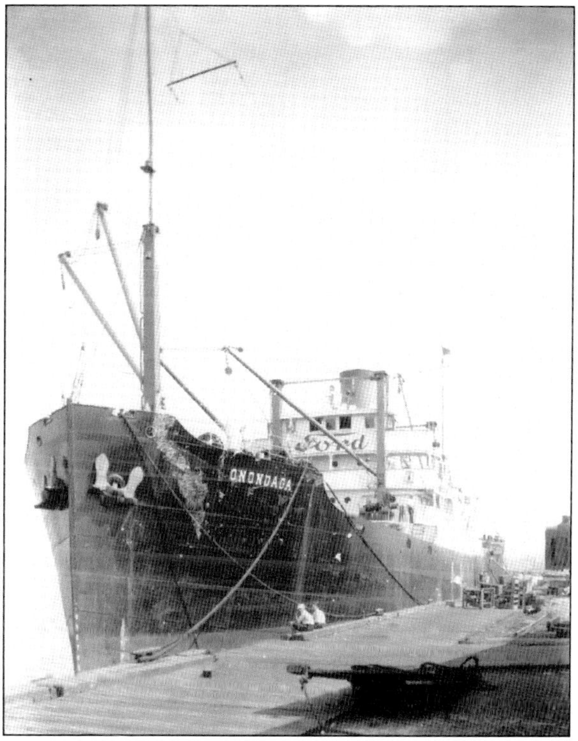

Travel by water has always influenced Hopewell, including the freighter *Onondaga*, shown docked in Hopewell. Ever since the days of captains John Smith, Francis Eppes, and others—not to mention the days of the depot during the Civil War—sea commerce has played a vital role for Hopewell and City Point. Though 80 miles from the Atlantic, Hopewell is an ocean port. Ships can travel from Richmond's port down the James River to Hopewell and the Chesapeake Bay. From there, ships can go anywhere in the world. In the early 1950s, about 350,000 tons of water freight per year passed through Hopewell. (Photograph courtesy of Jack Daniel.)

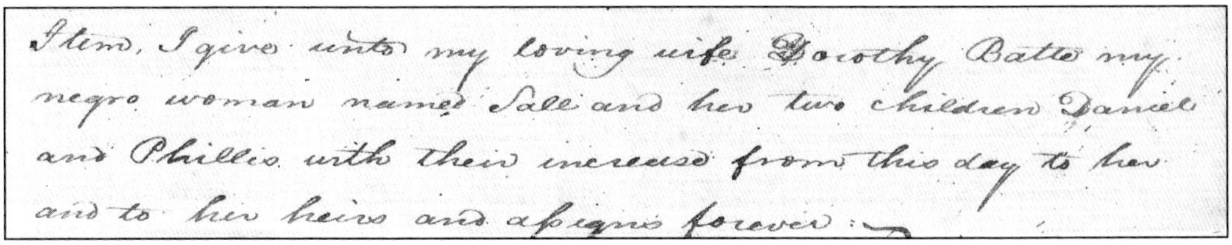

Item, I give unto my loving wife Dorothy Batte my negro woman named Salli and her two children Daniel and Phillis with their increase from this day to her and to her heirs and assigns forever :—

Slaves are given by name in this will. This section of Thomas Batte's will from September 17, 1787, states, "Item. I give unto my loving wife Dorothy Batte my negro woman named Salli and her two children Daniel and Phillis with their increase from this day to her and to her heirs and assigns forever." (Original document courtesy of Robert Gill and family.)

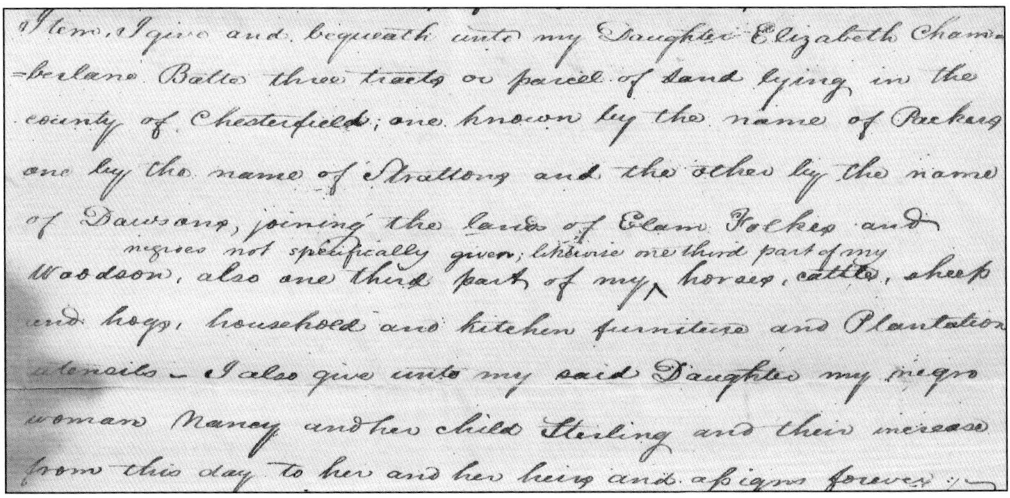

Item, I give and bequeath unto my Daughter Elizabeth Cham-berlane Batte three tracts or parcel of land lying in the county of Chesterfield; one known by the name of Packers one by the name of Strattons and the other by the name of Dawsons, joining the lands of Elam Folkes and Woodson, also one third part of my negroes not specifically given; likewise one third part of my horses, cattle, sheep and hogs, household and kitchen furniture and Plantation utensils — I also give unto my said Daughter my negro woman Nancy and her child Sterling and their increase from this day to her and her heirs and assigns forever :—

In another part of the will noted above, slavery was seen as both property and perpetual. The above reads, "Item, I give and bequeath unto my daughter Elizabeth Chamberlane Batte three tracts or parcel of land . . . also one third part of my negroes not specifically given; likewise one third part of my horses, cattle, sheep and hogs, household and kitchen furniture and Plantation utensils—I also give unto my said Daughter my woman Nancy and her child Sterling and their increase from this day to her heirs and assigns forever." (Original document courtesy of Robert Gill and family.)

This photograph shows Gen. Ulysses S. Grant's headquarters at City Point. Grant, using land of the Appomattox Manor as his headquarters, determined the overall strategy for ultimate Union victory. This Manor has a commanding view of City Point and its harbor. Grant's immediate goal was to cut the important rail lines surrounding Petersburg. Among the visitors in his City Point headquarters were Pres. Abraham Lincoln and his son Todd. (Photograph courtesy of the Library of Congress.)

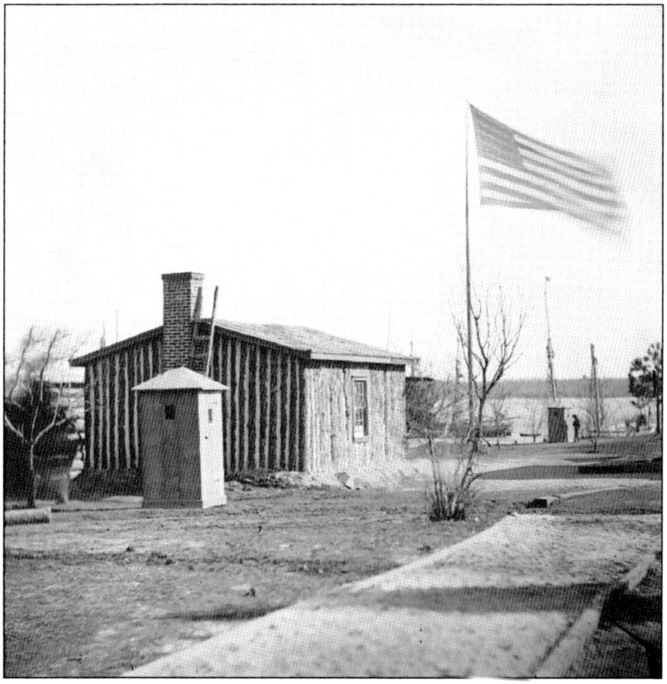

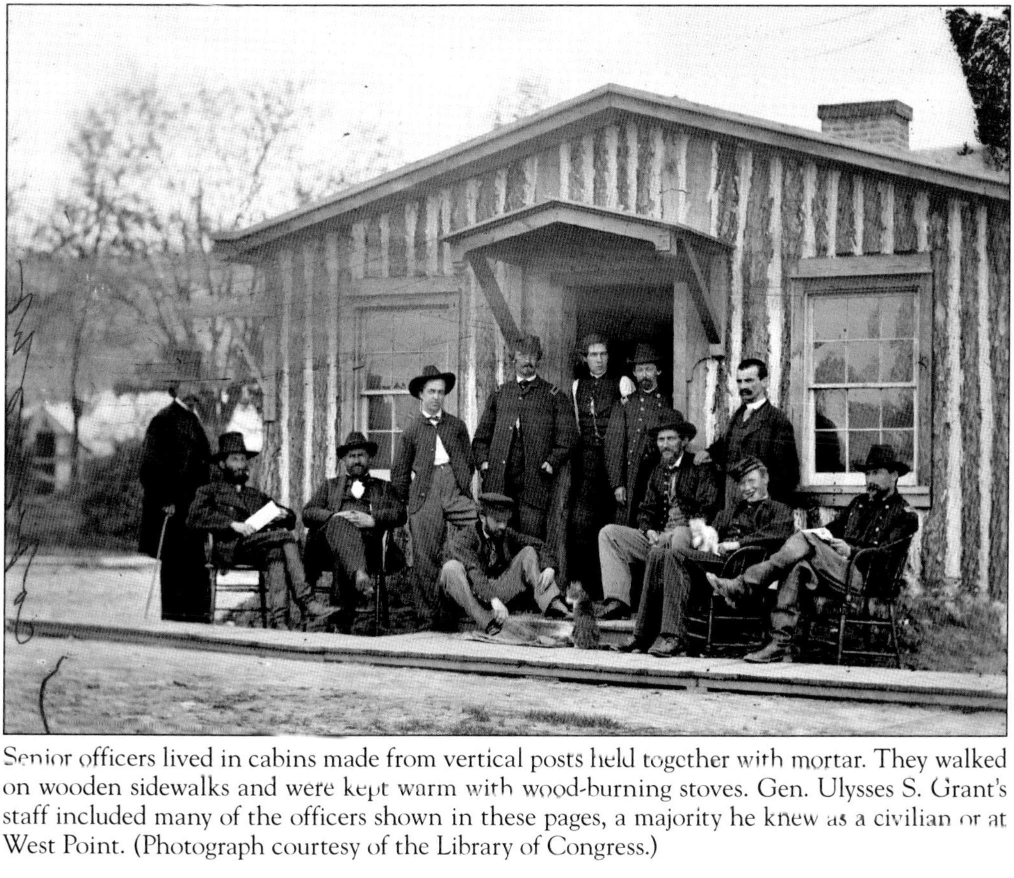

Senior officers lived in cabins made from vertical posts held together with mortar. They walked on wooden sidewalks and were kept warm with wood-burning stoves. Gen. Ulysses S. Grant's staff included many of the officers shown in these pages, a majority he knew as a civilian or at West Point. (Photograph courtesy of the Library of Congress.)

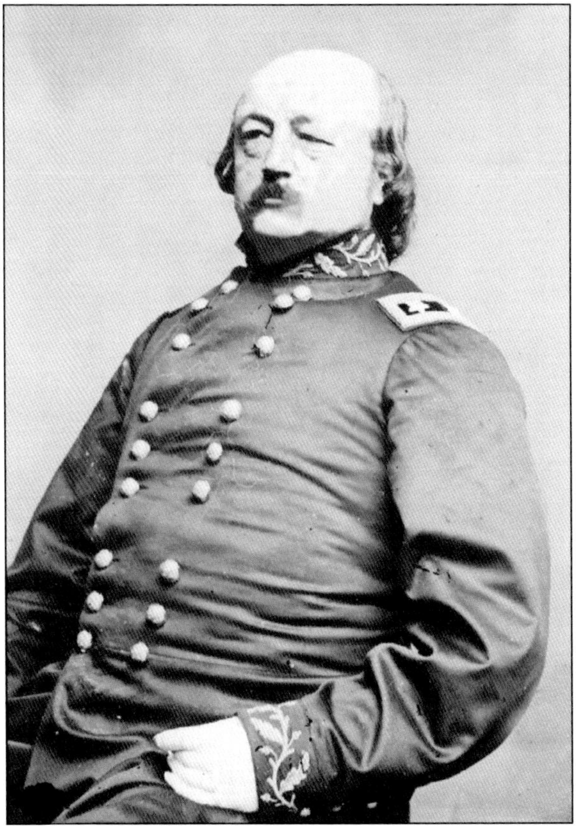

This photograph depicts Gen. Benjamin Butler, commander of the Army of the James (1818–1893). While Gen. Ulysses S. Grant commanded the Union army, Butler commanded the Army of James at City Point and was Grant's subordinate. In 1864, Butler commanded 18,000 troops assaulting Petersburg but was stymied by Confederate general Beauregard. At that time, he could not advance upriver any closer than Drewey's Bluff where even the famed USS *Monitor* could not pass. After the war, Butler was elected to the US House of Representatives and became the 33rd governor of Massachusetts. (Photograph courtesy of the Library of Congress.)

General Butler's staff is shown across the river from City Point. (Photograph courtesy of the Library of Congress.)

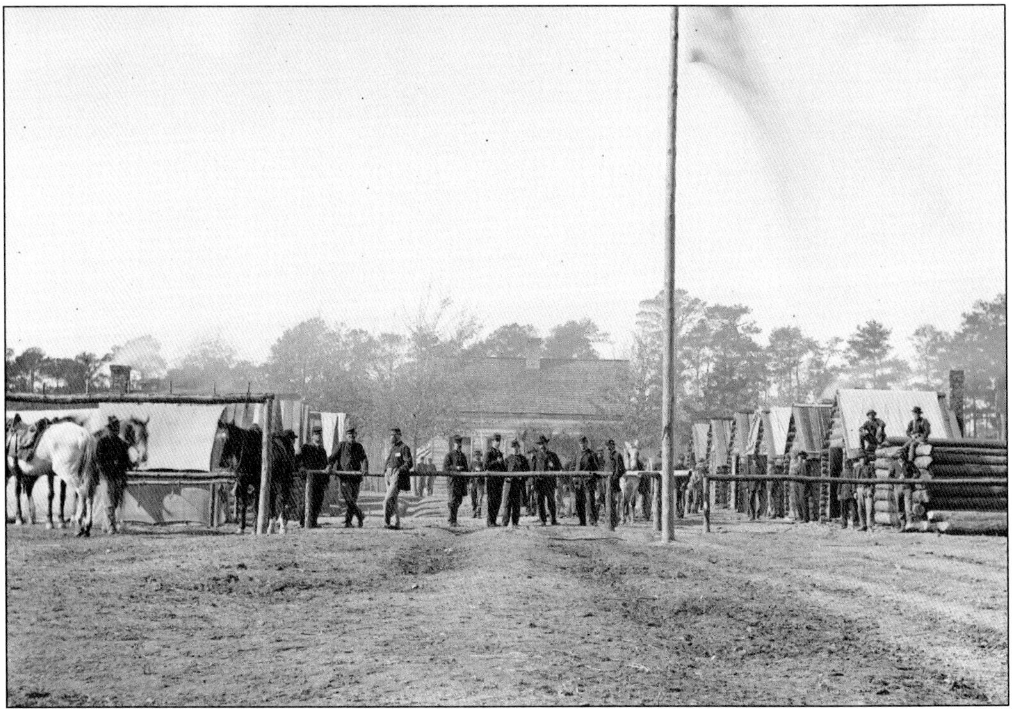

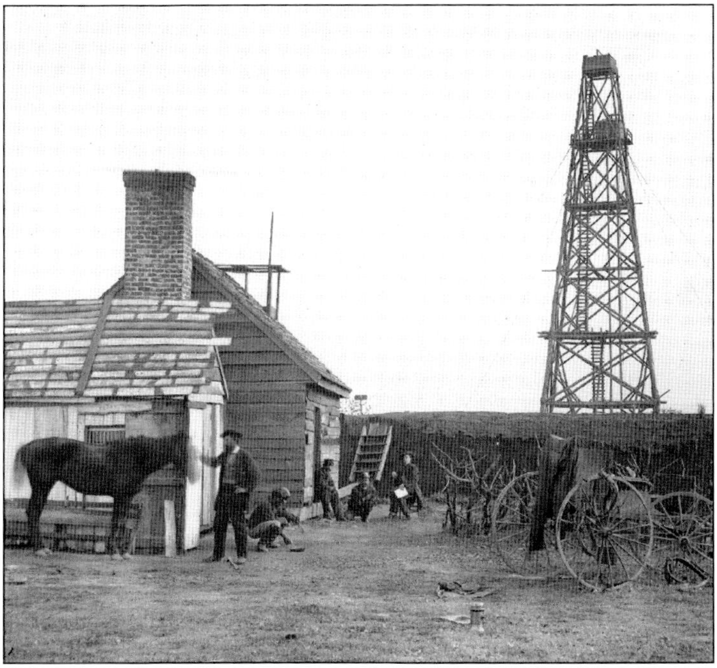

This signal tower was erected in the Bermuda Hundred section of the Appomattox (just across the river from Hopewell). Signal flags were waved to send messages from the towers. (Photograph courtesy of the Library of Congress.)

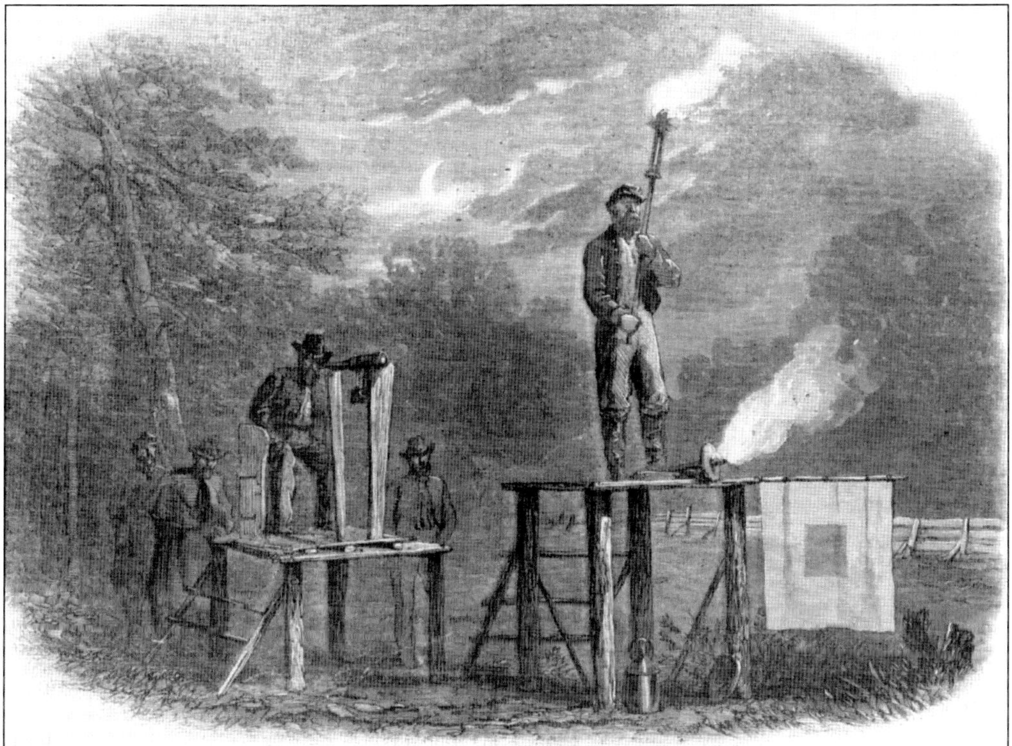

RMY OF THE JAMES—SIGNALING BY TORCHES ACROSS JAMES RIVER FROM GENERAL BUTLER'S HEAD-QUARTERS.—SKETCHED BY WILLIAM WAUD.—[SEE PAGE 734.]

General Butler's army used a variety of communications including telegraph and signal towers. Here, his army communicates the old-fashioned way—with signal fires. (Photograph courtesy of the Library of Congress.)

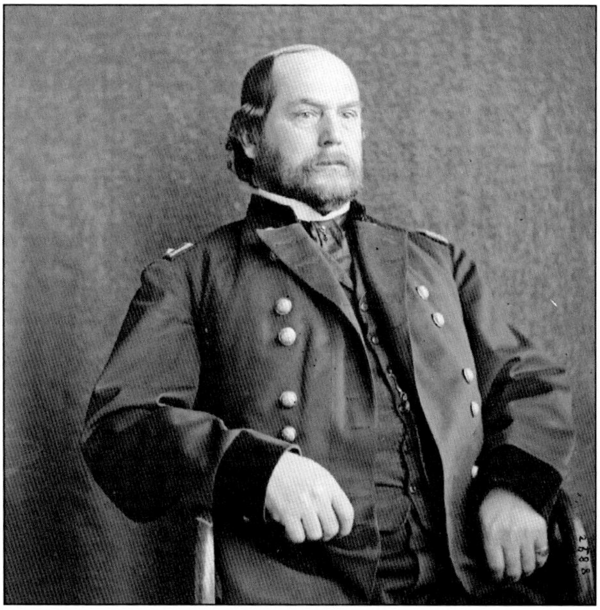

Gen. Rufus Ingalls, part of Grant's staff, built the depot at City Point. He entered West Point in 1839 where his plebe-year roommate was cadet Ulysses S. Grant. Upon graduation, Ingalls was posted to the Texas frontier. In 1848, he was appointed to the quartermaster department and sent to California for two years before that state entered the Union. He and Grant reunited in Fort Vancouver to help with Columbia River flood relief. Grant and Ingalls were together again in March 1864, when Ingalls served as Chief Quartermaster of the Army of the Potomac. (Photograph courtesy of the Library of Congress.)

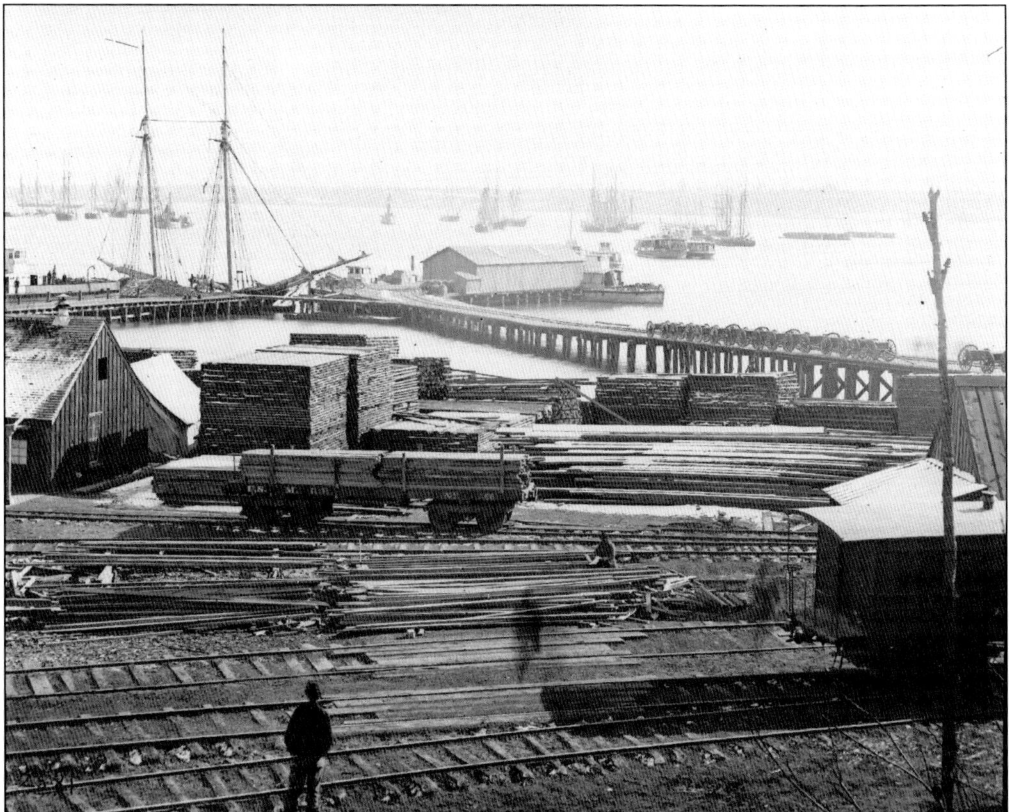

Part of Rufus's job was to outfit the army with weapons and powder. This photograph shows some barges designed for heavy hauling on a wharf built for munitions. Such barges played a role in the explosion described later in this book. (Photograph courtesy of the Library of Congress.)

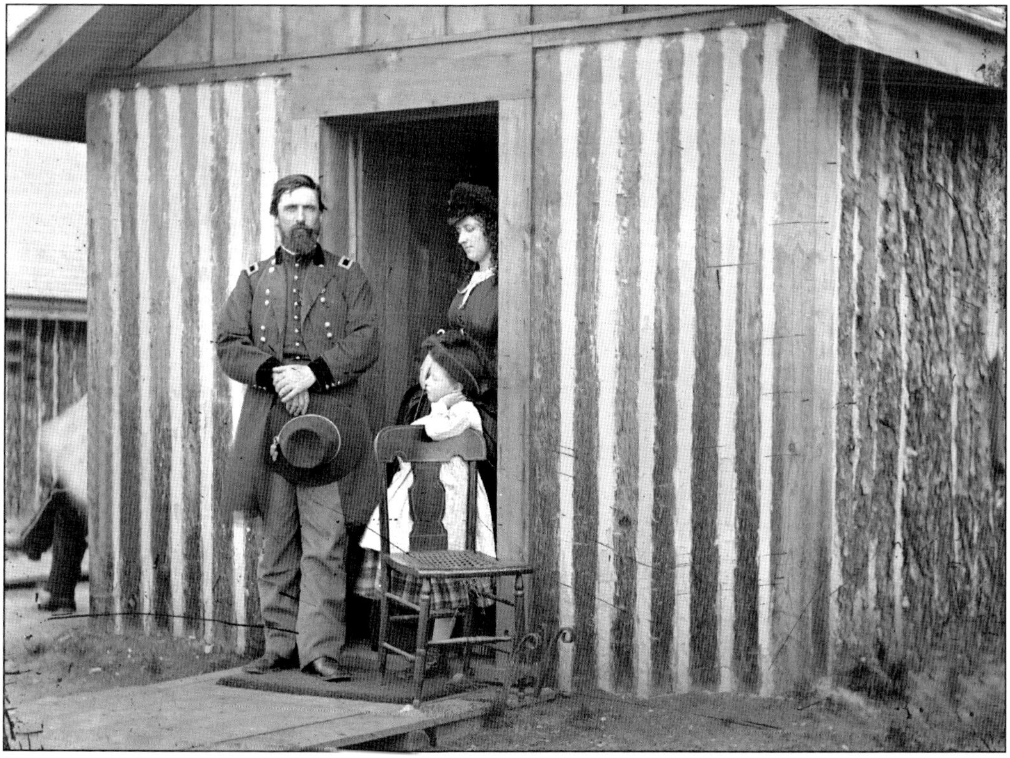

Brig. Gen. John Rawlins is shown with his family at City Point. Rawlins was among the other major Union leaders to gather at City Point. He and General Grant were longtime friends. They first met when Grant, the future commander in chief of the Army of the Potomac, was working in a leather goods store run by Rawlins's brother in Galena, Illinois. After the war, Grant appointed Rawlins his Secretary of War (www.arlingtoncemetery.net). (Photograph courtesy of the Library of Congress.)

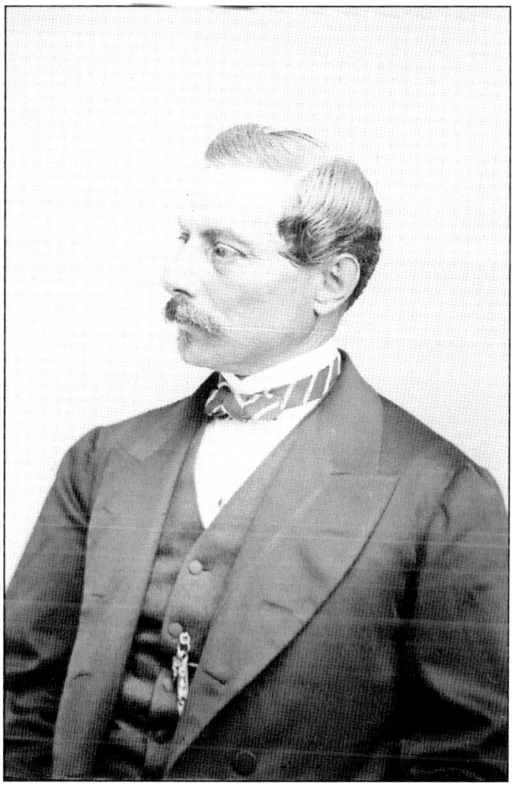

Commanding the Confederate forces in Petersburg was Gen. Butler's opposite, Gen. P.G.T. Beauregard, a Louisianan and Renaissance man. He was an inventor, writer, officer, and politician. Victorious at the First Battle of Bull Run (Manassas), he commanded troops at Shiloh and the Siege of Corinth in northern Mississippi. In Petersburg, he successfully thwarted Union assaults in that city during 1864. After the war, he became a railroad executive and leader in the Reform Party, which fought for the civil rights of freed slaves. (Photograph courtesy of the Library of Congress.)

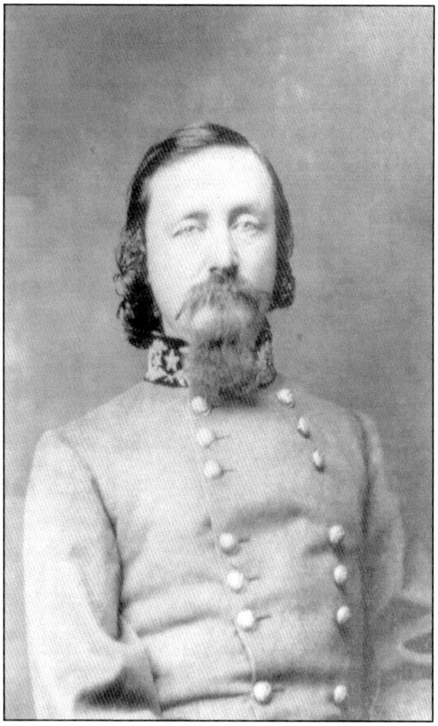

Whatever happened to Maj. Gen. George Pickett after Pickett's Charge? The famed major general was well known for his charge, along with North Carolinian General Pettigrew, at Gettysburg. Pickett was Beauregard's subordinate at Petersburg, commanding forces that guarded the South Side Railroad. (Photograph courtesy of the Library of Congress.)

What about the civilians at City Point? When the Union captured City Point, many fled their homes. This photograph shows civilians' abandoned buildings being recycled. The home and outbuildings are being used by the Union army to stable horses. (Photograph courtesy of the Library of Congress.)

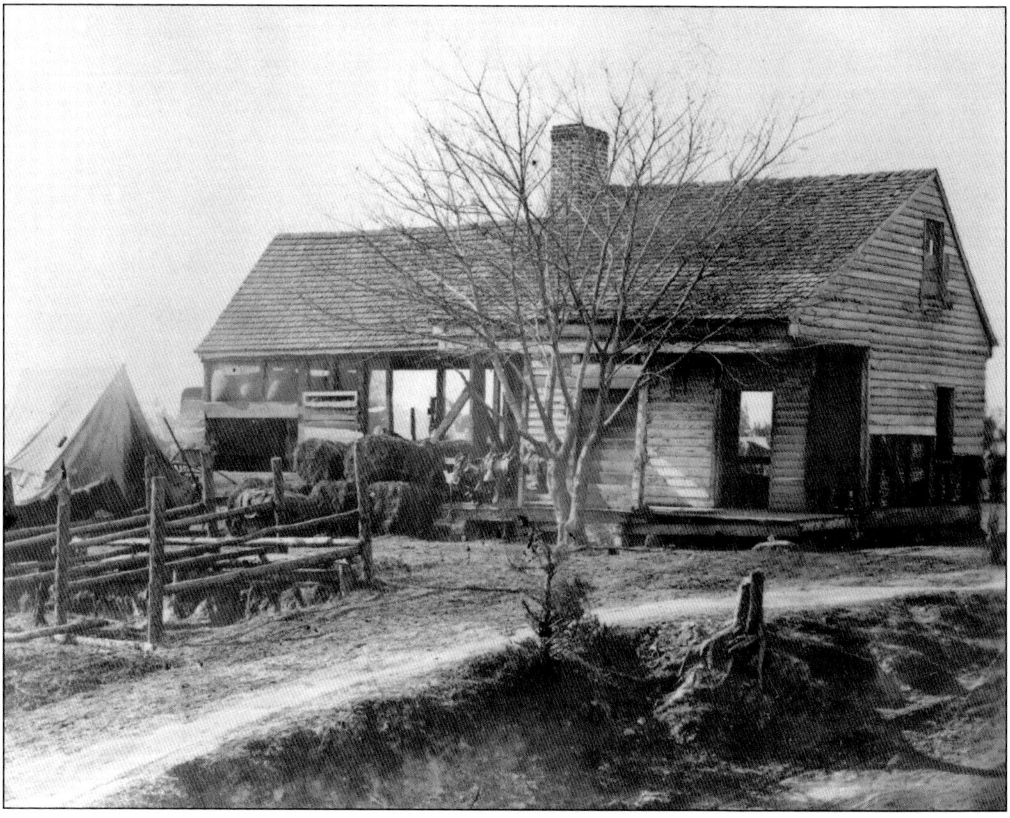

This drawing shows another reaction to Union troops. Some City Point civilians did not flee. Here, Union troops gather water as they are fired upon by City Point residents. The Union soldiers beat a hasty retreat. (Drawing by R. Waud; photograph courtesy of the Library of Congress.)

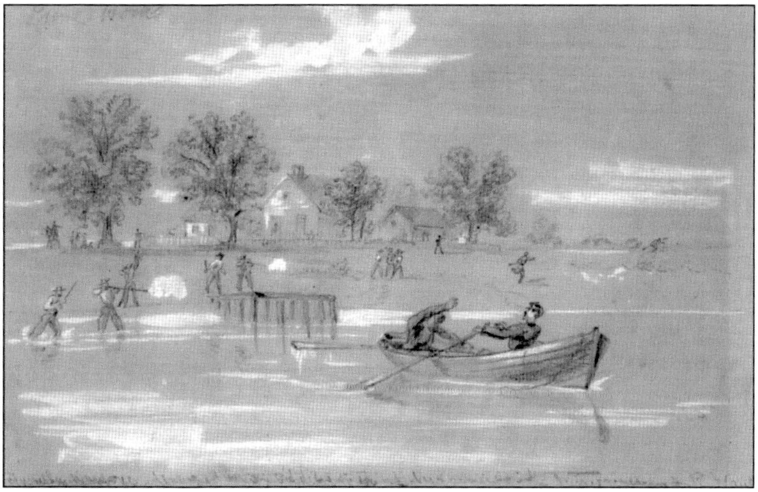

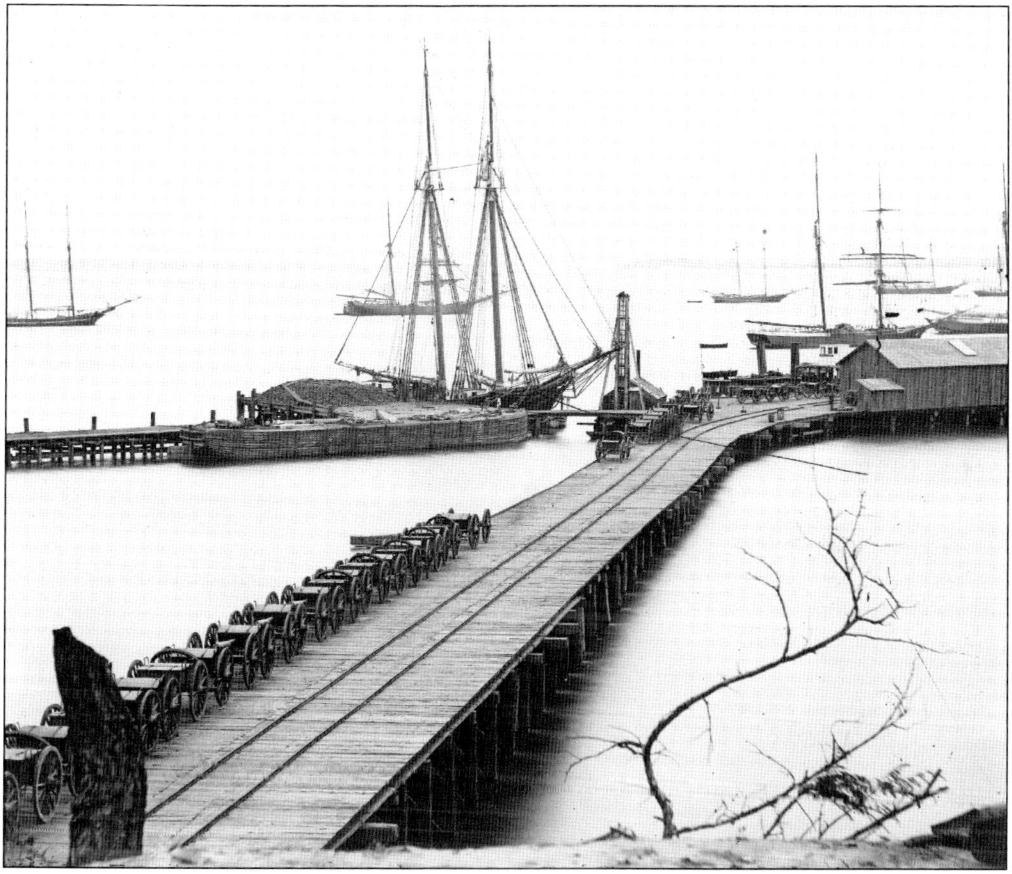

Lincoln had his death dream in the waters just off City Point. In the spring of 1865, he waited for war news west of Petersburg while aboard the *River Queen* off City Point. He had a dream in which he walked into the Capitol and heard weeping. He asked a soldier standing guard who had died? The soldier answered, "The President." A week later, Lincoln was assassinated. This picture of a schooner off City Point's artillery wharf evokes the scene of his dream. (Photograph courtesy of the Library of Congress.)

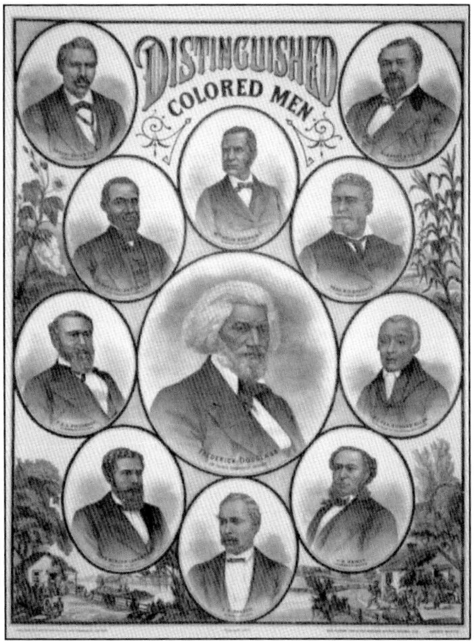

John Mercer Langston (1829–1897) is pictured at the lower left. He recruited soldiers for the US Colored Troops after that force was authorized by the Union in 1863. Many of these soldiers fought at City Point and Petersburg. Along with Confederate general William Mahone (who led troops at Petersburg), Langston went on to help lead the Readjuster Party. He also led Virginia State University and won a seat in Congress, becoming the first African American congressman from Virginia. The center photograph is of Frederick Douglass, the renowned reformer. (Photograph courtesy of the Library of Congress.)

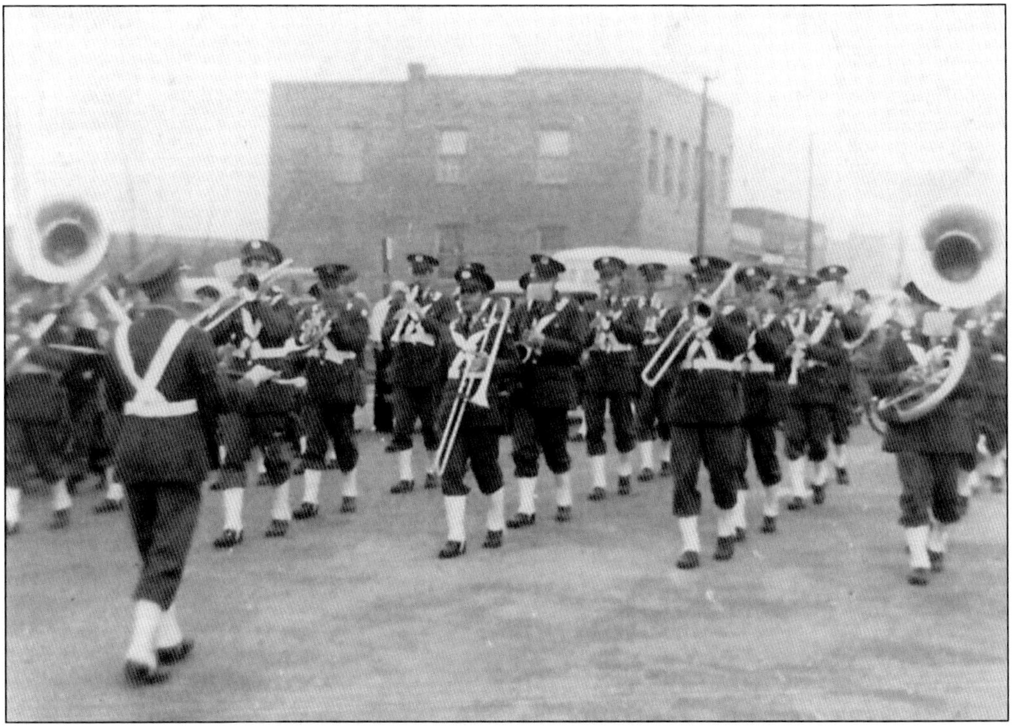

Fort Lee, formerly Camp Lee, has been and continues to be important to the people and the economic and social aspects of Hopewell. During World War I, Hopewell was an embarkation point for entry into Europe, and the base housed 65,000 troops at that time. After World War I, that number dropped severely, as did the population of Hopewell. But by 1952, the population of the base rose to 19,000. Fort Lee is now a major training base, which also houses the Quartermaster Museum and the Army Women's Museum. (Photograph courtesy of the Appomattox Regional Library.)

Typical of industrious, ingenuous, and poor but patriotic immigrants, Pasquale and Maria Basile are shown with children (from left to right) Lena, Jeff, Tony, and Mary (in front). Pasquale emigrated from Italy to the United States in 1907 and came to Hopewell in 1915 during the boom years. Pete, as people called him, became a prominent barber and opened a shop downtown. (Photograph courtesy of Millie Basile.)

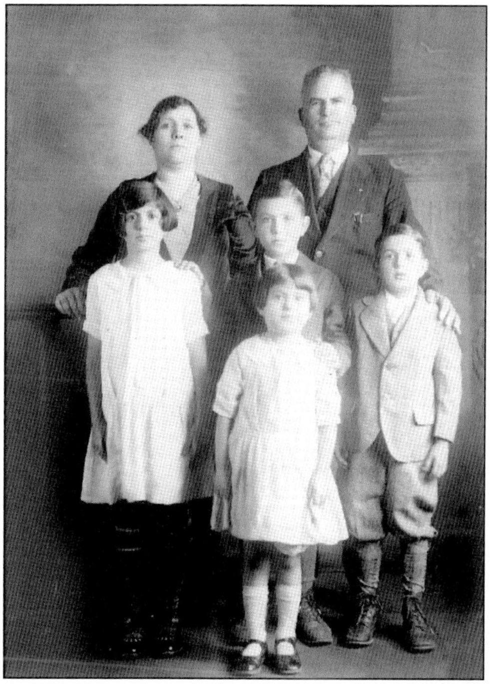

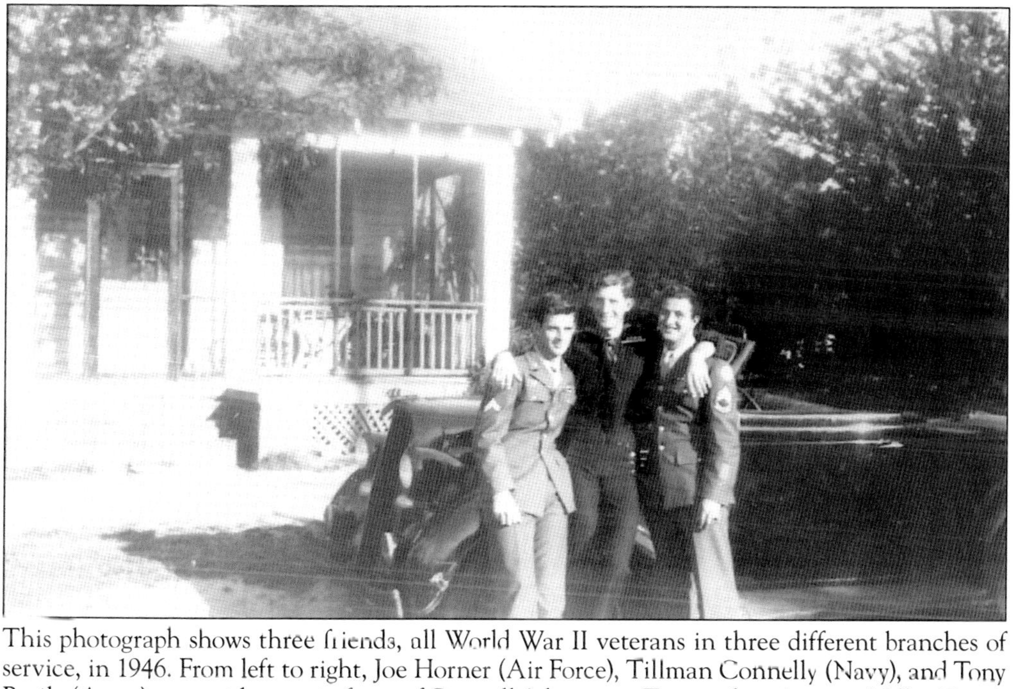

This photograph shows three friends, all World War II veterans in three different branches of service, in 1946. From left to right, Joe Horner (Air Force), Tillman Connelly (Navy), and Tony Basile (Army) pose with a car in front of Connelly's home on Twenty-first Avenue. Millie, Tony's future wife, and Tony used to ride in the car's rumble seat. Horner is said to have invented the flip-top openings on crush-proof cigarette boxes. Fame followed persistence and in the Pacific theater in World War II, many GIs from the Hopewell–Fort Lee area were surprised to see Tony's O.K. Barber Shop on the Pacific island of Guadalcanal. He cut the hair of servicemen there. (Photograph courtesy of Millie Basile.)

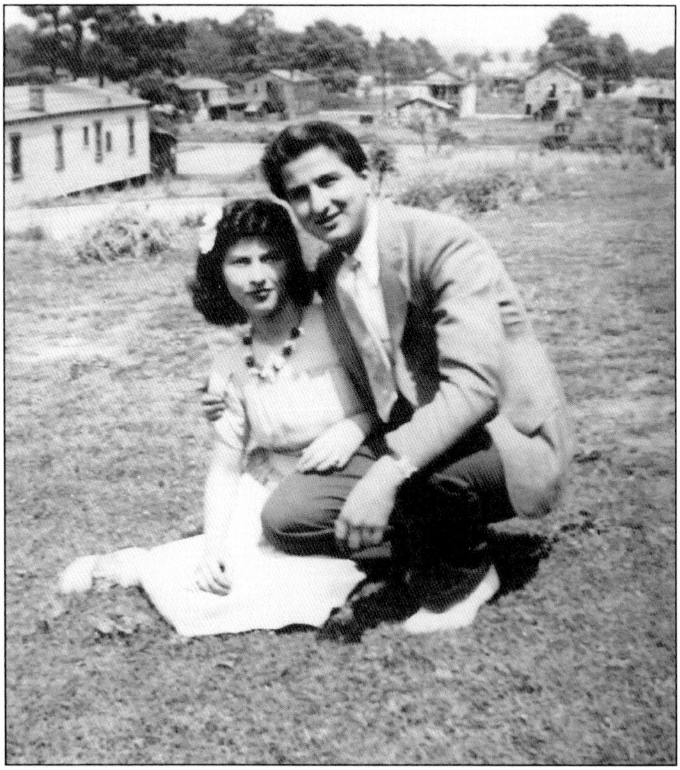

Tony Basile and his sister Mary are shown in 1941. Tony, son of immigrant barber Pete Basile, followed in his father's footsteps and became a barber. (Photograph courtesy of Millie Basile.)

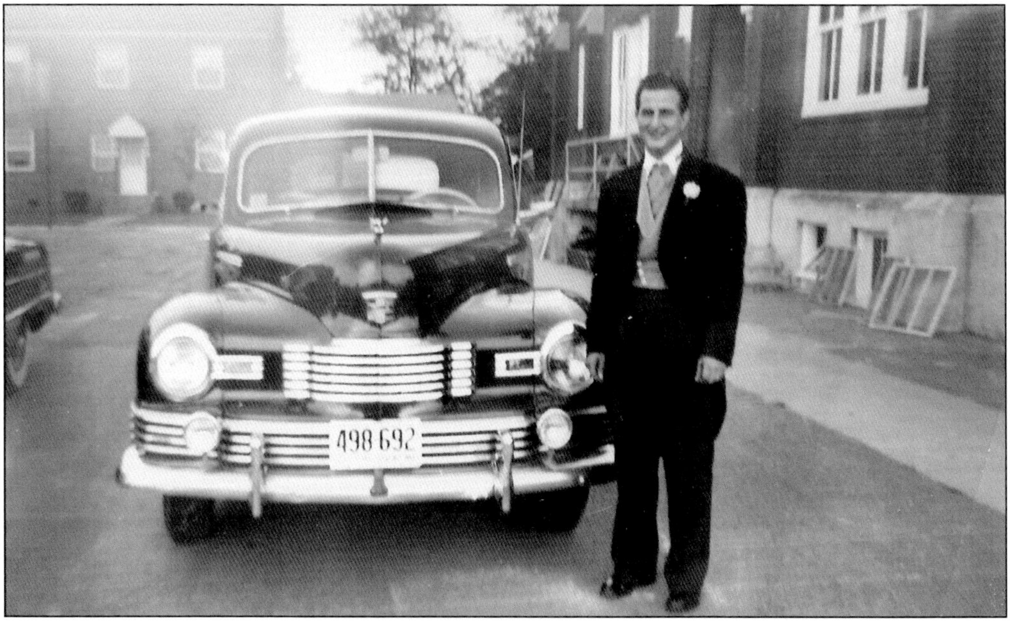

Tony Basile and his car are photographed in front of St. James Roman Catholic Church around 1954. Basile picked up his father's trade as a barber the old-fashioned way—by learning at his father's feet (actually his elbow). His apprenticeship did not last long; Basile was cutting hair by the time he was 10 years old. He and Millie became prominent residents in Hopewell. (Photograph courtesy of Millie Basile.)

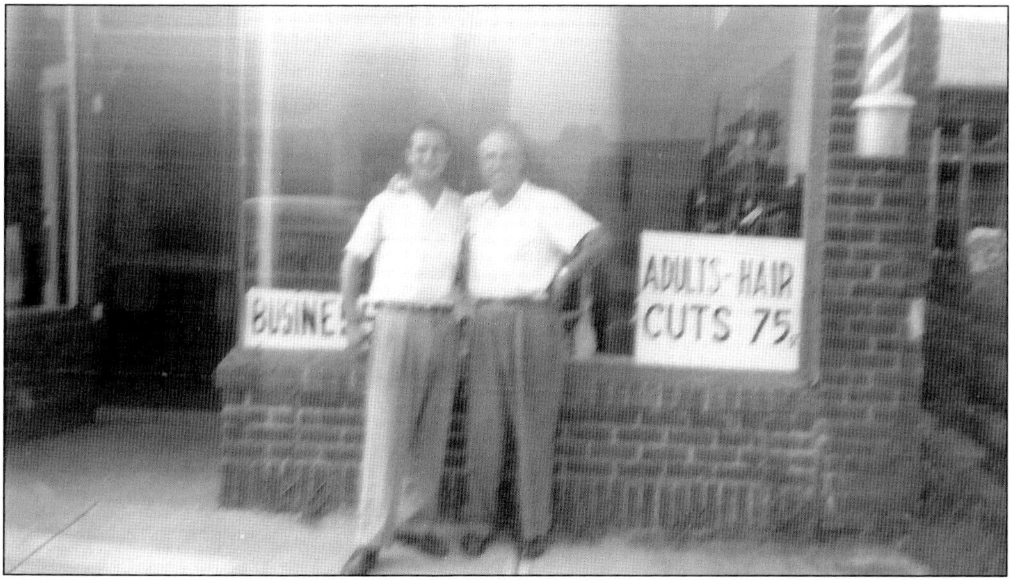

Pictured are Tony Basile and his cousin Frankie around 1955 in front of Basile's barbershop at 909 City Point Road. Basile operated barbershops on Main Street, City Point Road, and later from his home at 2208 Grant Street. (Photograph courtesy of Millie Basile.)

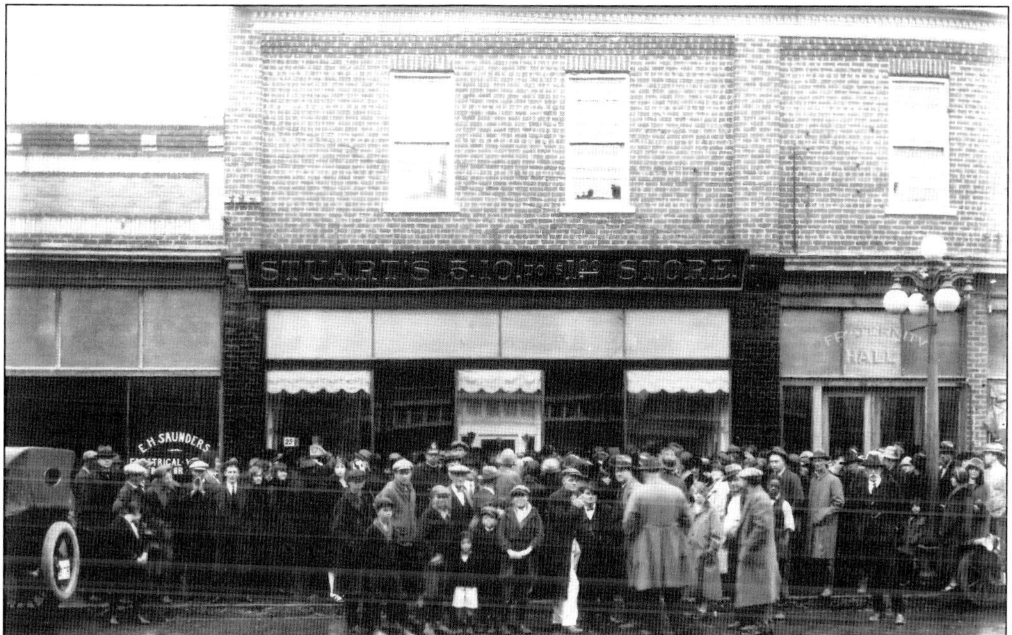

In this photograph, taken before the end of World War I, immigrants line up in front of Stuart's store to learn English at the fraternity hall. To the left is the E.H. Saunders electrical store, which still does business in Hopewell. (Photograph courtesy of Jack Daniel.)

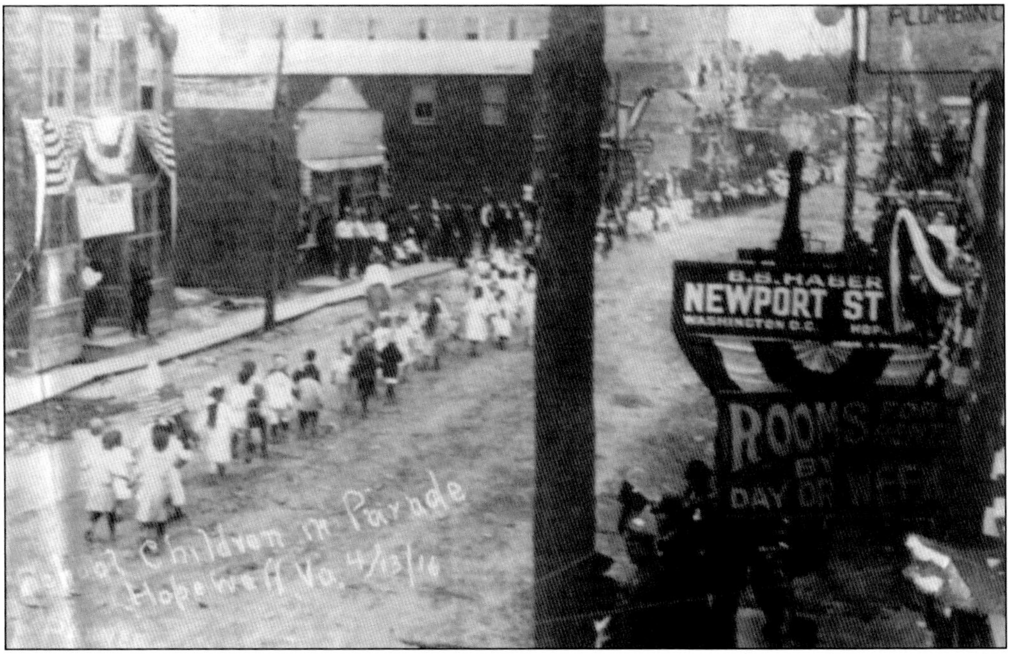

In this 1916 photograph, young people walk in a parade. Children have played prominent roles in Hopewell, including caring for the area. Hopewell began one of the first state Police-Fire Boys Clubs, and 250 mothers once collected $2,000 in a single hour for the March of Dimes. By 1952, about one-quarter of all church members were children. (Photograph courtesy of the Appomattox Regional Library.)

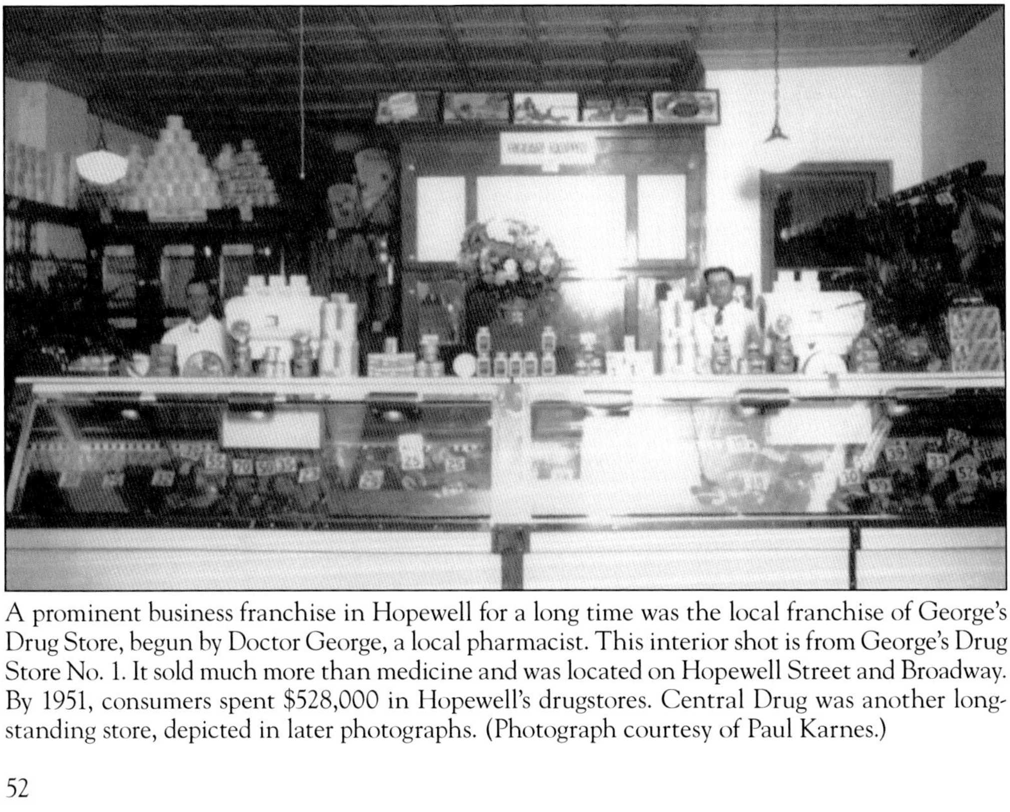

A prominent business franchise in Hopewell for a long time was the local franchise of George's Drug Store, begun by Doctor George, a local pharmacist. This interior shot is from George's Drug Store No. 1. It sold much more than medicine and was located on Hopewell Street and Broadway. By 1951, consumers spent $528,000 in Hopewell's drugstores. Central Drug was another long-standing store, depicted in later photographs. (Photograph courtesy of Paul Karnes.)

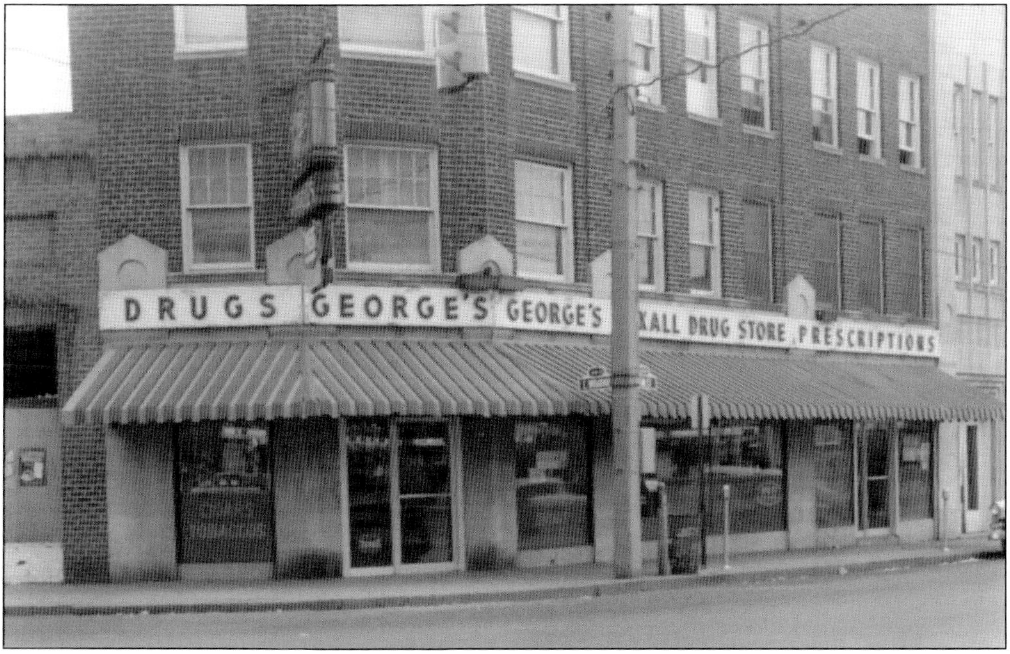

This is George's Drug Store No. 2. This second store was located on Main Street and Broadway. These photographs were taken in the days when telephone numbers had only four digits. Store No. 1's number was 2370, and Store No. 2 could be reached by dialing 5676. (Photograph courtesy of Jack Daniel.)

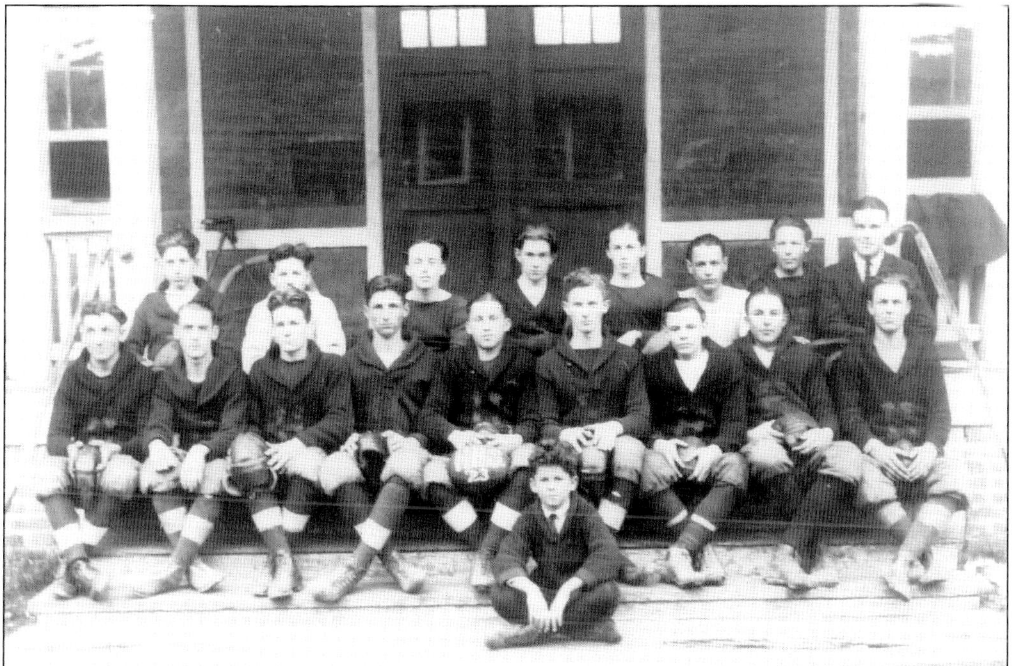

According to the *2009 Hopewell Public Schools Alumni Directory*, Hopewell football began to compete interscholastically in 1923. Pictured is that team. The equipment is quite different from what is used today. (Photograph courtesy of the Appomattox Regional Library.)

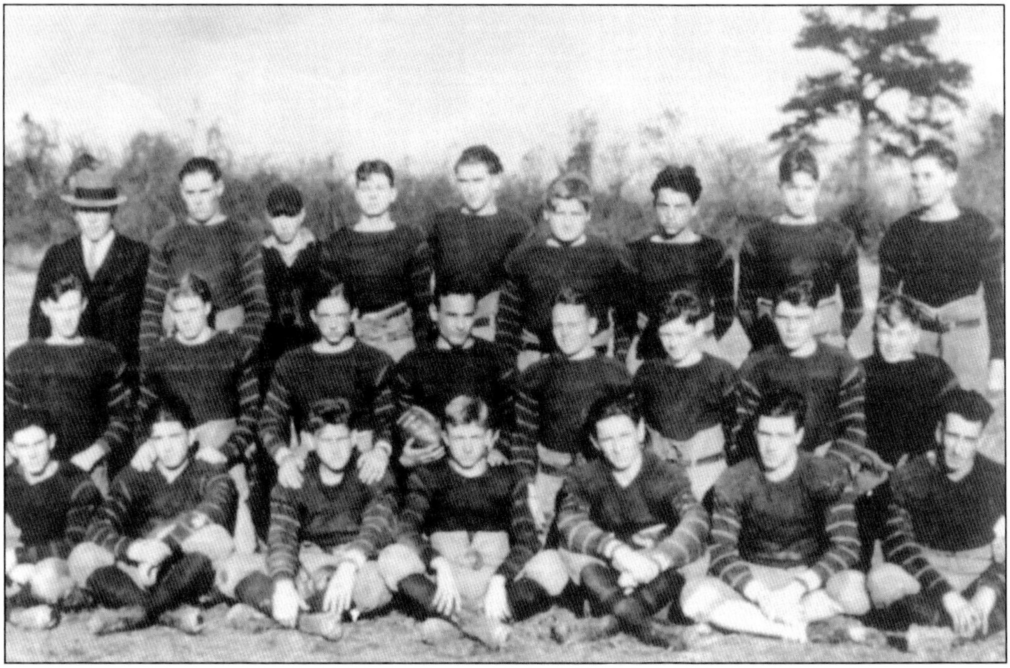

The 1927 football team is pictured. In the late 1940s, a farsighted Hopewell High School coach began the Hopewell Quarterback Club, which sponsored football teams in lower grades. This gave instruction and experience to the youth, affording stronger teams by the time they reached high school. The legacy of this early preparation consistently produces some of the best teams in the state. (Photograph courtesy of the Appomattox Regional Library.)

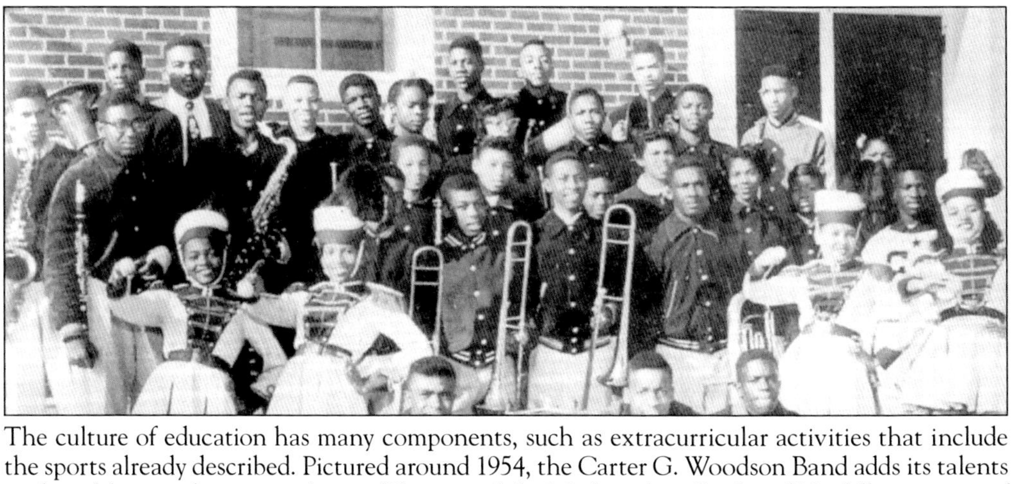

The culture of education has many components, such as extracurricular activities that include the sports already described. Pictured around 1954, the Carter G. Woodson Band adds its talents to the athletic and artistic cultures. (Photograph by Modern Arts Studio of Norfolk, courtesy of Juanita Chambers.)

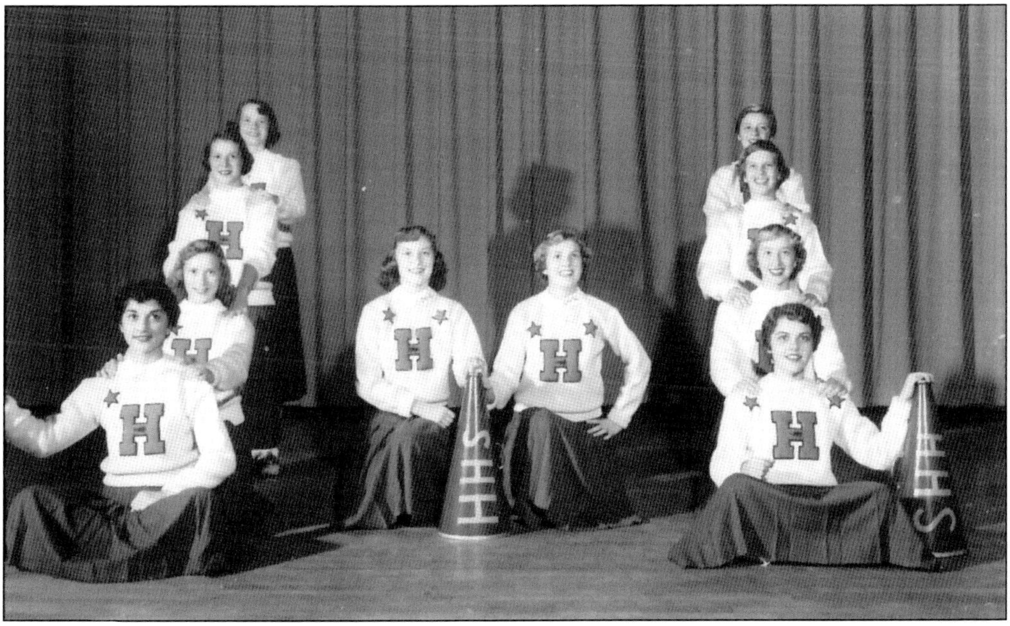

Women have always played an important role in high school extracurricular activities, including their own teams in basketball as early as 1923, softball in 1935, and field hockey in 1946. Here, the cheerleading squad continues the tradition in 1956. (Photograph courtesy of Hopewell Public Schools.)

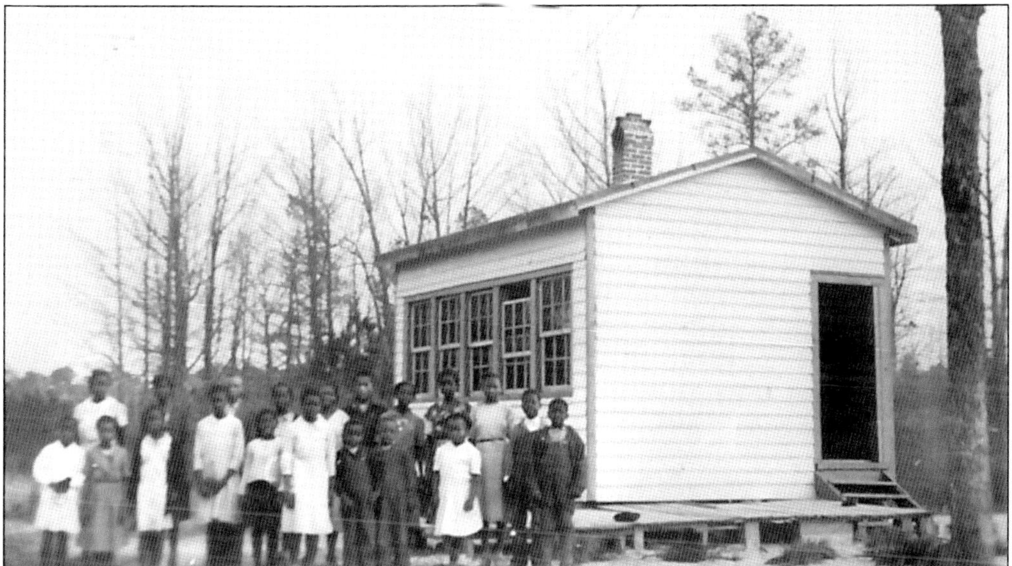

In the era of racial segregation, African Americans were educated in separate facilities. Here, a class of African American students gathers outside an unnamed school. According to the 2009 *Hopewell Public Schools Alumni Directory*, formal education of African Americans can be dated to 1916 when DuPont organized training so that African Americans could sign their names on paychecks. The local YMCA building was first used. Eventually, DuPont chose a location behind what is now fire station No. 1 on Station Street to build a school, which taught students through the eighth grade. (Photograph courtesy of Hopewell Public Schools.)

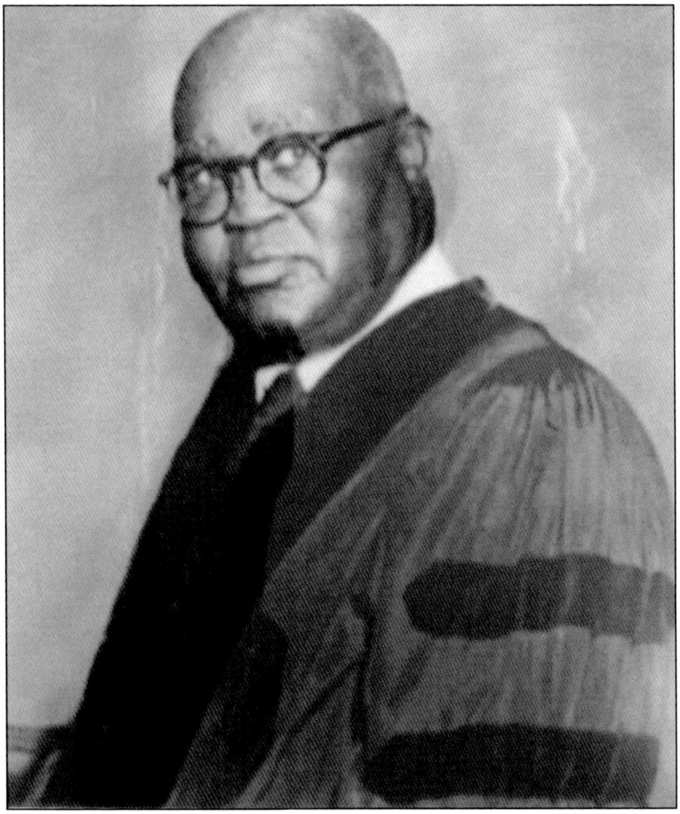

Rev. Samuel Perry was the instructor at the Carter G. Woodson School's earlier location, now designated fire station No. 1. This school offered instruction through the eighth grade and had an enrollment of around 80. (Photograph courtesy of Juanita Chambers.)

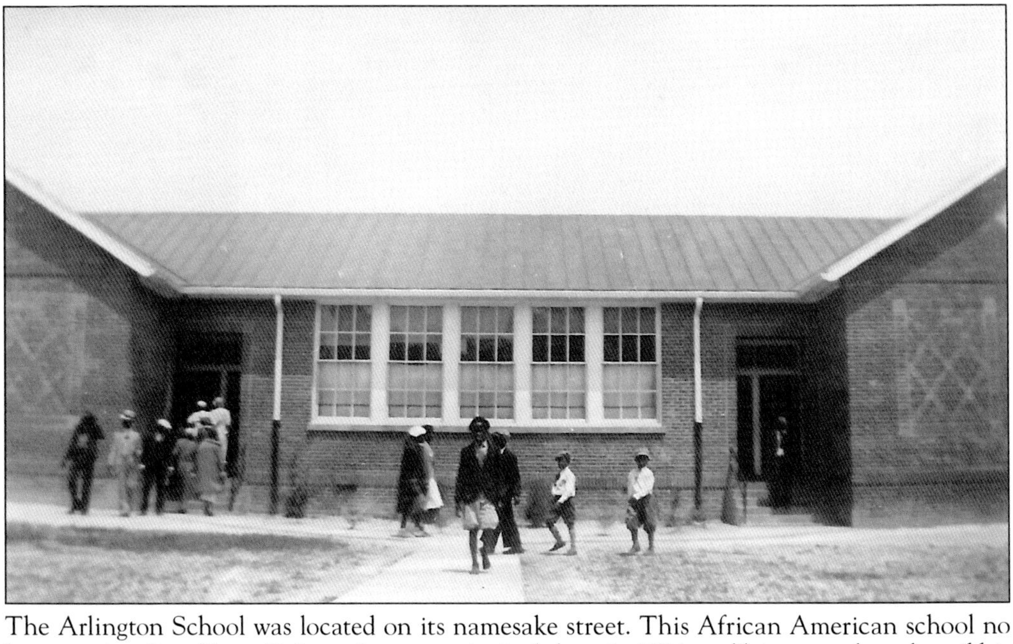

The Arlington School was located on its namesake street. This African American school no longer exists. Rev. Harry E. James became principal there in 1924, and his tenure lasted until his retirement in 1946. He passed away one year after he retired. (Photograph courtesy of Hopewell Public Schools.)

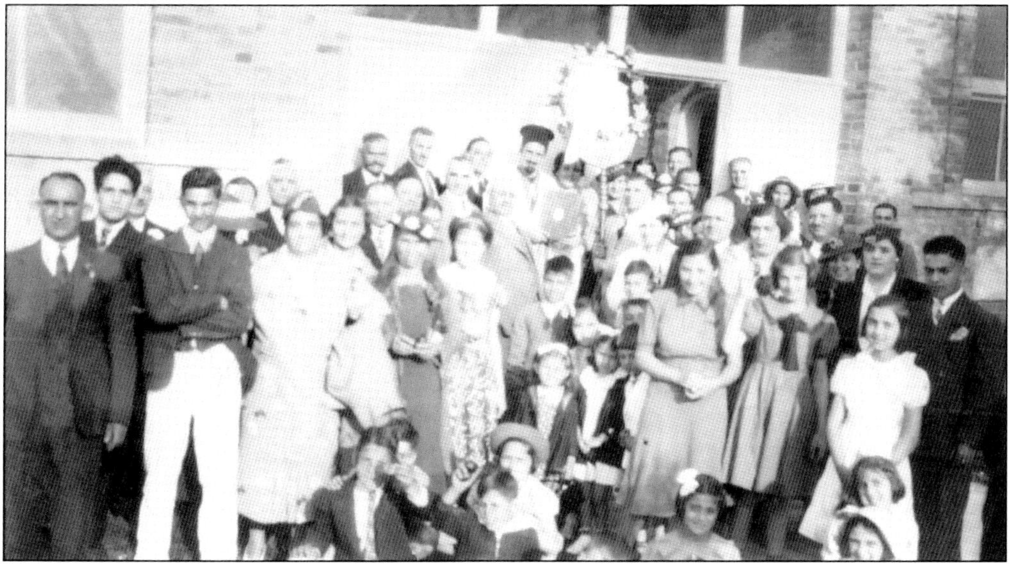

The Greek community nurtured both its spiritual and cultural heritage. It formed the American Hellenistic Educational and Progressive Association to foster Greek cultural heritage, including dances, festivals, and memorializing Greek Independence Day. The Greek Festival is still celebrated and open to the public. Given the profusion of flowers on the standard (to the right of the clergy) and the colored eggs that several of the young people are holding, this photograph must have been taken during an Easter celebration at the original St. Elpis Greek Orthodox Church. The smiling boy at the front center is clutching one of the eggs, which were dyed red. (Information courtesy of Homer Eliades; photograph courtesy of the Appomattox Regional Library.)

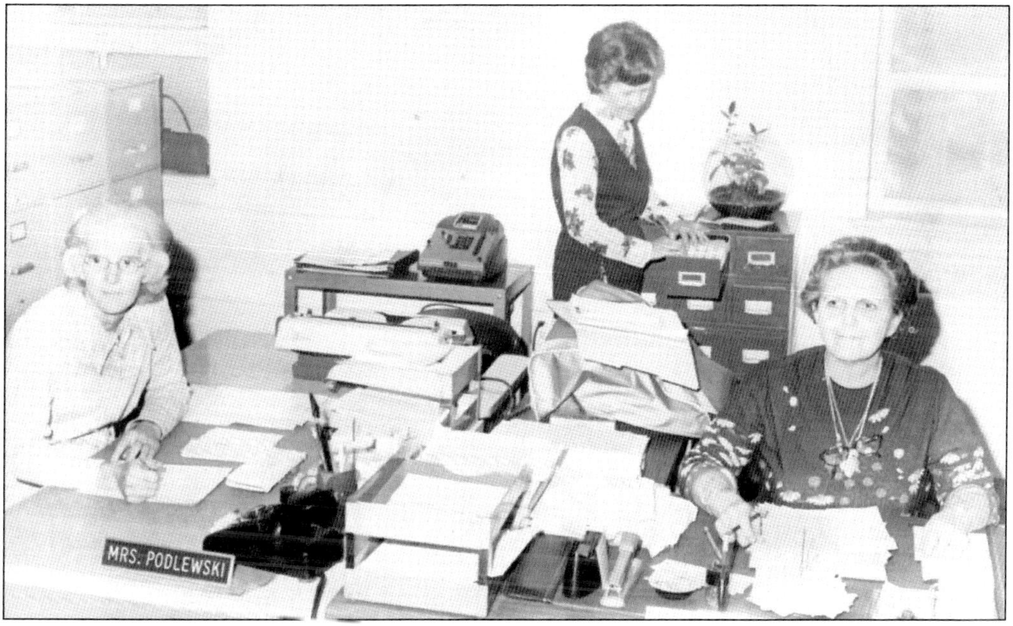

It takes more than teachers and administrators to run a school. In this photograph, from left to right, are Marie Podlewski, Doris Hughes, and Ellen Gill, who worked in the school system for 20 years. Gill's husband, Roland, is noted elsewhere in this book. (Photograph courtesy of Hopewell Public Schools.)

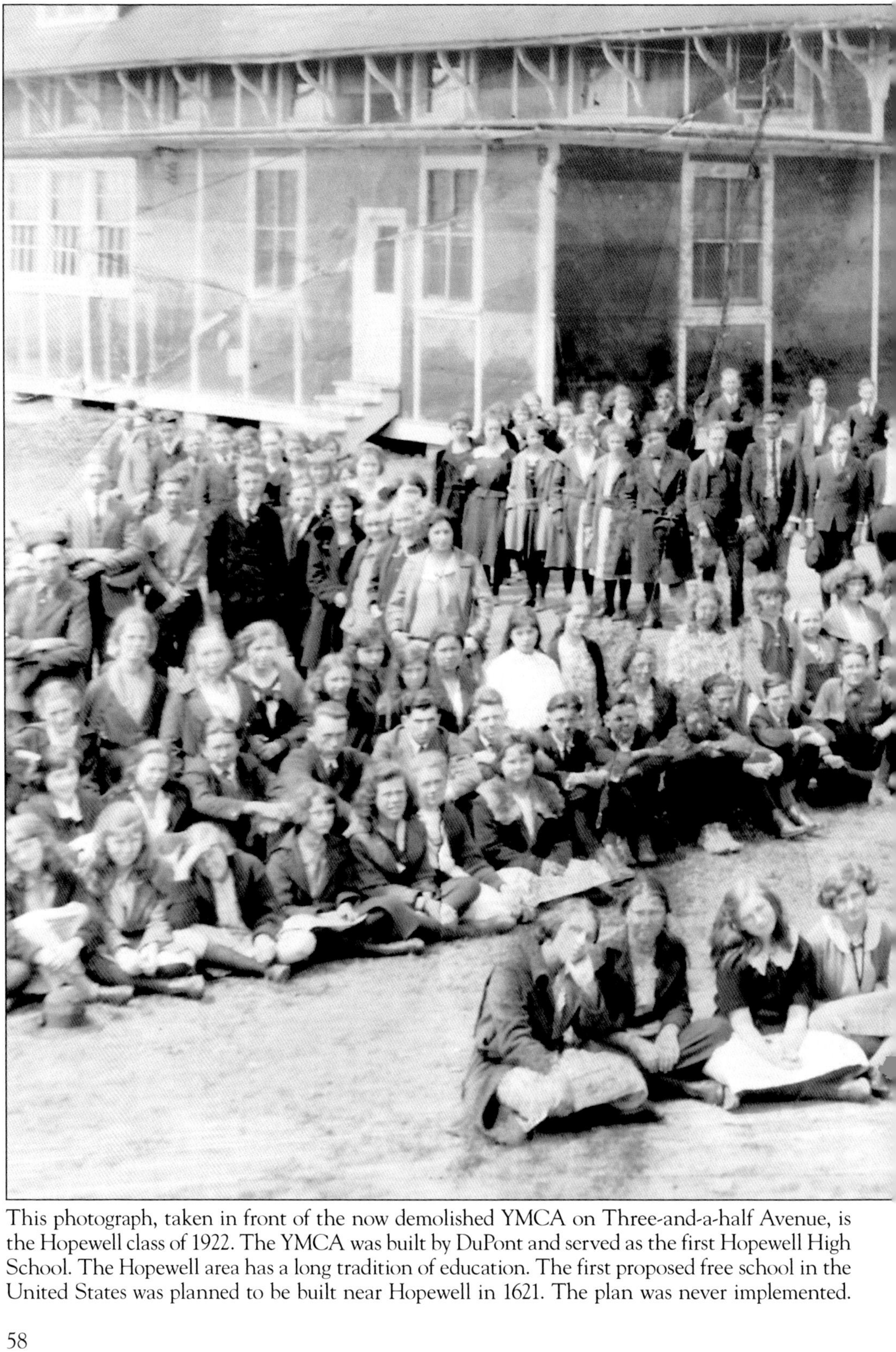

This photograph, taken in front of the now demolished YMCA on Three-and-a-half Avenue, is the Hopewell class of 1922. The YMCA was built by DuPont and served as the first Hopewell High School. The Hopewell area has a long tradition of education. The first proposed free school in the United States was planned to be built near Hopewell in 1621. The plan was never implemented.

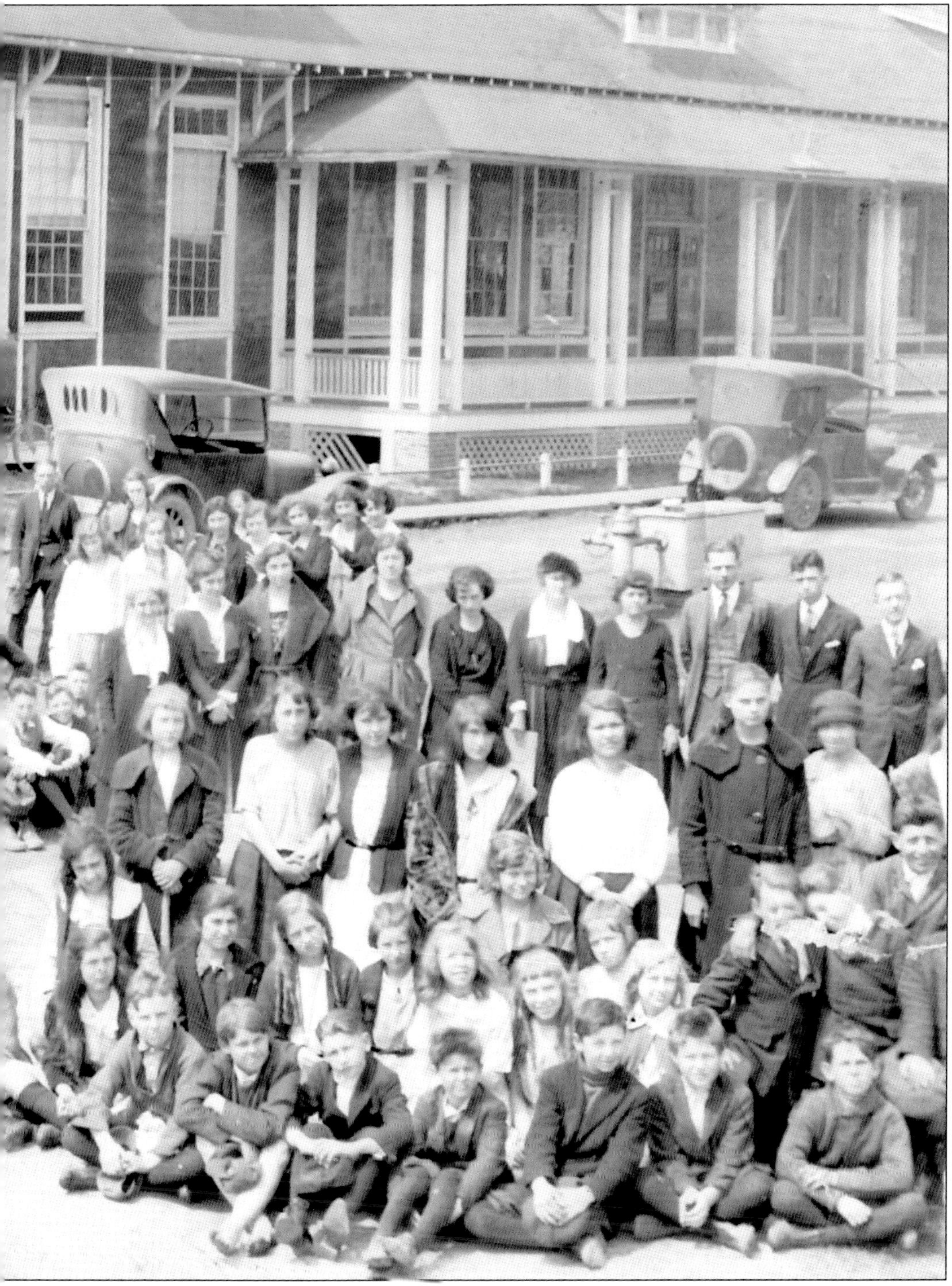

Rev. Patrick Copeland was the headmaster, and a later Hopewell school was named after him. Since the early days, students have taken a hands-on approach to their education and school life. As early as 1928, a student government was formed and in the year 2000, the school began its literary publication, the *Paragon*. (Photograph courtesy of the Hopewell Public Schools.)

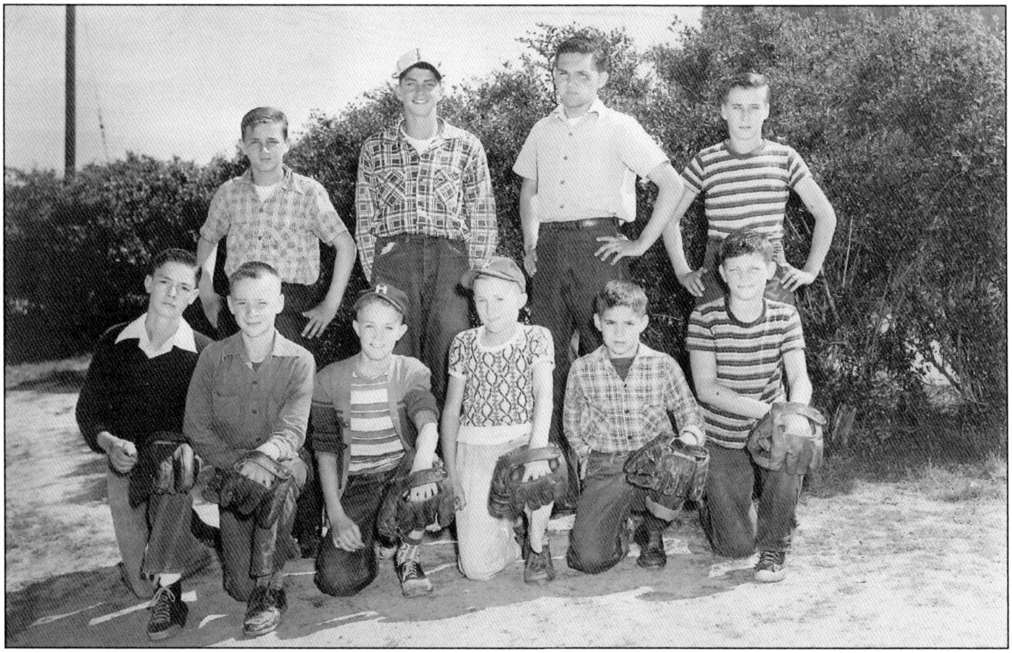

This is a group portrait of the DuPont School Baseball Club. These young men formed an informal group and played at the local school. They include a young man who later played professional baseball for the Philadelphia Phillies. (Photograph courtesy of Paul Karnes.)

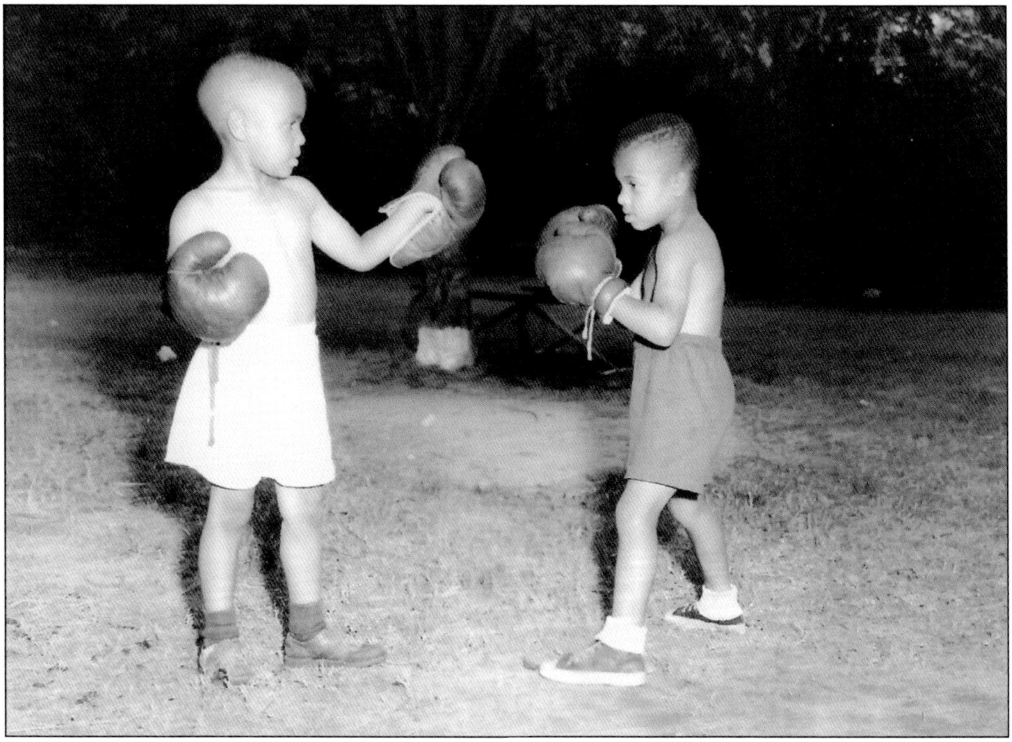

Young boxers practice their pugilistic skills, probably in one of the local parks. (Photograph courtesy of Jack Daniel and the *Hopewell News*.)

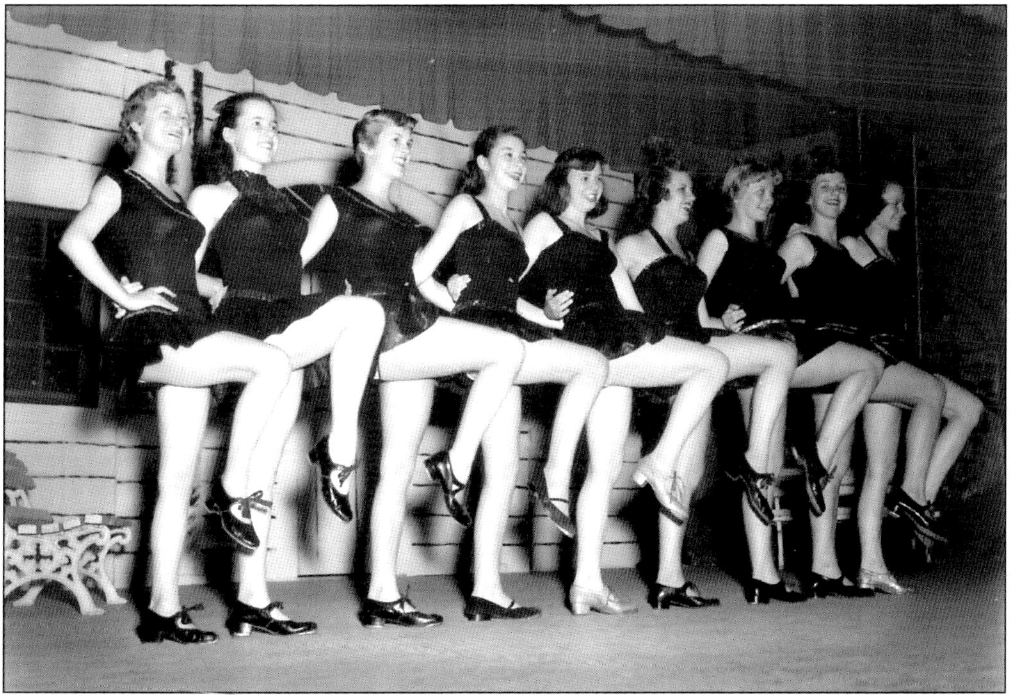

High school students kick up their heels in a dramatic production around 1955. (Photograph courtesy of Jack Daniel and the *Hopewell News*.)

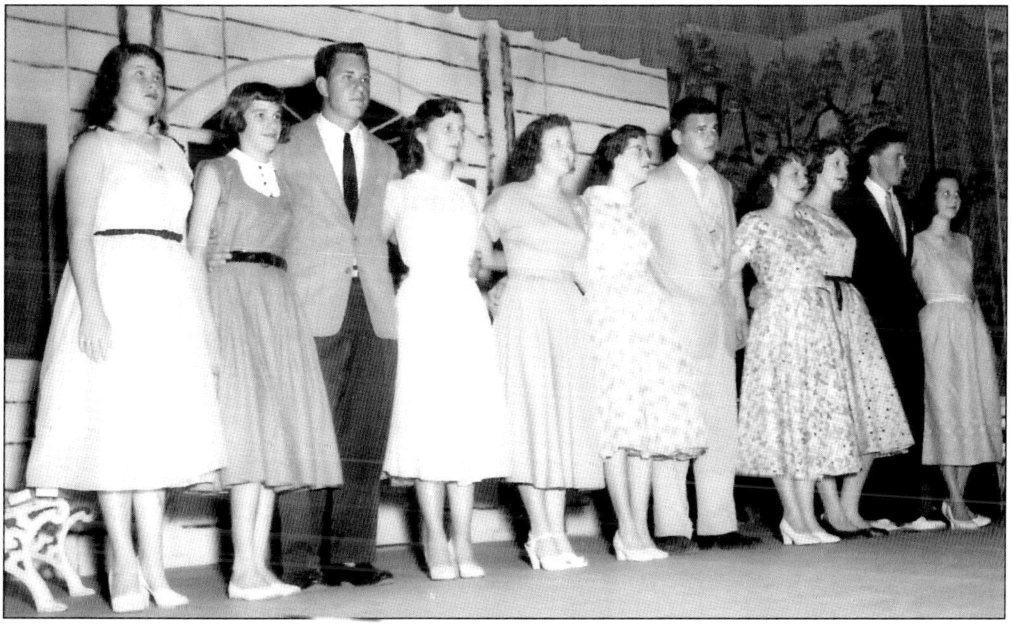

High school students stage a dramatic production during the 1954–1955 school year. The set looks the same for the production in the previous photograph. Note the metal and wooden bench (lower left) in both photographs.This promised to be quite a play. Jack Daniel, a major contributor to this book, is fifth from right. (Photograph courtesy of Jack Daniel and the *Hopewell News*.)

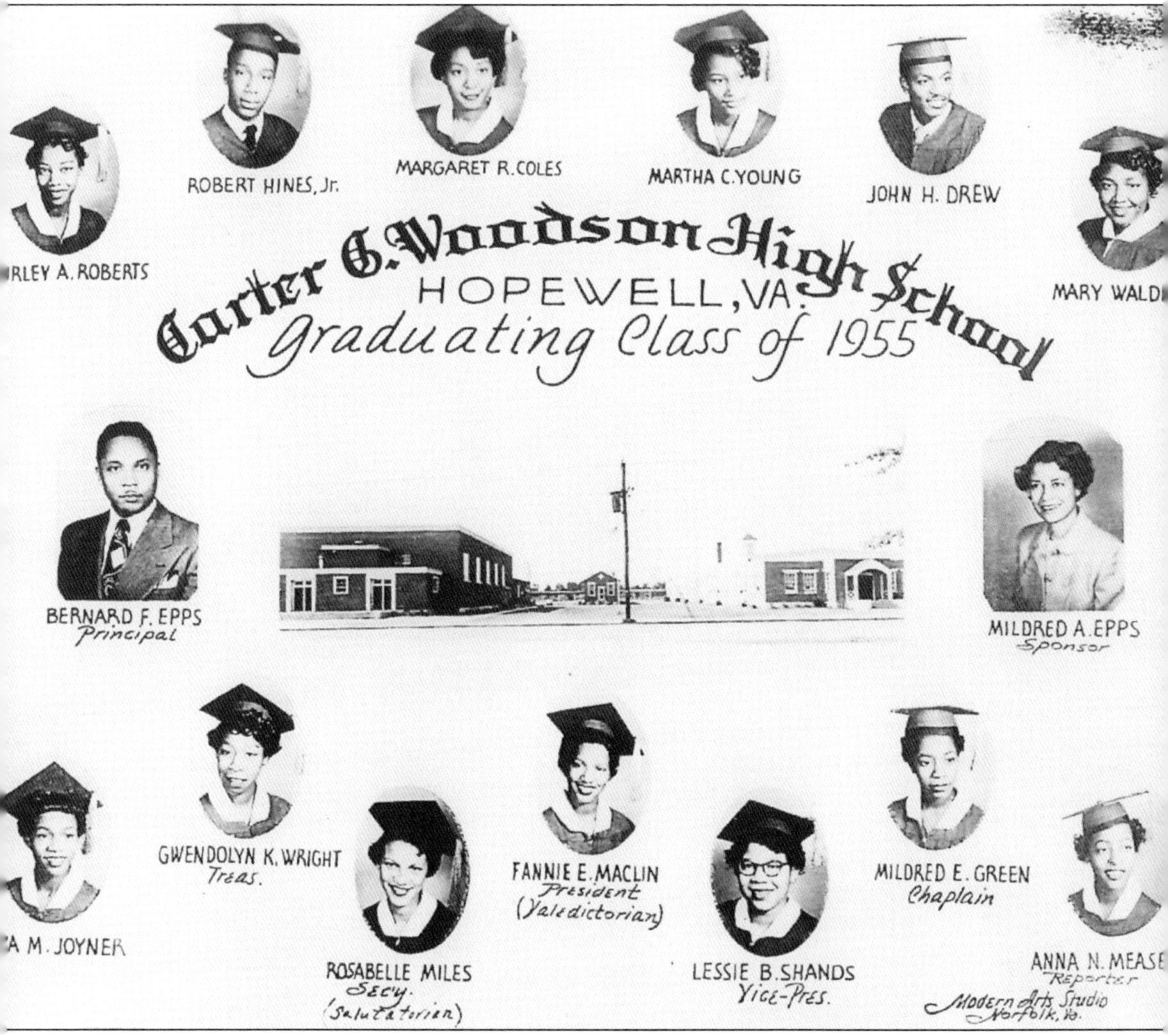

The Carter G. Woodson School class of 1955 is shown in the yearbook. Bernard Epps was the principal that year. This photograph shows the school discussed earlier. In this graduating class of 13, Mildred Epps served as the sponsor with Fannie Maclin as president and valedictorian and Lessie Shanks as the vice president. Rosabelle Miles was honored as the secretary and salutatorian, Gwendolyn Wright was the treasurer, and Anna Mease was the class reporter. The class chaplain was Mildred Green. Epps's tenure as Carter G. Woodson School's principal ran from 1946 through 1971. At the beginning of his tenure, the school had a student enrollment of 351, seven elementary teachers, and four high school teachers. There were 13 members of this graduating class, and as educational integration occurred in the 1960s, the final all–African American graduating class for Carter G. Woodson was in 1968. (Photography by Modern Arts Studio of Norfolk, courtesy of Juanita Chambers.)

The marbles champion was Robert Howard, shown in about 1950. He later became an Eagle Scout and a commander in the US Navy. His father worked in human resources for the Hercules Powder Company in Hopewell. (Photograph courtesy of Paul Karnes.)

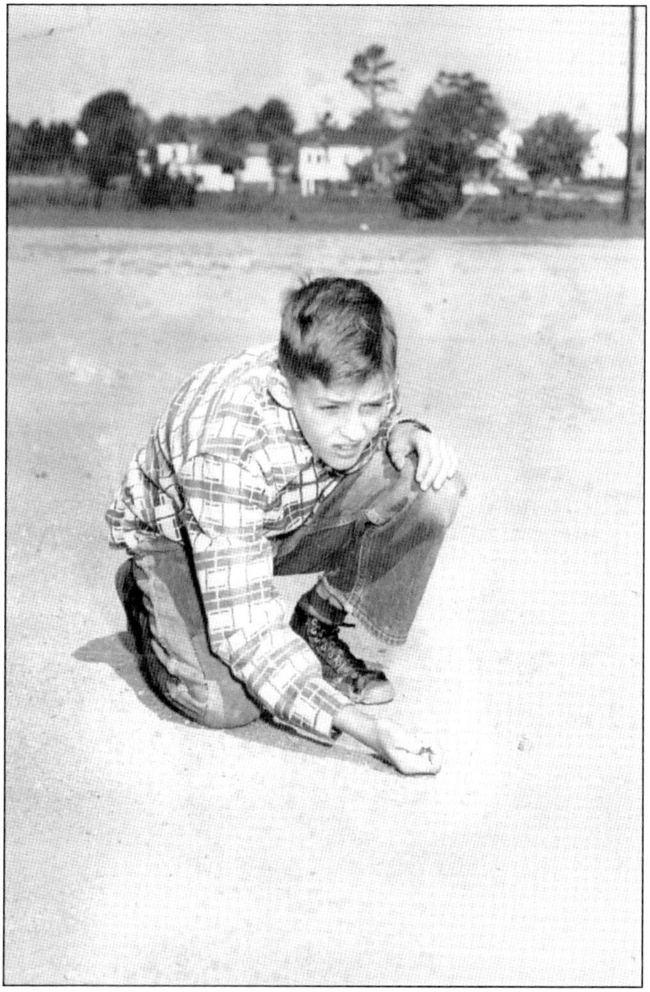

Young people have fun no matter the weather extremes in Hopewell. Around the time this local swimming pool was photographed (1951–1952), almost 4,000 young people used it. (Photograph courtesy of Jack Daniel and the *Hopewell News*.)

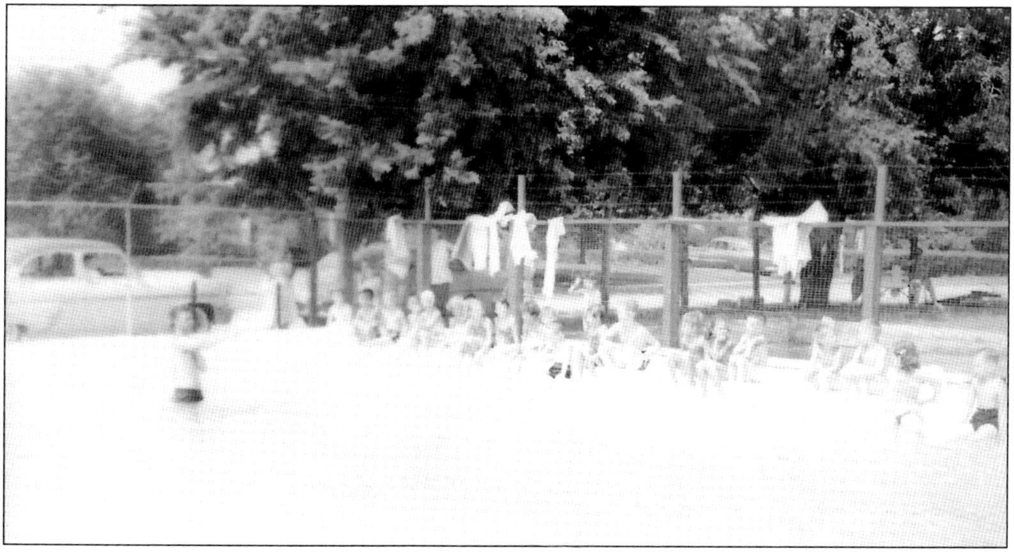

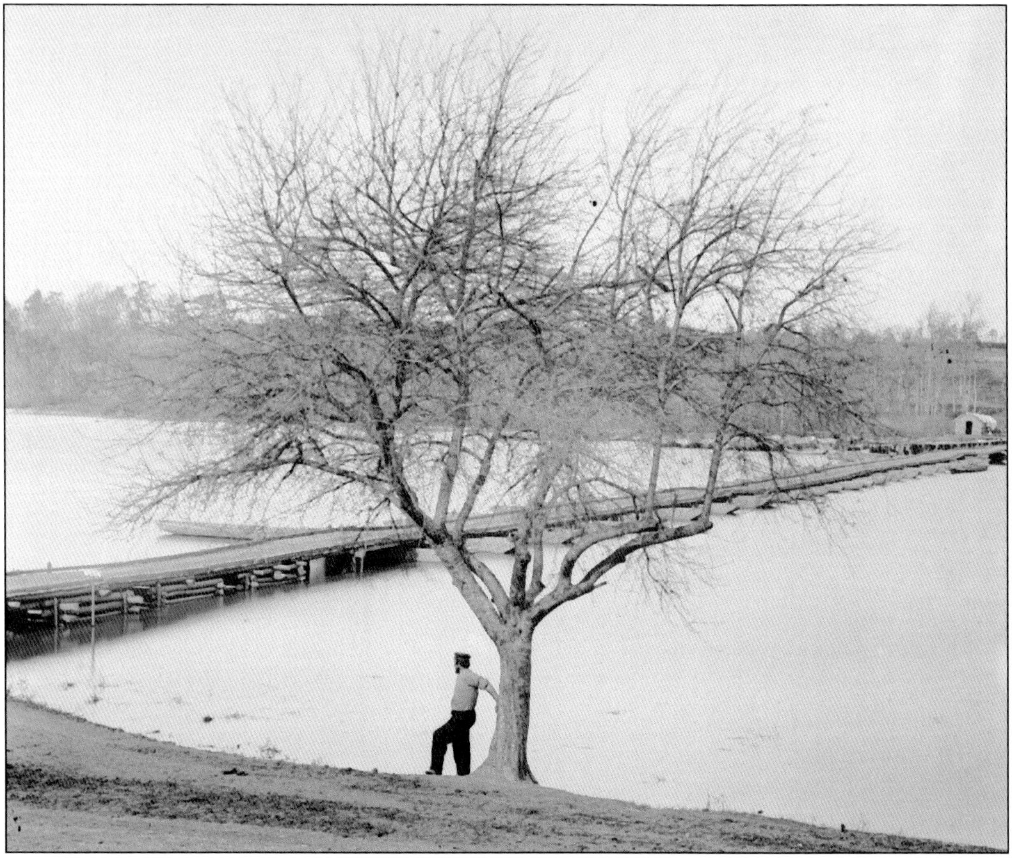

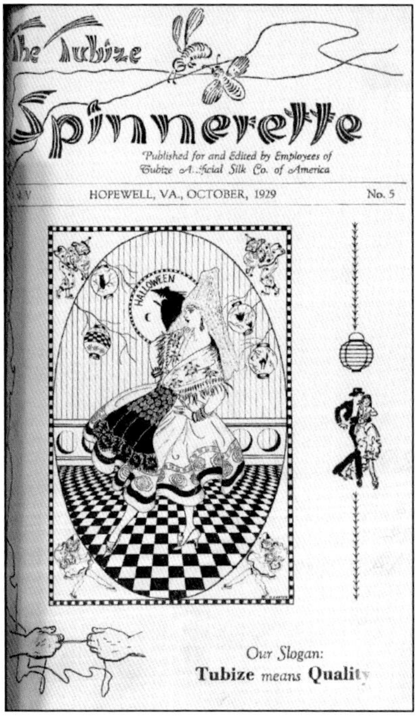

Hopewell is a place for recreation and free association, even in incongruous situations. This man seems to be enjoying his ease, even during wartime. Taken around the time of the Siege of Petersburg, this photograph shows the pontoon bridges that crossed the Appomattox. The composition of the photograph, with the focus upon the lone man leaning against the solitary tree, suggests not so much an engineer scrutinizing the pontoons, but the creative process of an artist or inventor. (Photograph courtesy of the Library of Congress.)

A whimsical—even magical—rendering of an image connected to Hopewell is illustrated by this fanciful cover of the 1929 Halloween issue of the Tubize *Spinnerette*. Complete with a witch, bat, and owl, this cover evinces a playful, yet elegant picture of Halloween and those who celebrate it. A couple apparently dressed for a rumba or waltz adds to the graceful, sophisticated air of the cover illustration. This company magazine was published from 1925 to 1934. (Magazine courtesy of Appomattox Regional Library.)

Three

PRODUCTS AND IMAGINATION

Hopewell's products include both items and ideas. Products are more than things. They arise from imagination and determination. Even before history was written, Hopewell's inhabitants adapted the environment just as they adapted to it. The Native Americans around Hopewell adapted to and adopted from this land. They scraped canoes from logs with nothing more than fire and shells. They strategically burned forestland to increase crop productivity and enriched their diet by adopting squash, corn, and beans from other lands. The English settlers adopted the local use of tobacco into a major economy and cultural activity. English entrepreneurs adopted City Point's harbor and riverbanks into tobacco terminals. During the Civil War, the Union Secret Service at City Point translated information into tactical advantage. General Grant developed the tactical use of City Point's harbor, spy-driven information, and the disciplined use of railroads to achieve a strategic victory. Later, US chemists and entrepreneurs from DuPont created massive industries and transportation networks at Hopewell–City Point. Later, Tubize Artificial Silk Company created fine artificial silk from chemicals. Other industries came, including an attempt in the late 1800s at a sturgeon packing plant and a fine china manufacturing plant.

The military has continued to have a strong presence in Hopewell. In 1912, the E.I. DuPont de Nemours and Company built a dynamite plant on 800 acres at City Point and enlarged the plant in 1914 to supply guncotton, an ingredient in smokeless powder during World War I. Fort Lee (formerly Camp Lee) swelled and dipped in population during and after wartime and is currently a major military base.

People invest themselves in a place, and a place invests itself in the people. Both are changed in that process. The following photographs show how Hopewell's products included information, military intelligence, religious and spiritual inspiration, goods, immigration, education, and values. A place impacts people and products, just as people and products impact a place. Images, in turn, capture attitudes, imaginations, and aspirations.

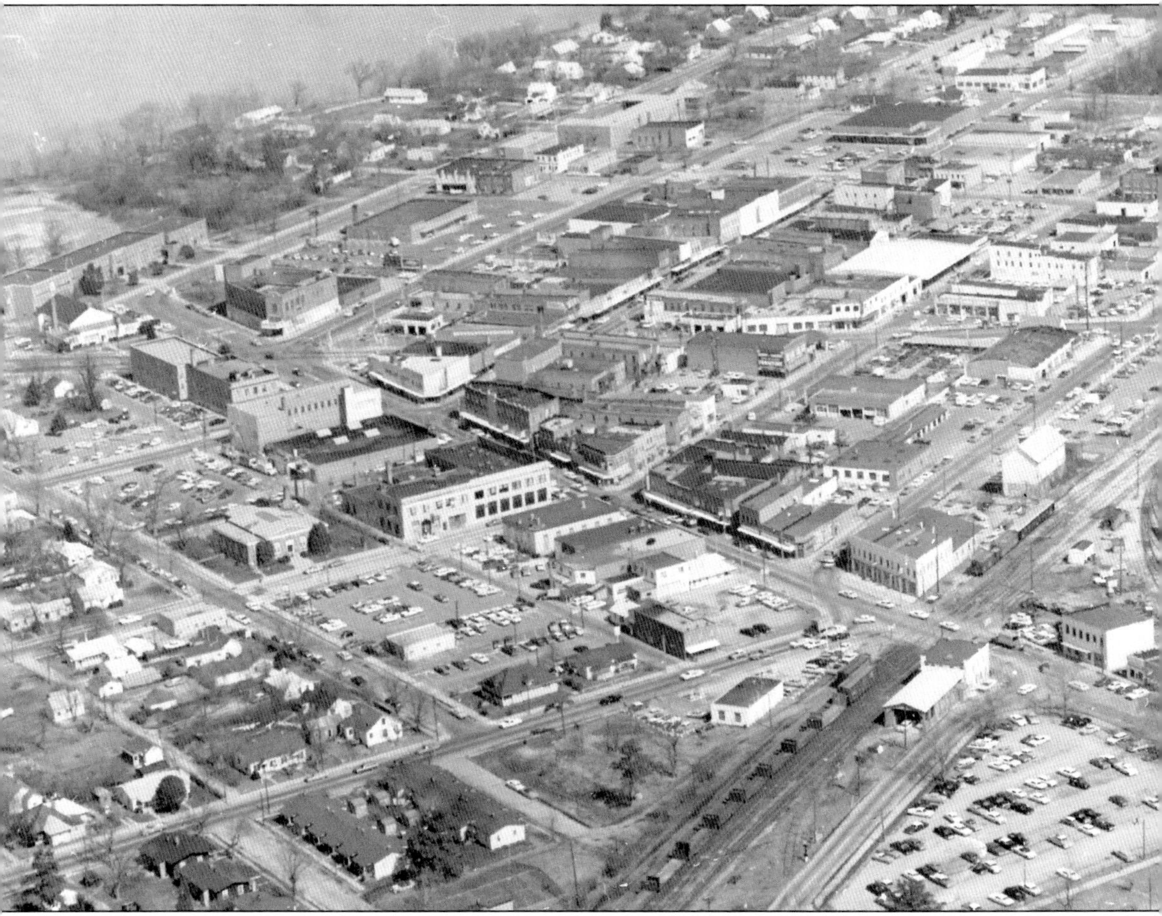

While Hopewell's products include both things and imagination, this aerial photograph of Hopewell in the 1960s offers a broad perspective of the town. Running through the center of this photograph is Main Street. This street ends to the far left at the now demolished Patrick Copeland School, with ball fields in back toward the James River. This school was named after the Reverend Patrick Copeland, who headed the first free school in the new Colonial territories. The whitish structure across the street on the far left is the United Service Organizations (USO). It later became the parks and recreation building. The Beacon Theater sits one block to the right. Moving right another block, metal-covered sidewalks are visible on the right side of the street. One block to the right on the left side of the street is the State Planter's Bank, and the Pioneer Federal Bank sits catty-corner. (Photograph courtesy of Jack Daniel and the *Hopewell News*.)

Hopewell has a long history of adaptation and innovation. In the photograph of this 1590 etching by DeBry and White, Virginia Native Americans make their boats by burning out the inside of logs and scraping them with shells. (Photograph courtesy of the Library of Congress.)

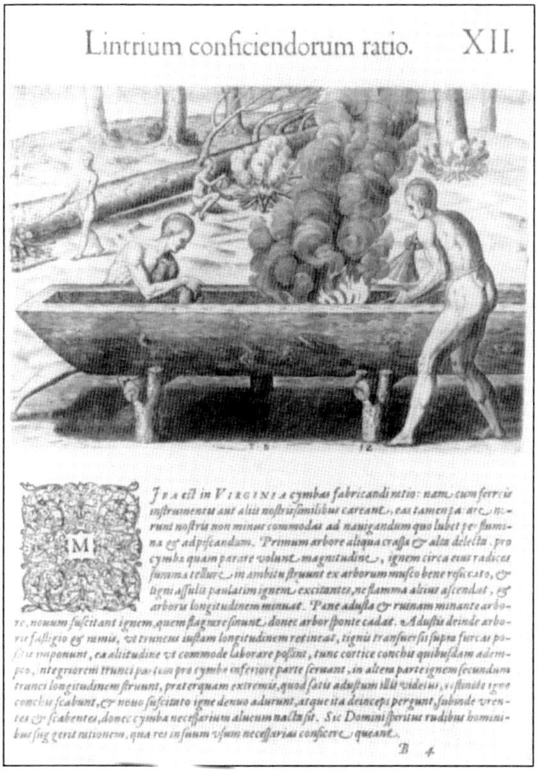

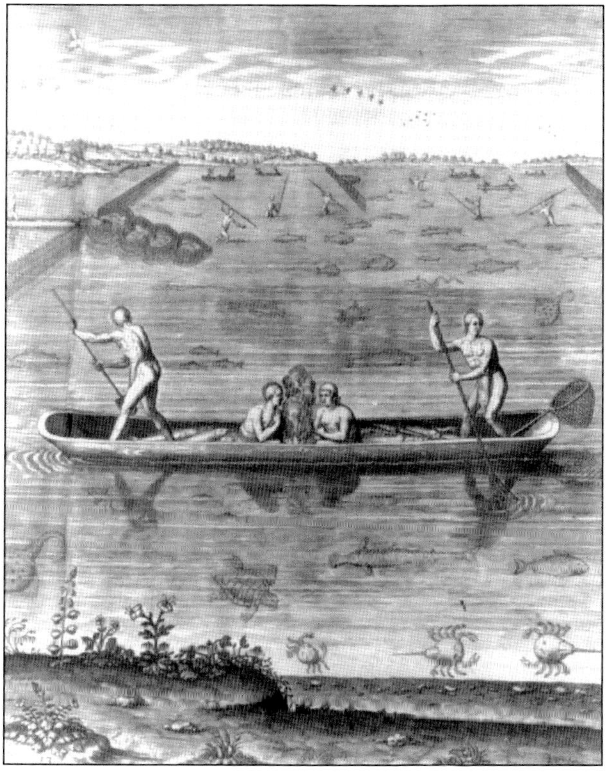

In this 1590 DeBry and White graphic, Virginia Native Americans are depicted fishing in several ways; some stand in the river and spear fish and others use a canoe. Note the depictions of the varieties of fish in the transparent water. Some seem rather fanciful. Villagers appear to be smoking the fish they have already caught right in the canoe. Fishing, hunting, and farming were among the main lifeways of the Powhatan Confederacy. (Photograph courtesy of the Library of Congress.)

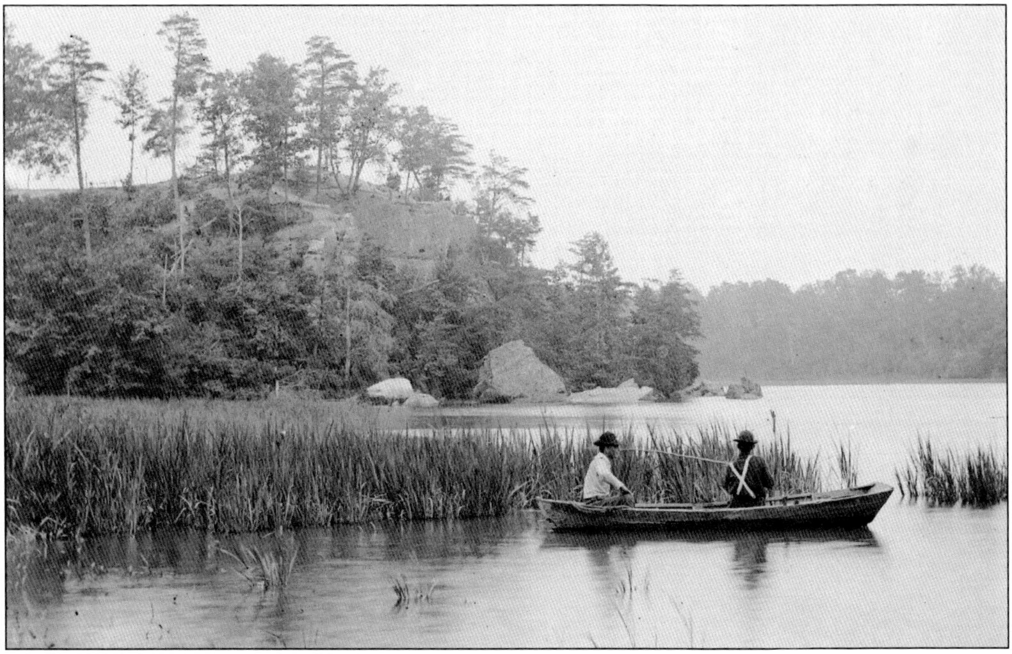

The methods of fishing have not really changed much as this photograph from about 1866 demonstrates. Taken near Bermuda Hundred (near Hopewell), this photograph shows how people have used boats for both pleasure and acquiring food for centuries. Now there are marinas and boat launches along both the James and Appomattox Rivers near Hopewell. (Photograph courtesy of the Library of Congress.)

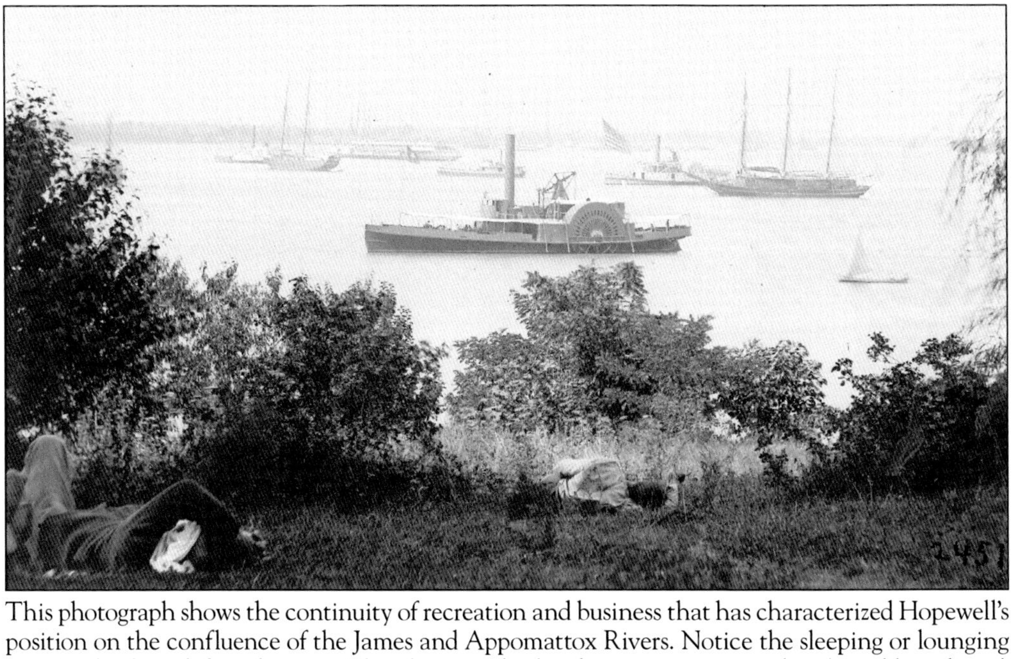

This photograph shows the continuity of recreation and business that has characterized Hopewell's position on the confluence of the James and Appomattox Rivers. Notice the sleeping or lounging men in the front left and center. The photograph also depicts a transport ship (possibly military) along the river. These various roles of the rivers—recreational, mercantile, and strategic—are part of Hopewell's history and culture. (Photograph courtesy of the Library of Congress.)

In the 1930s, Hopewell expanded its strategic and recreational capacity into the so-called third dimension of airspace. Its airport, described in some detail near the end of this book, was the scene of air shows during which daredevil pilots barnstormed in their flying machines. This advertisement for an August 16, 1939, air show makes a creative comparison between a dining menu and the menu of the air show. The fare at an air show included such delicacies as "tail spin salad," "gas tank tea," "Chinese Duck (one wing lo)," and "slide slip yams." (Photograph courtesy of the Appomattox Regional Library.)

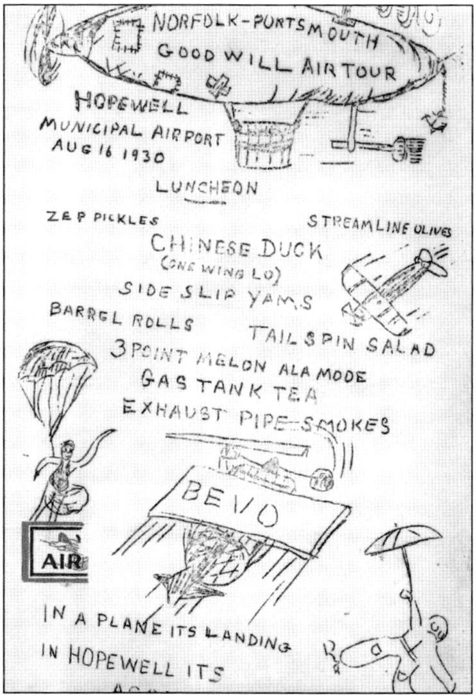

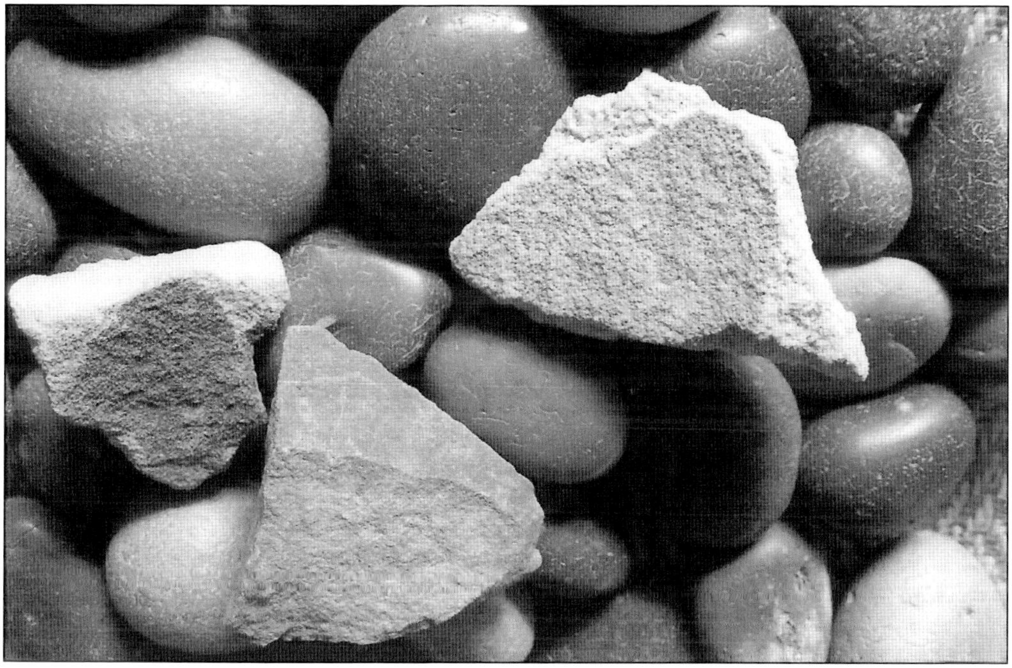

Anyone who walks in City Point–Hopewell is likely to tread on history everywhere. Roland Gill, of Hopewell, suggested the author walk the banks of City Point and scoop up ballast stones, which were rounded stones stored deep inside hulls to add weight and, thus, stability to tall sailing ships. These stones were collected by the author, as were pottery shards that were perhaps left hundreds of years ago by Native Americans along the banks of the Appomattox River. (Photograph courtesy of Laura Lee Duncan.)

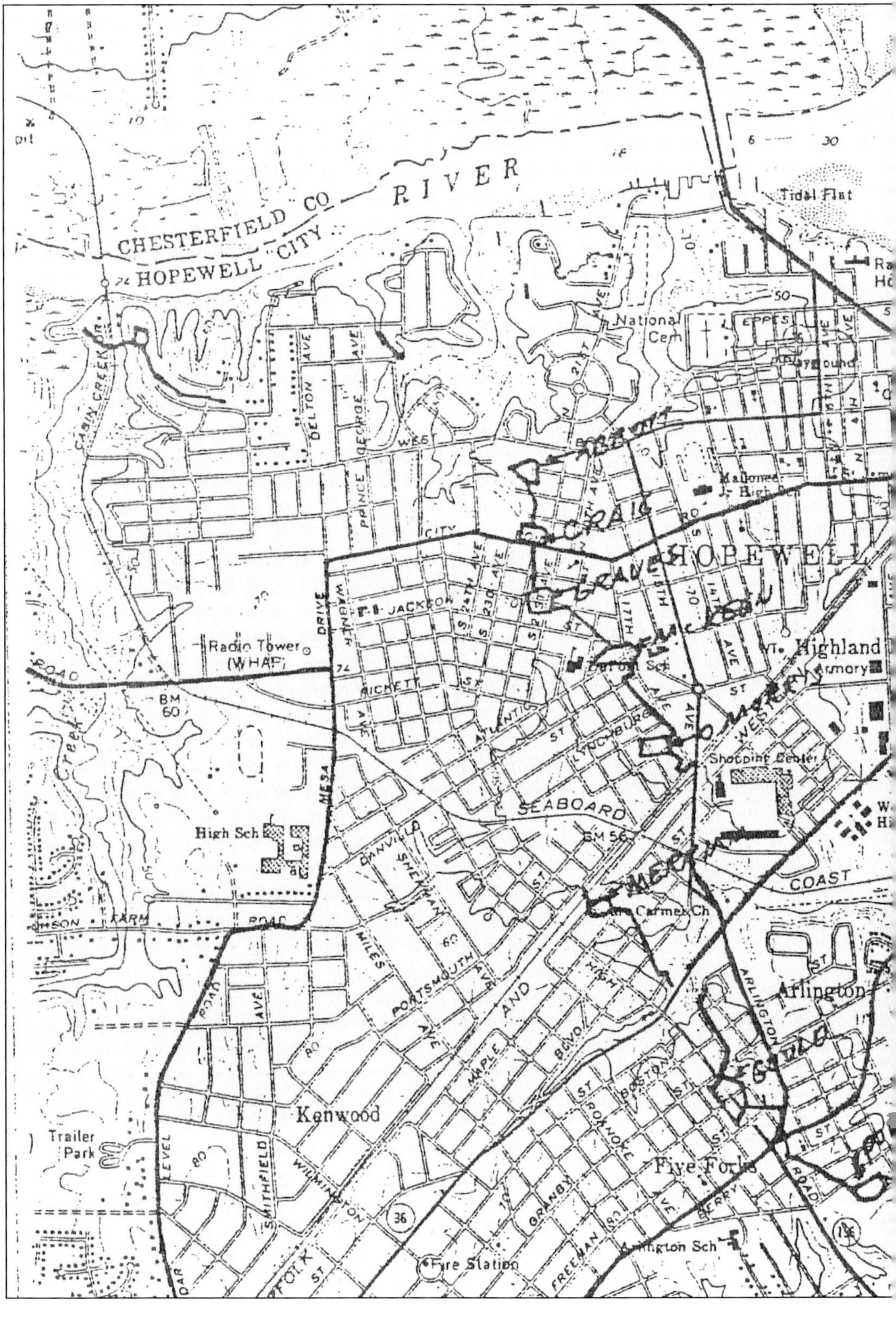
CHESTERFIELD CO
HOPEWELL CITY
RIVER
Tidal Flat
CABIN CREEK DR
National Cem
EPPES
Playground
DELTON AVE
PRINCE GEORGE AVE
WEST
CITY
HOPEWELL
JACKSON
WAGNER AVE
MESA DRIVE
Radio Tower (WHAP)
ROAD
BM 60
RICKETT ST
ATLANTIC
LYNCHBURG
SEABOARD
BM 56
Shopping Center
Highland
Armory
COAST
High Sch
FARM
ROAD
DANVILLE
SHERMAN
MILES
PORTSMOUTH AVE
MAPLE
AND
HIGH
BLVD
ARLINGTON
Arlington
Kenwood
Trailer Park
LEVEL
SMITHFIELD
WILMINGTON
BOSTON
ROANOKE
GRANBY
FREEMAN
Five Forks
BERRY
Arlington Sch
Fire Station
36

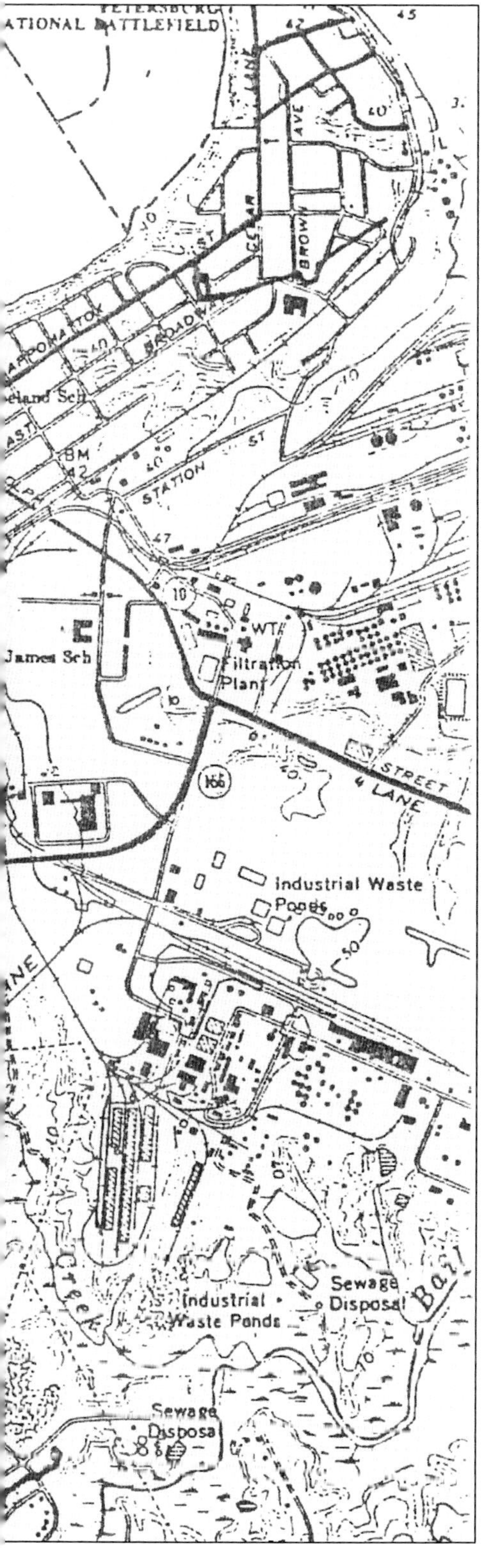

When Union troops captured City Point, the Confederacy wanted it back. So Union commanders placed a string of forts to guard the vital port and depot. This map, drawn by Johnny Altman, is similar to the one shown in the first chapter, except for one crucial innovation. Where the earlier image showed a topographical outline of the forts, this graph is laid upon a street map of Hopewell. Allowing for reasonable changes in scale, the forts can be located with a couple of blocks in current Hopewell. Fort Abbott (next photograph) was located near the current West and Twenty-first Streets. (Map courtesy of Johnny Altman Sr.)

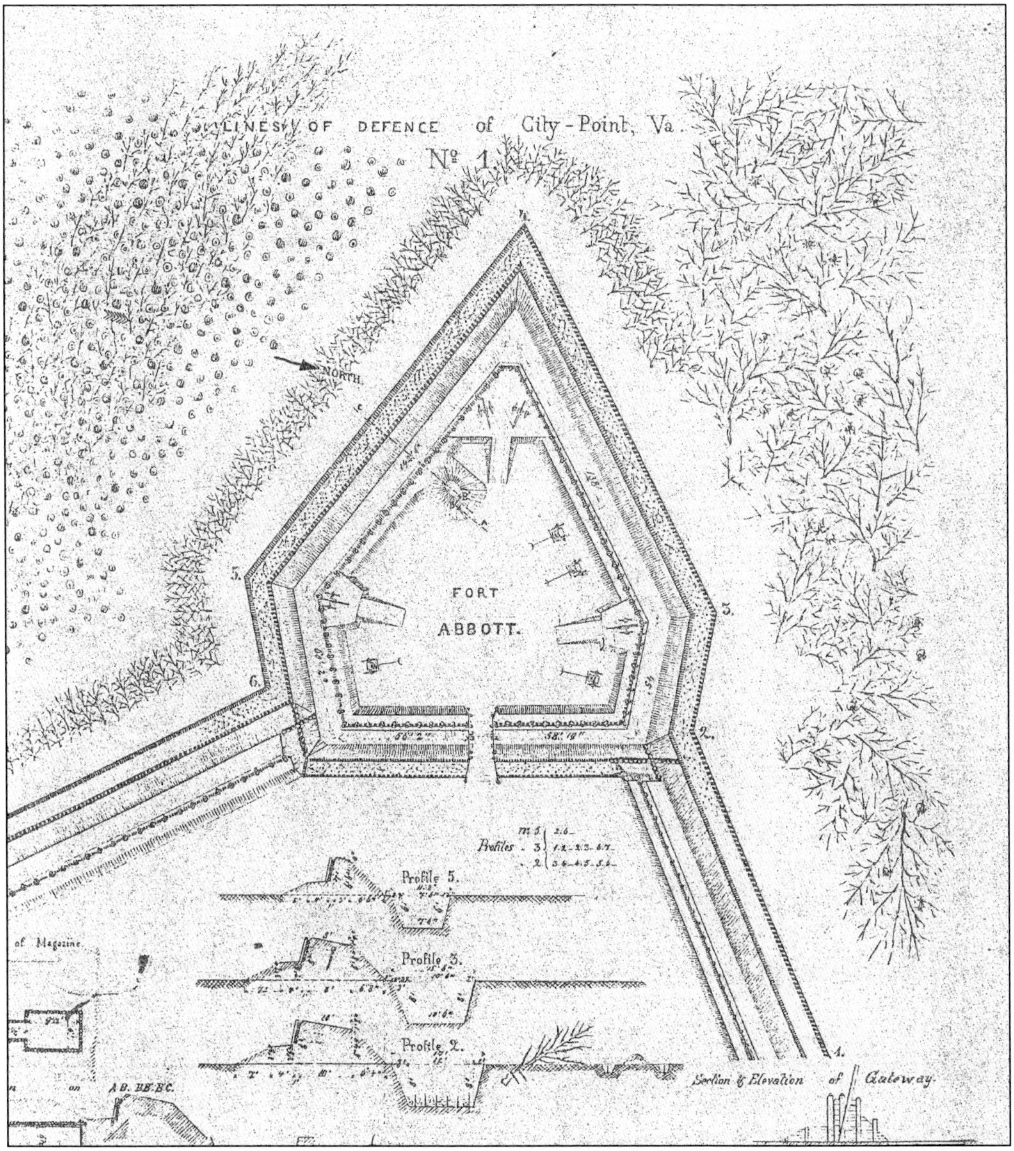

Fort Abbott, among others, defended City Point. Originally, the main point of this fort would have been shifted left, toward the Confederate forces arrayed in Petersburg. The approximate dimensions of this five-sided fort are given, clockwise from top: point 4 to point 3 measures 138 feet; point 4 to point 5 measures 142.5 feet; point 5 to point 6 measures 60 feet; point 3 to point 2 measures 45 feet; and point 6 to point 2 is 115 feet. (Drawing courtesy of Paul Karnes and the Library of Congress.)

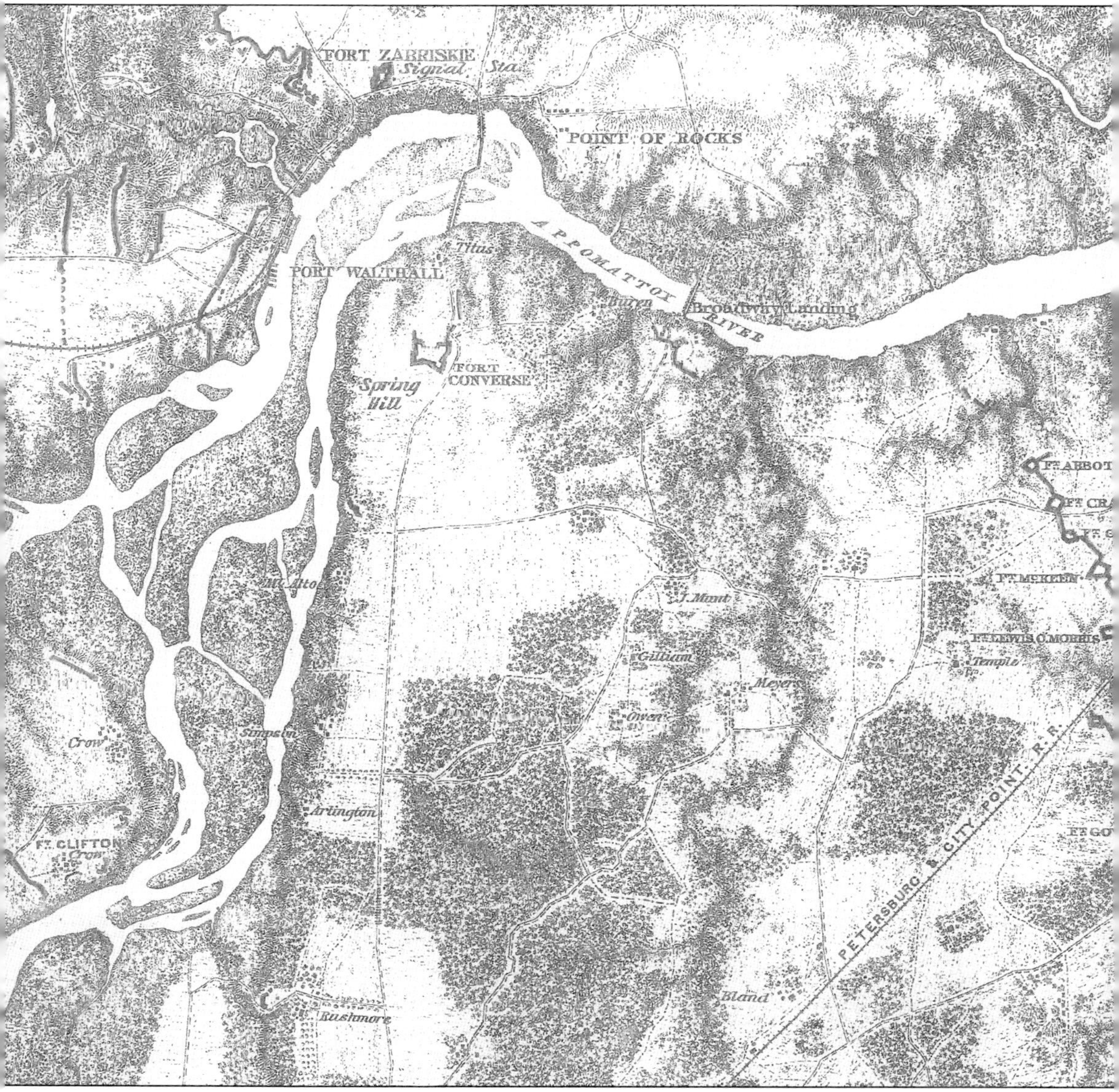

To the west of Fort Abbott, the Confederate army defended Petersburg under Gen. P.G.T. Beauregard. Petersburg was a pivotal rail line, forming a hub that ultimately supplied Richmond from feeder rail lines all over the South. The Confederate commanders and politicians knew very well the necessity of keeping Petersburg in Confederate control. The Appomattox River is to the top of the map, with the Petersburg and City Point Railroad to the bottom. The site of Fort Abbott can be seen to the east (middle right) of the map. Fort Abbott and the other forts were designed to stop activities such as the Beefsteak Raid in September 1864. In that raid, Confederate cavalry outmaneuvered Union forces to steal a large herd of cattle. Fort Converse and Broadway Landing can be seen in the north near Spring Hill. To the north of Port Walthall and across the Appomattox River is the Fort Zabrinskie signal station. (Map and information courtesy of Johnny Altman Sr.)

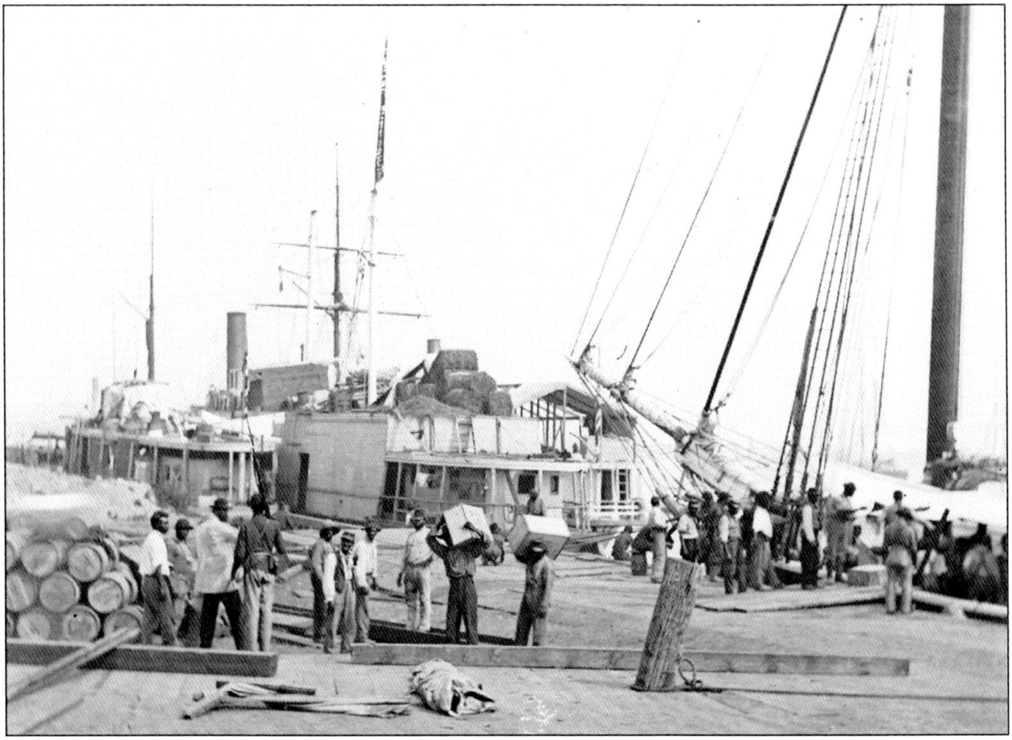

This is a good close-up of the enormity of the ships, the wharves, and those who unloaded Union supplies. (Photograph courtesy of the Library of Congress.)

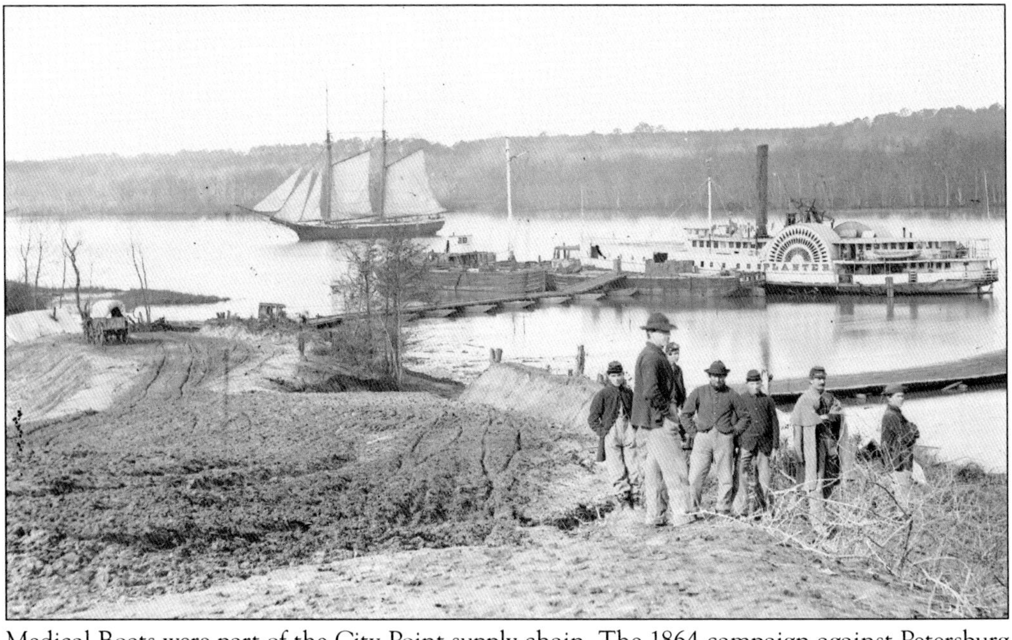

Medical Boats were part of the City Point supply chain. The 1864 campaign against Petersburg and the surrounding Richmond defenses was ghastly and costly for both sides. City Point, as the focal point for all supplies in this campaign, was a logical place for medical facilities. (Photograph courtesy of the Library of Congress.)

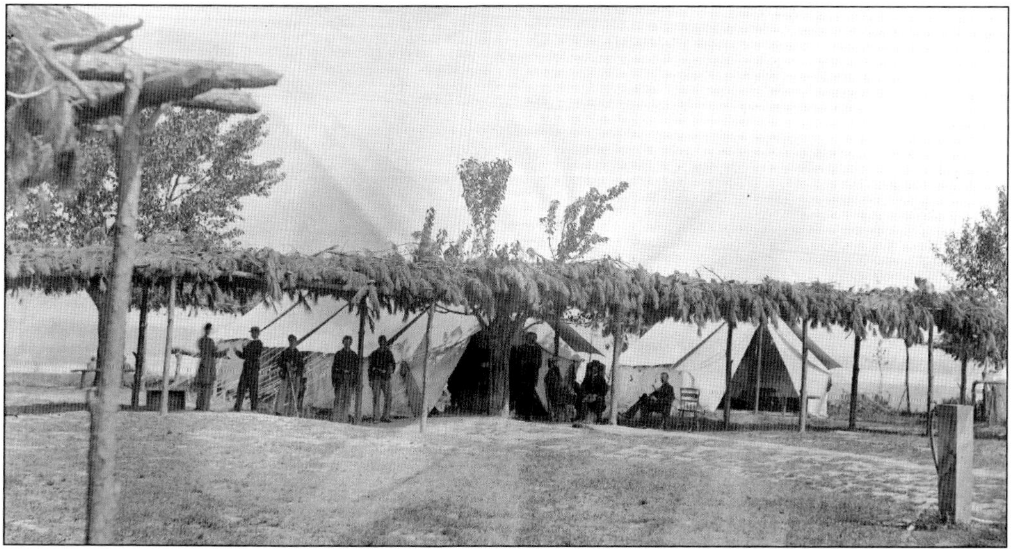

City Point also housed the general hospital. National Park Service data divides the battles for Petersburg into the campaign of June 15–18, 1864, and the entire Siege of Petersburg. In the short campaign, 62,000 Federal soldiers and 42,000 Confederate soldiers were engaged. This campaign cost the Union 8,150 casualties and the Confederates 3,236. That was just the beginning. The total Siege of Petersburg left the Confederates with 28,000 casualties and the Union with 42,000 dead. (Photograph courtesy of the Library of Congress.)

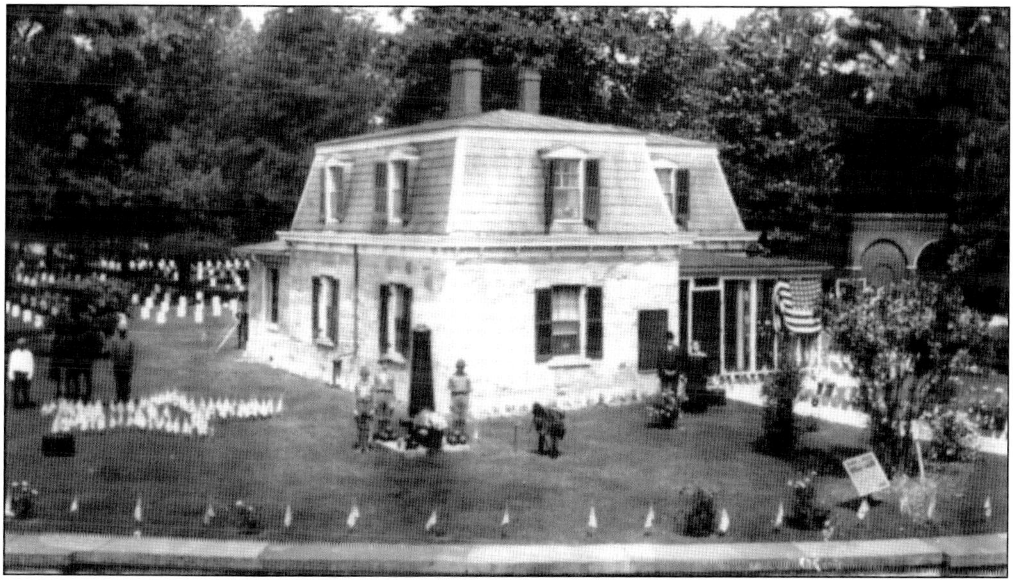

Regrettably, the state of medical care during the Civil War was such that a relatively minor wound might prove fatal. Additionally, the use of large-caliber lead bullets in rifled muskets and 19th-century grenades and artillery, including heavy mortars, conspired to make the death rate among combatants very high by today's standards. Many of the Union dead were transferred to this National Cemetery off West Broadway and Eleventh and Twelfth Streets. This photograph from about 1950 shows Boy Scouts standing on the center monument, possibly during a Memorial Day celebration. The graves, cemetery, stone wall in front, and other structures shown are still there. (Photograph courtesy of Jack Daniel and the *Hopewell News*.)

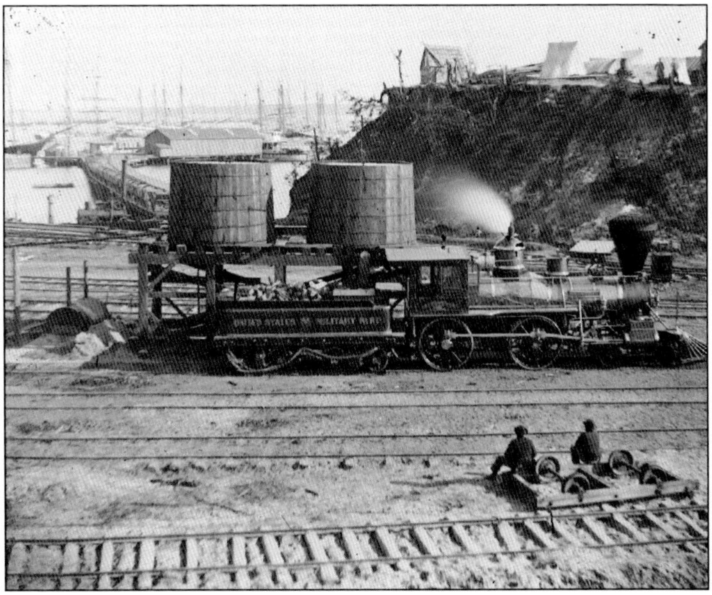

This photograph shows the careful choreography of logistics at City Point during the Civil War. Ships bring troops and supplies to the wharfs (top of photograph) and crews and teamsters off-load them to rail lines or to waiting wagons. (Photograph courtesy of the Library of Congress.)

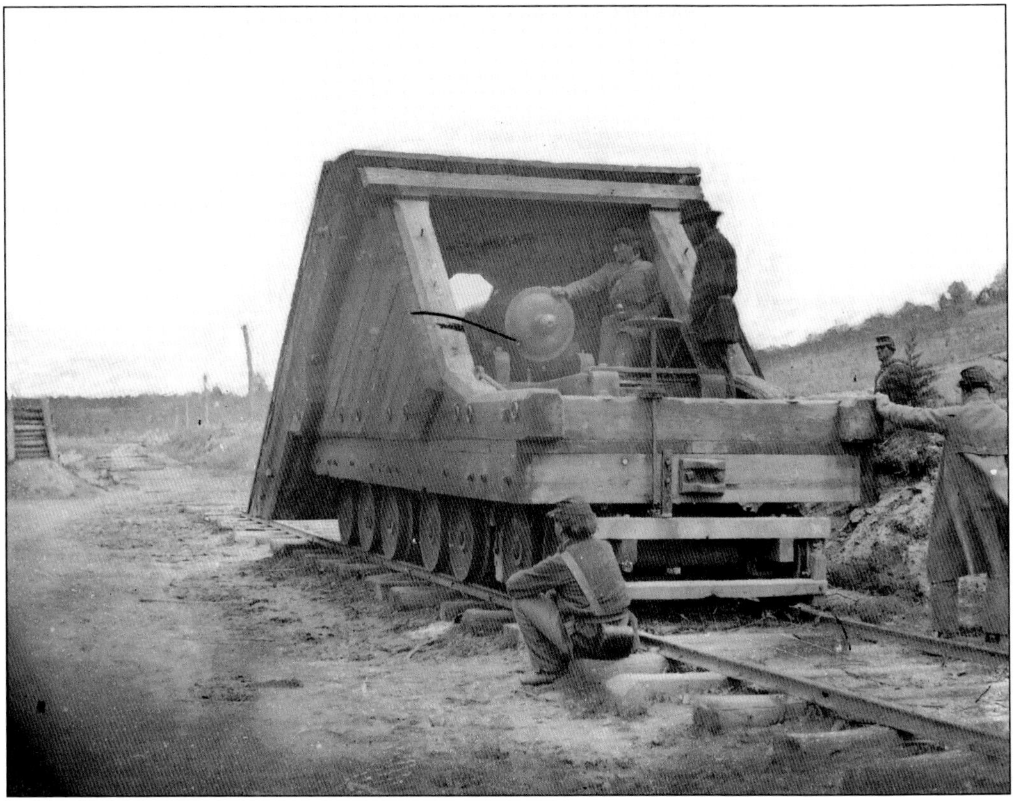

Railroad guns were used toward the end of the war. One famous railroad gun, a 13-inch mortar that lobbed 200-pound shells into Petersburg from as far away as three miles, was nicknamed the "Dictator" or the "Petersburg Express." This gun is on display at the Petersburg Battlefield Park outside of Hopewell. This kind of gun was prescient to the siege warfare of World War I, where great siege guns mounted on rail lines were used. (Photograph courtesy of the Library of Congress.)

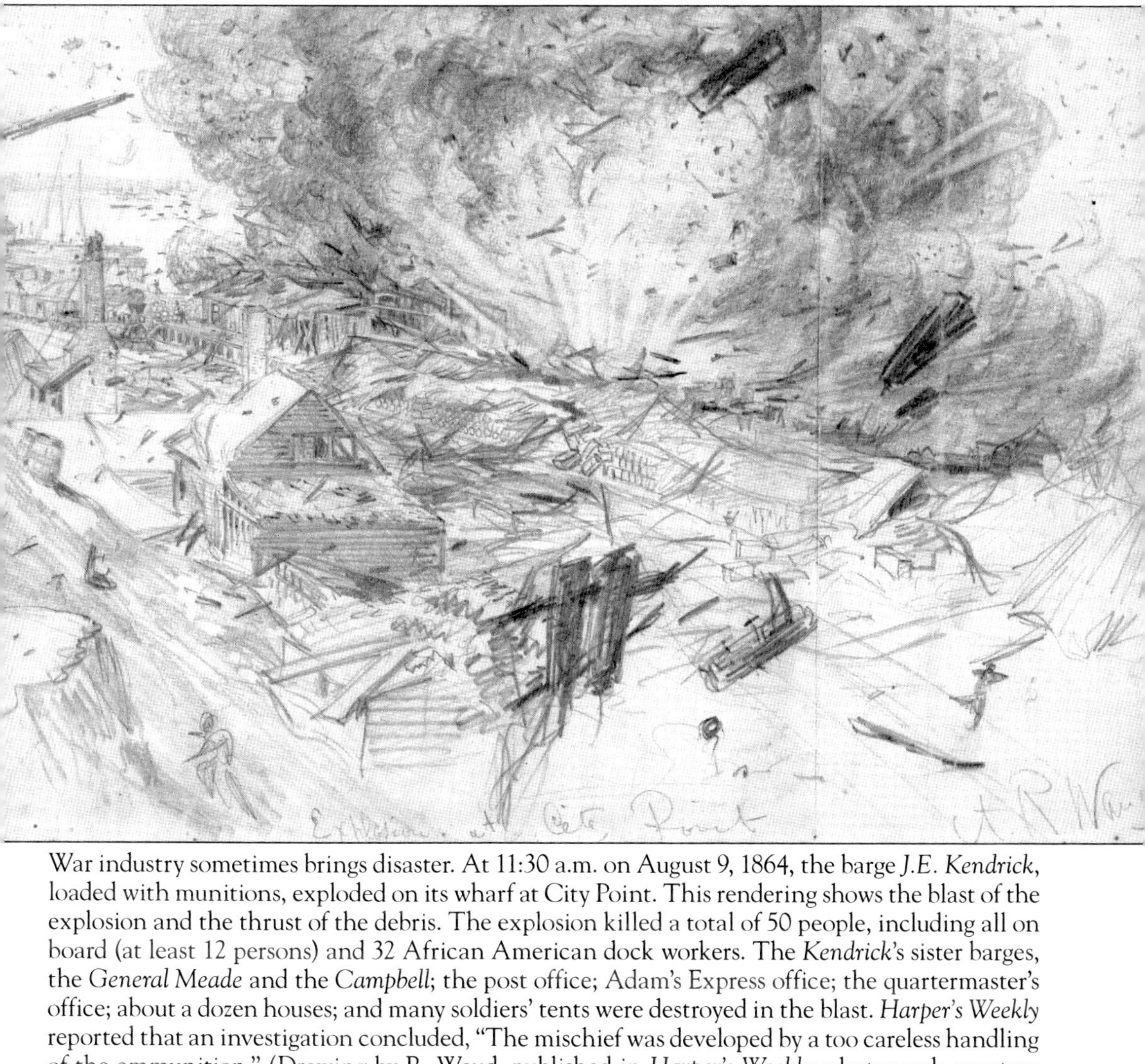

War industry sometimes brings disaster. At 11:30 a.m. on August 9, 1864, the barge *J.E. Kendrick*, loaded with munitions, exploded on its wharf at City Point. This rendering shows the blast of the explosion and the thrust of the debris. The explosion killed a total of 50 people, including all on board (at least 12 persons) and 32 African American dock workers. The *Kendrick*'s sister barges, the *General Meade* and the *Campbell*; the post office; Adam's Express office; the quartermaster's office; about a dozen houses; and many soldiers' tents were destroyed in the blast. *Harper's Weekly* reported that an investigation concluded, "The mischief was developed by a too careless handling of the ammunition." (Drawing by R. Waud, published in *Harper's Weekly*; photograph courtesy of the Library of Congress.)

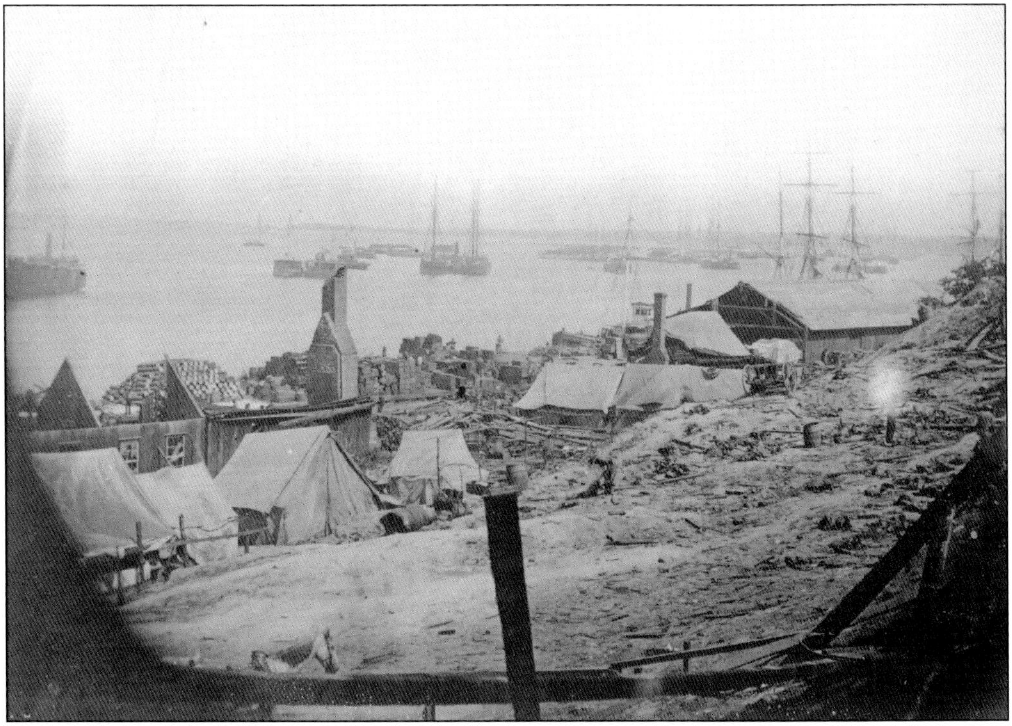

This August 1864 photograph shows the post-explosion effects. The captain of the *J.E. Kendrick* was not on board at the time of the accident, and an after-incident investigation was conducted. Eyewitnesses reported that muskets, shells, bolt heads, and wood planking rained down for a mile all around the explosion. The August 27, 1864, issue of *Harper's Weekly* reported that the air was "piled thick with ruinous fragments." (Photograph courtesy of the Library of Congress.)

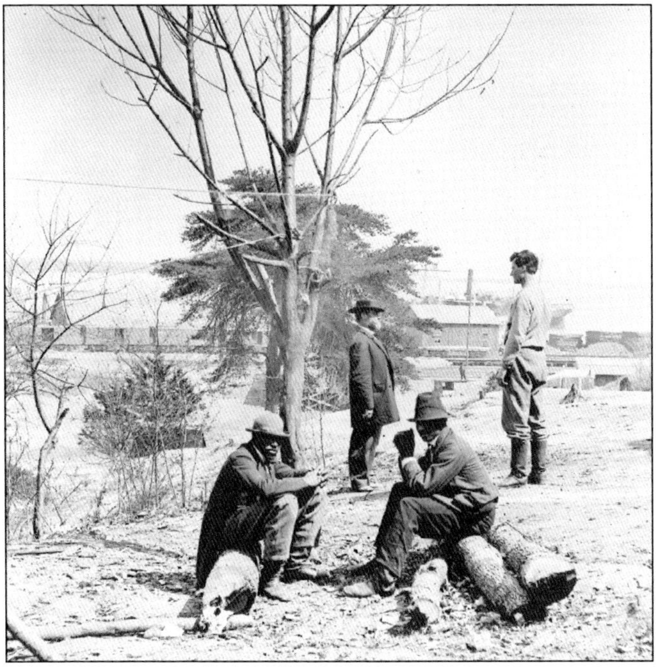

Hopewell also saw an explosion of military intelligence. This photograph shows scouts at the headquarters in City Point. According to Jim Rada (www.suite101.com), the first hires of the Secret Service were sometimes as colorful as their first boss, William Wood, was brave. Wood distinguished himself in the Mexican-American War. The first recruits (not pictured) included an individual who was already counterfeiting money in New Jersey, another who was a forger, and a third who was then imprisoned in Chicago. (Photograph courtesy of the Library of Congress.)

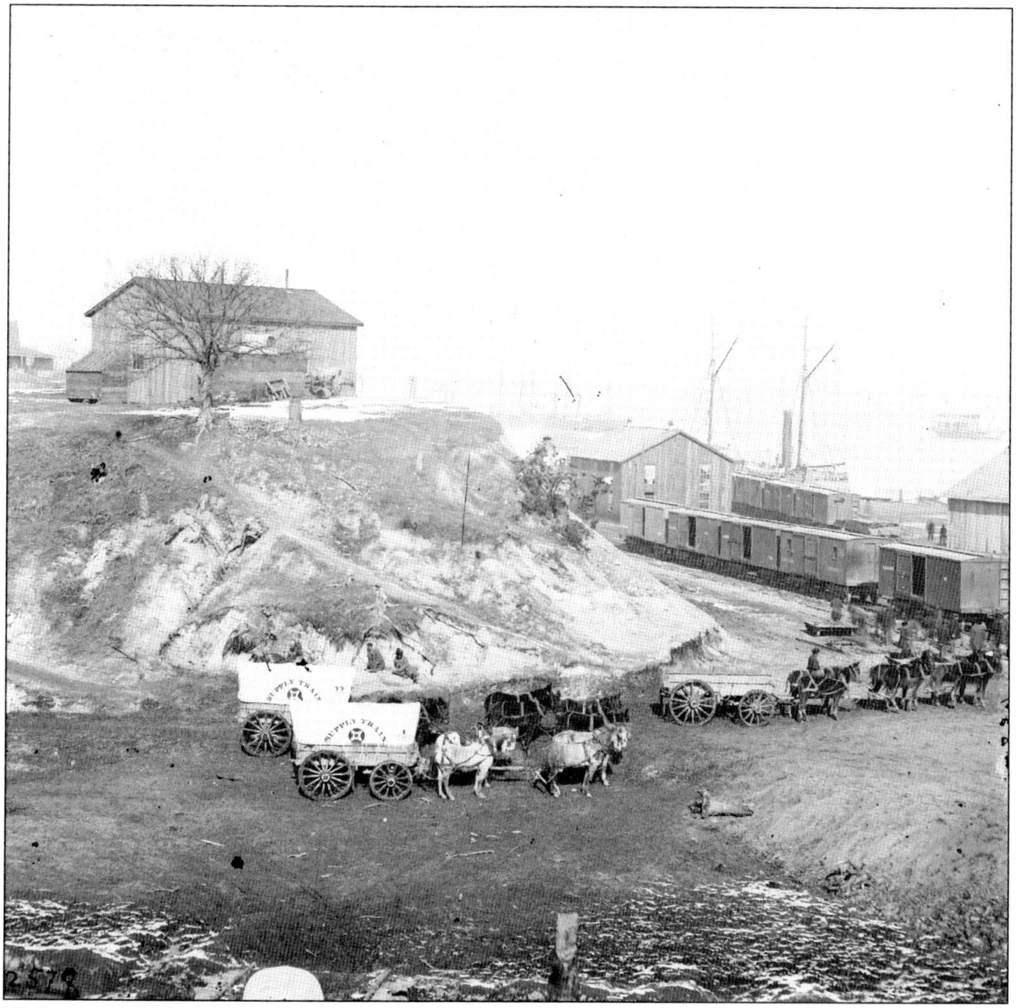

This photograph shows Gen. Marsena Patrick's headquarters and ordnance wharf at City Point. Perhaps the grandfather of the Secret Service, Patrick was born in upstate New York and led soldiers against Stonewall Jackson during the Shenandoah Valley Campaign. Units under his command saw action in Antietam, and later, Patrick was appointed the provost marshal of the Army of the Potomac. Gen. Joseph Hooker asked Patrick to create the Bureau of Military Information, a network of spies. Gen. Ulysses S. Grant appointed Patrick to provost marshal over all of the armies massed against Richmond. Never losing his love for agriculture, Patrick headed the New York State Agriculture Society after the war. He then served as that state's agriculture commissioner. (Photograph courtesy of the Library of Congress.)

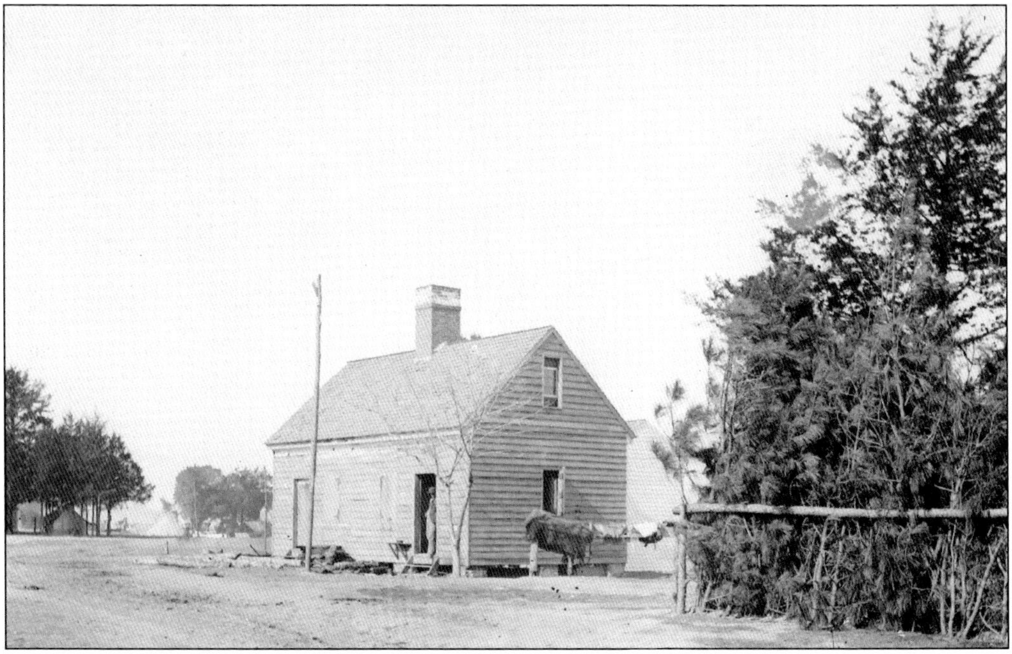

This is the headquarters of the Secret Service at City Point. If the grandfather of the Secret Service was General Patrick, then the father was surely William P. Wood. When Union Secretary of War Edward Stanton asked Wood, then-superintendent of the Old Capital Prison System, to begin an intelligence service, the first goal was counterfeiting. Wood, a hero of the Mexican-American War, wanted to stop the counterfeiting of Union money and promoted the counterfeiting of Confederate money (Jim Rada, www.suite101.com). The Confederacy would no longer supplement its resources with fake Union money and the Union's currency would not be harmed by counterfeit bills. (Photograph courtesy of the Library of Congress.)

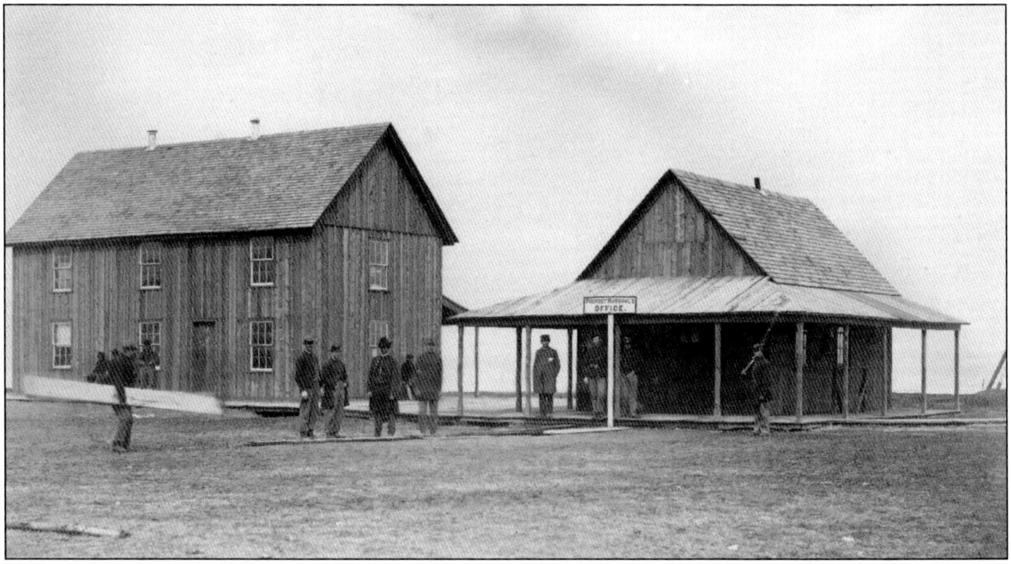

Uncovering the right military intelligence at the right time is useless unless it can be shared with the right people at the right time. What secrets must have passed inside the walls of this City Point post office during the Civil War! (Photograph courtesy of the Library of Congress.)

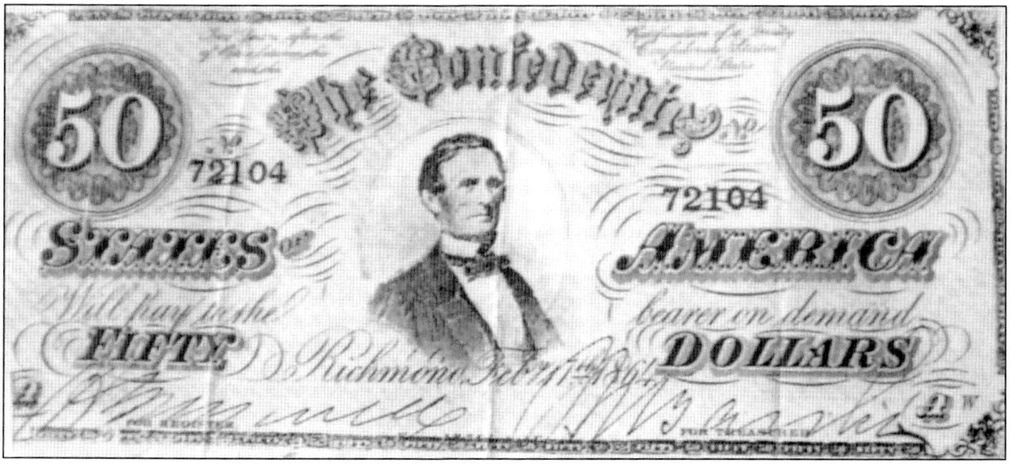

This counterfeit Confederate bill was probably made in the North to destabilize its adversary's economy. The serial numbers on the upper right and left can be tracked on the Internet as counterfeit. (Currency courtesy of Robert Gill and family.)

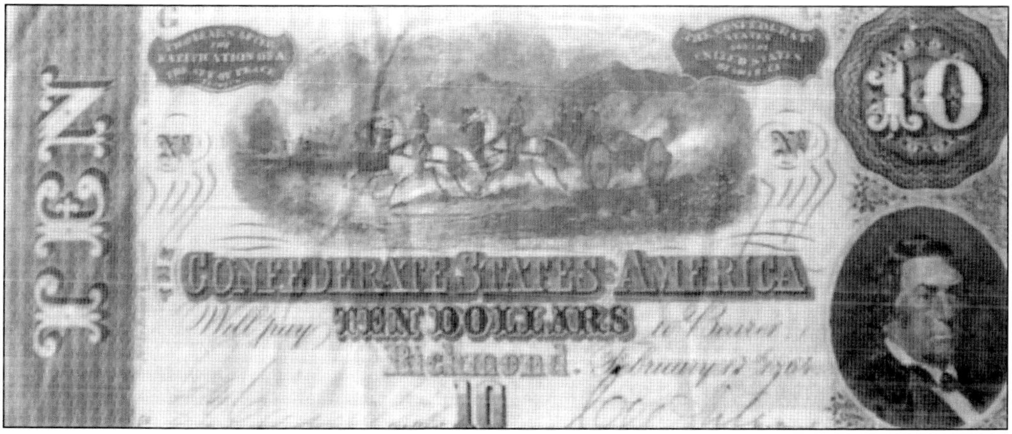

This is genuine Confederate currency. Both notes were found wrapped in a money belt by Roland Gill as a young man while he plowed a field across the river from Hopewell. It is said that nurse Clara Barton, founder of the Red Cross, worked in a field hospital near where the bills were discovered. (Currency courtesy of Robert Gill and family.)

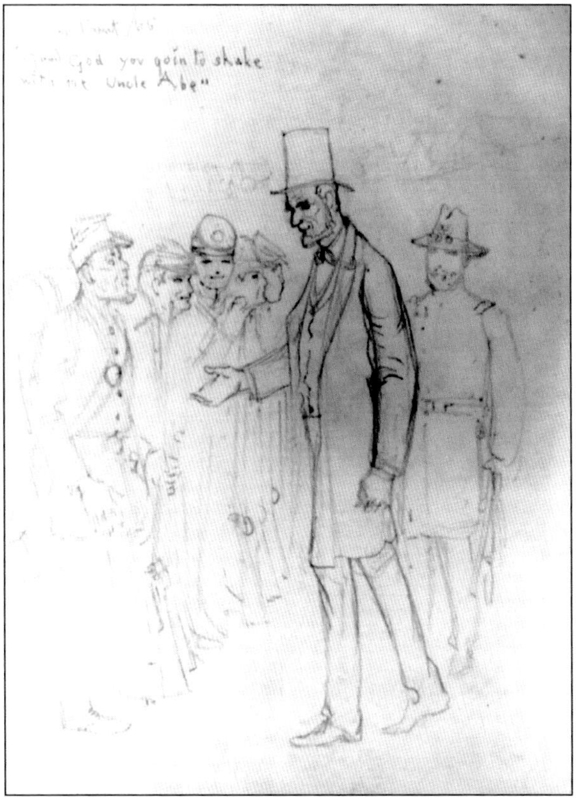

On March 20, 1865, General Grant sent a telegram to President Lincoln saying, "Can you not visit City Point for a day or two? I would like very much to see you, and I think the rest would do you good." In this sketch by Charles Wellington (1841–1926)—which reads, "Good God, you goin to shake with me, Uncle Abe"—the president is shown reaching out his hand to a Union soldier. (Photograph courtesy of the Library of Congress.)

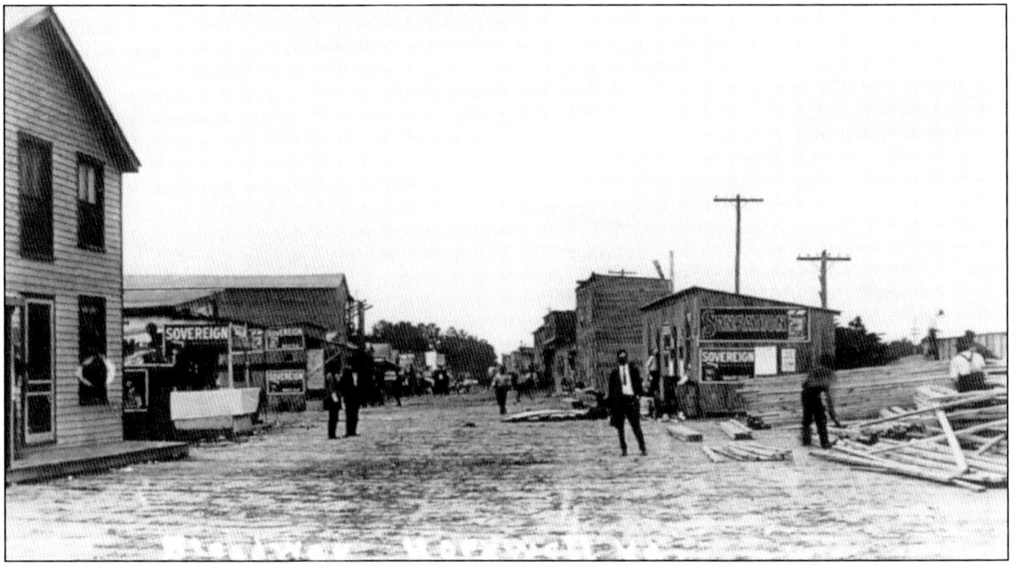

This photograph from about 1914 may have been taken a short time after the previous photograph, as the streets seem wider and treeless. Communication poles are visible in the background. Sovereign and Sensation cigarette advertisements figure prominently in this photograph. In the August 30, 1913, issue of the *Daily Kentucky New Era*, a full-page advertisement offers a free scarf pin and two cash coupons (worth half a penny each) for every 5¢ pack of Sovereign cigarettes purchased. (Photograph courtesy of the Appomattox Regional Library.)

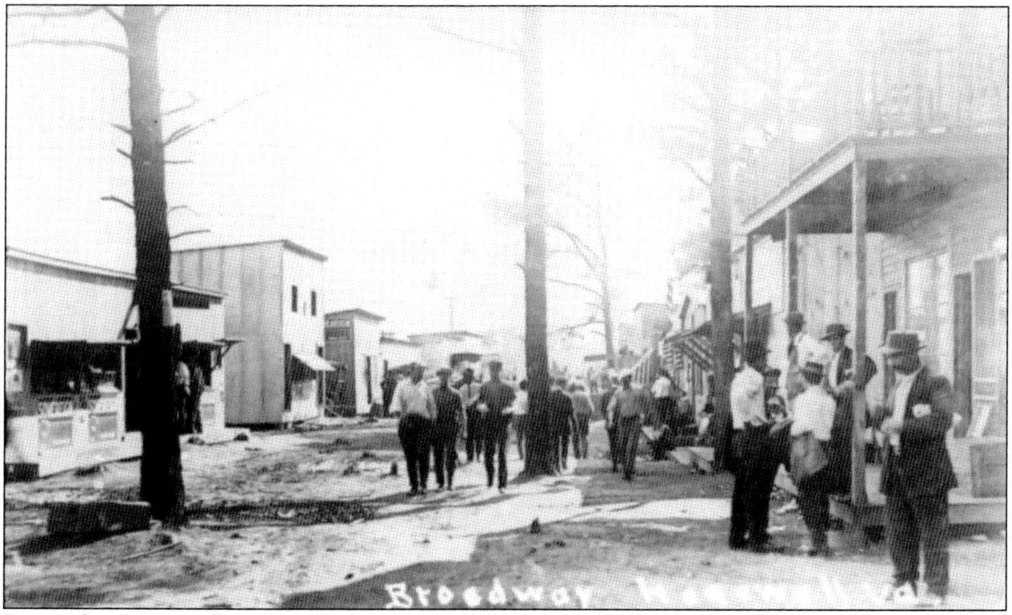

Pictured is a Hopewell street scene from around 1913. A year earlier, DuPont had bought an initial 800 acres and would later purchase an additional 1,600 acres to make dynamite and guncotton as Europe headed for war. By 1915, the area's population grew from a few hundred to several thousand. In this photograph, trees stand uncut in the middle of the road. Raised, wooden sidewalks lift pedestrians' feet off the dirt and mud. (Photograph by A. Robbins, courtesy of the Appomattox Regional Library.)

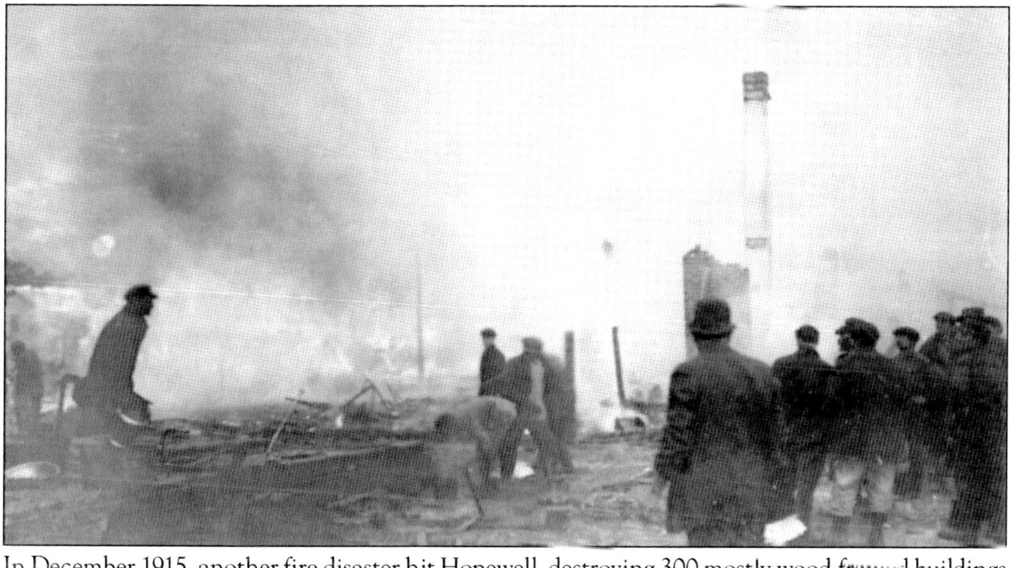

In December 1915, another fire disaster hit Hopewell, destroying 300 mostly wood-framed buildings in the heart of downtown Hopewell. When the fire burned itself out around 8:00 p.m., most of the downtown was gone. The damage estimates were $300,000—in 1915 terms. Immediately after the fire, Hopewell was rebuilding. The fire was not the real story. The real story was the remarkable reconstruction, which was completed using brick and included an enhanced fire-fighting apparatus, both of which resulted in vast improvements. In the year after the fire, Hopewell built its first hospital, and the community and businesses continued to grow. (Photograph by A. Robbins, courtesy of the Appomattox Regional Library.)

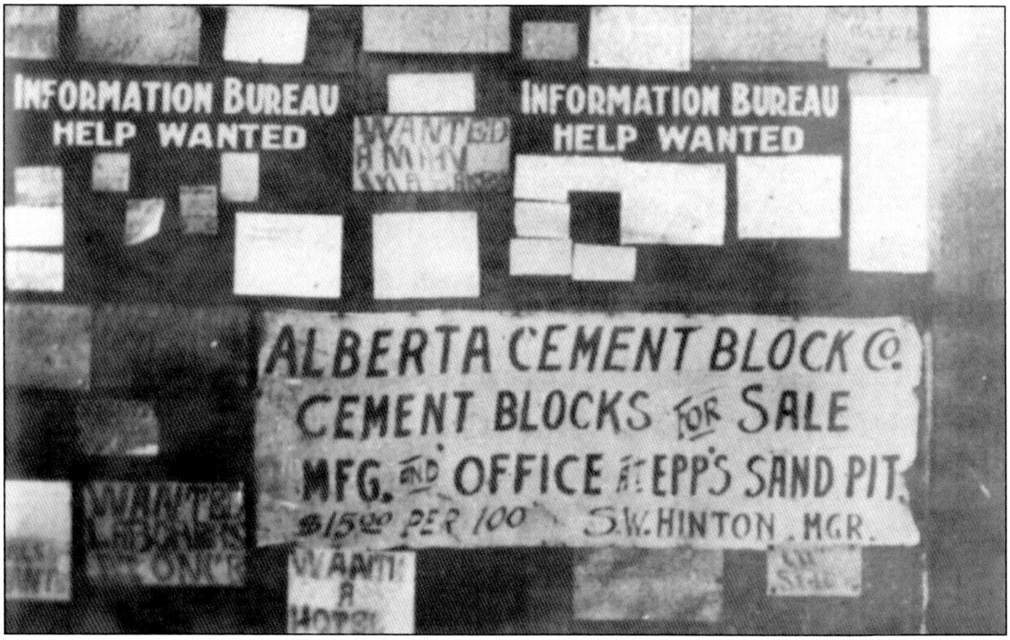

This "Information Bureau" from around 1915 was a place to post help-wanted advertisements. Notices included "Wanted laborers at once" and "A man in a bakery." After the fire, building and recovery followed swiftly. Europe was fighting the "war to end all wars," and the guncotton DuPont produced was part of that war effort. (Photograph courtesy of the Appomattox Regional Library.)

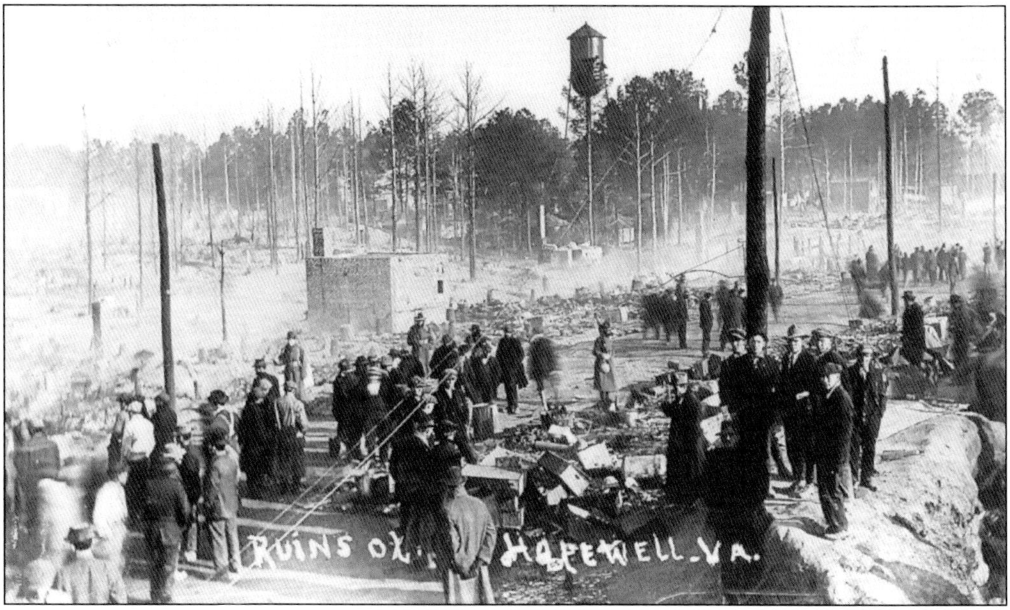

Hopewell rebuilt and rose from the ashes. This photograph shows thriving business in mostly brick buildings. Looking closely reveals trolley tracks. Between 1949 and 1952, fire damage to buildings amounted to around $24,000 (compared to the 1915 estimated cost of $300,000) and damages to the contents was around $46,000. Between 1925 and 1951, the assessed value of properties within the city increased 500 percent to $30.5 million. Automobiles were also becoming widespread. (Photograph by A. Robbins, courtesy of Jack Daniel.)

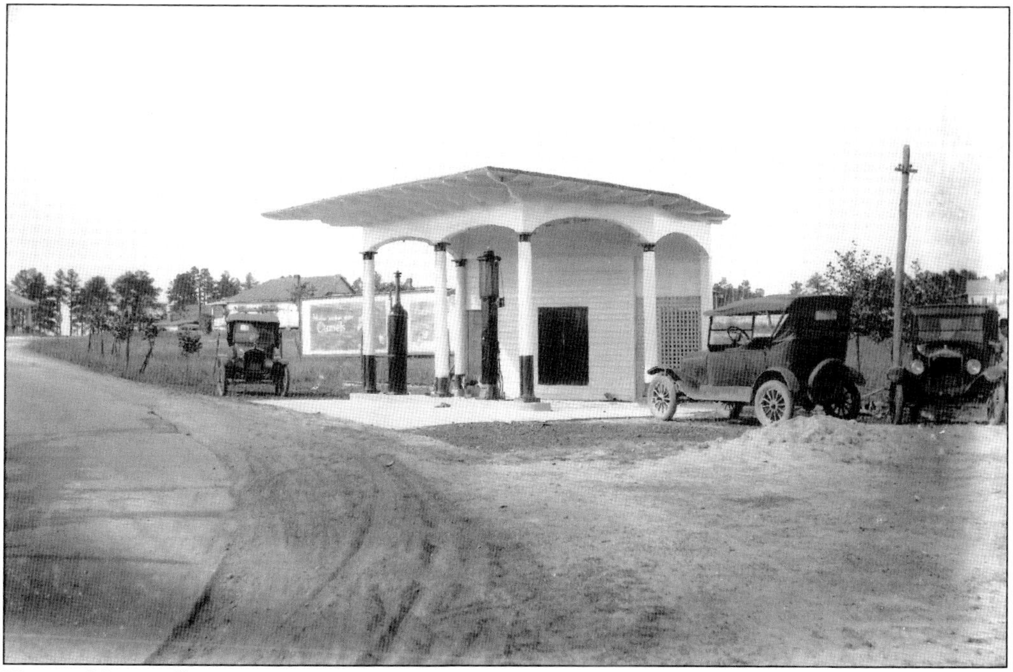

Here, a Hopewell gas station uses gravity pumps to provide fuel. Customers could see through the glass tanks and know exactly how much gas they were getting. In the background, a billboard advertises a brand of cigarettes still available today. (Photograph courtesy of Jack Daniel.)

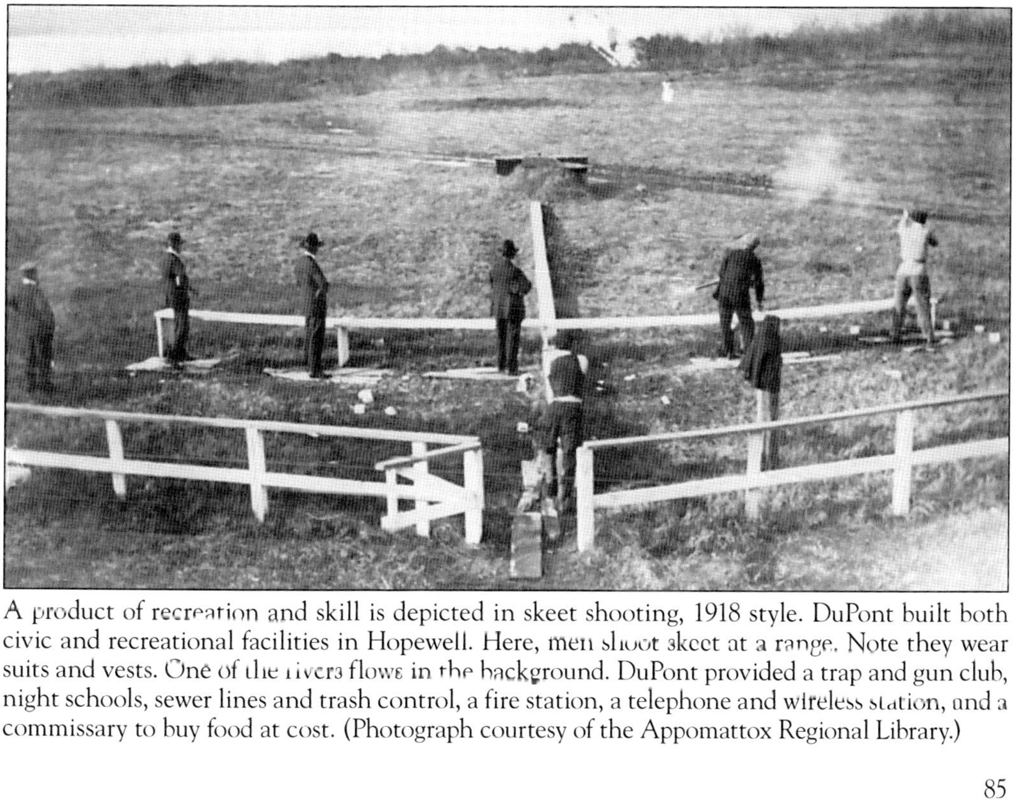

A product of recreation and skill is depicted in skeet shooting, 1918 style. DuPont built both civic and recreational facilities in Hopewell. Here, men shoot skeet at a range. Note they wear suits and vests. One of the rivers flows in the background. DuPont provided a trap and gun club, night schools, sewer lines and trash control, a fire station, a telephone and wireless station, and a commissary to buy food at cost. (Photograph courtesy of the Appomattox Regional Library.)

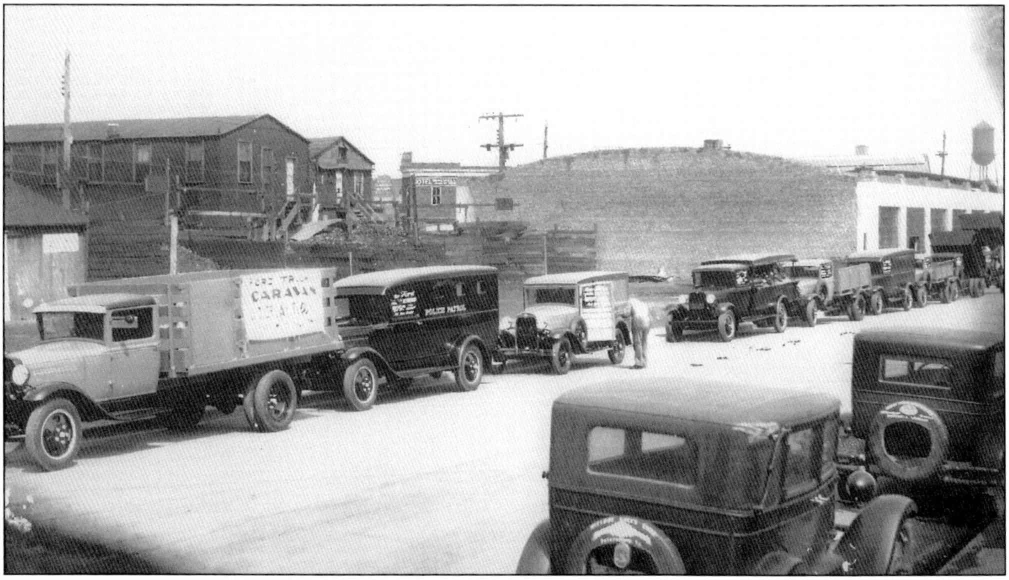

Cars, some for sale, line City Point and Broadway, two important streets in Hopewell. To the left, the sign on the truck advertises a truck sale "today." The vehicle behind it reads "Police Patrol" and is selling for $975. In the background is the rear of the Hotel Hopewell. (Photograph courtesy of Paul Karnes.)

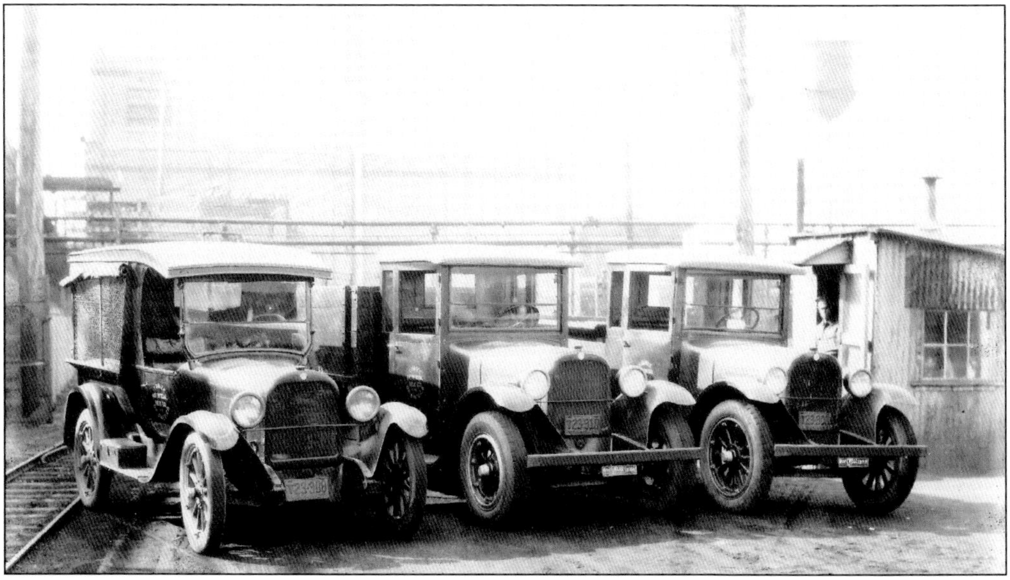

After the boom years came the bust years. Immediately after the armistice of World War I, Hopewell was reduced to a few hundred people. Some of Hopewell's residents, however, would not give up and began a precursor to the chamber of commerce. They helped convert the near-abandoned DuPont facilities to other industries, including the Stamscott Company (before the Hercules Powder Company), the Hummel-Ross Fiber Corporation (later a part of Continental Can, Inc.), and the Tubize Artificial Silk Company, whose trucks are shown above. By 1920, a total of 11 new companies planned to open or were already operational in Hopewell. The Tubize Chatillon Corporation, a Belgian company, built a rayon plant in Hopewell to manufacture artificial silk. The physical plant cost $10 million dollars in 1915. (Photograph courtesy of Jack Daniel.)

The next few images illustrate the variety of means and motivations for Hopewell manufacturing and imagination. Production is sometimes related to patriotism. This *Splinters* issue, from the explosive-making DuPont plant in Hopewell, shows Uncle Sam in front of the factory. The cover, which reads, "Hopewell—it's up to you," is dated September 1917, only five months after the United States declared war on Germany. The DuPont *Splinters* magazine was published between 1917 and 1918. (Magazine courtesy of the Appomattox Regional Library.)

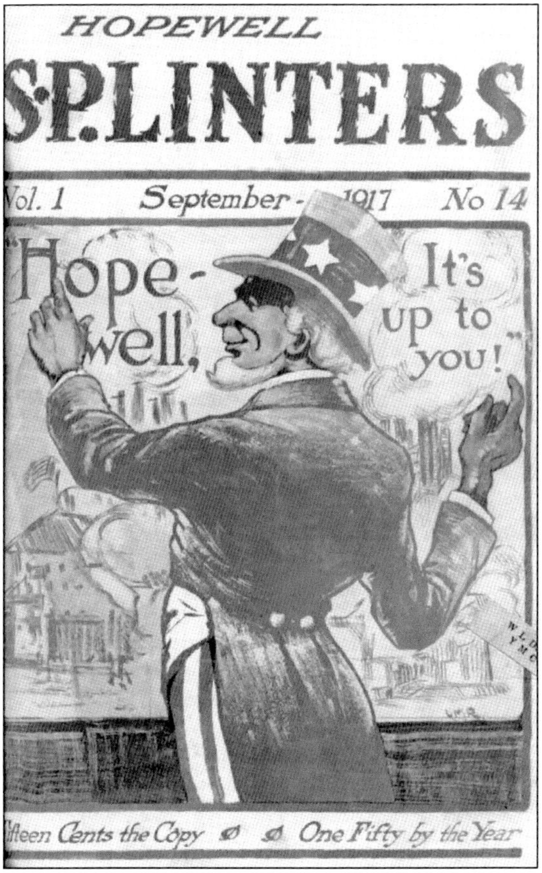

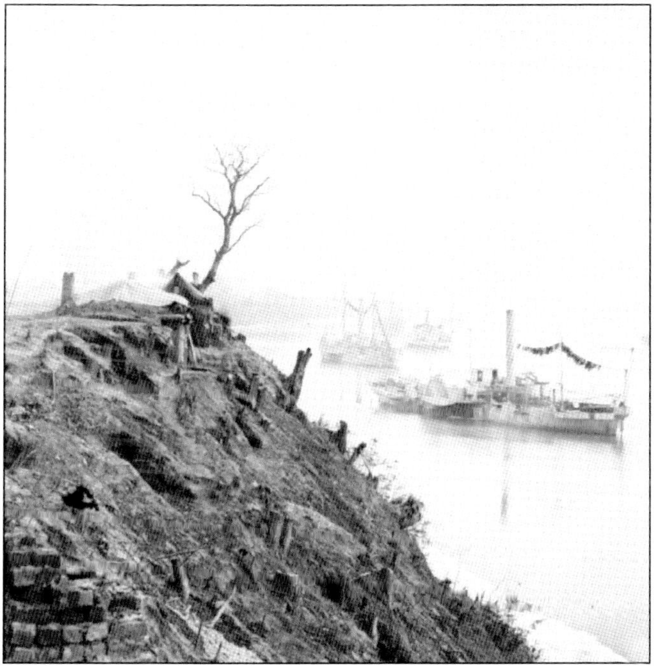

Just as DuPont pioneered explosives, Hopewell had seen many innovations during the Civil War. All five of the side-wheel paddleboats visible in this photograph (from about 1864) show single, enormous smokestacks, not sails. Additionally, the river seems choked with such support vessels. One might wonder if the days of supposed chivalrous, single-person combat (much discussed with the advent of machine guns) had already been replaced by overwhelming technological advancement and logistical support. (Photograph courtesy of the Library of Congress.)

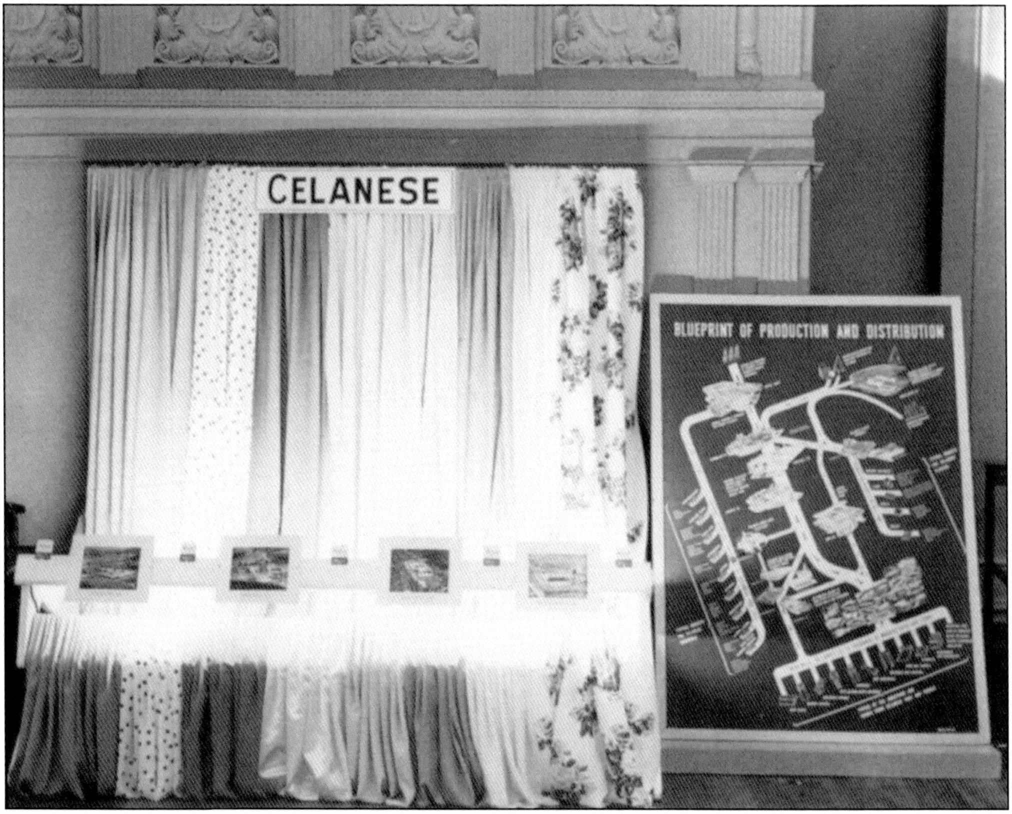

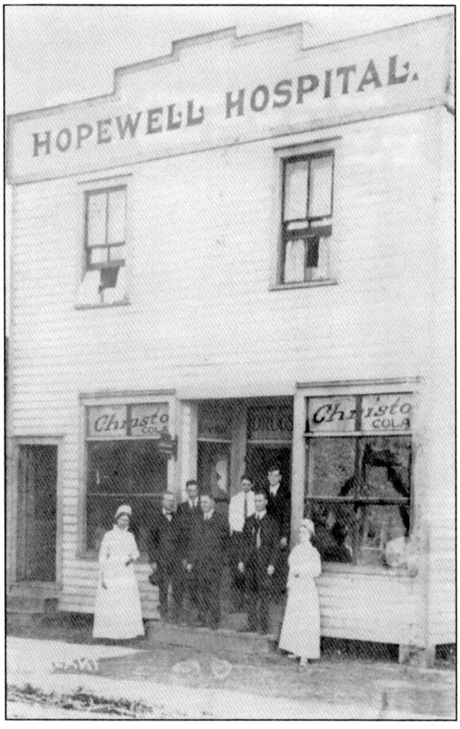

This photograph is of a Celanese Corporation display, providing a "blueprint of production and distribution." Draped behind the display are samples of its products. The bottom of the display shows photographs of its plants in Staunton (far left), Narrows (second from left), Hopewell, and Bridgewater (far right). At the bottom right of the photograph, the display charts, "From mills, the fabrics go to thousands of manufacturers and stores." (Photography courtesy of the *Hopewell News*, photograph courtesy of the Appomattox Regional Library.)

Rebuilding Hopewell meant both bodies and buildings. Hopewell's early hospital is shown with nurses standing outside. A soda advertisement also appears. This hospital, built in 1917, stands amid a long tradition of health care in the area. Mount Malady, the first English hospital in America, was founded at Henricus a few miles upriver from Hopewell. (Photograph courtesy of Jack Daniel.)

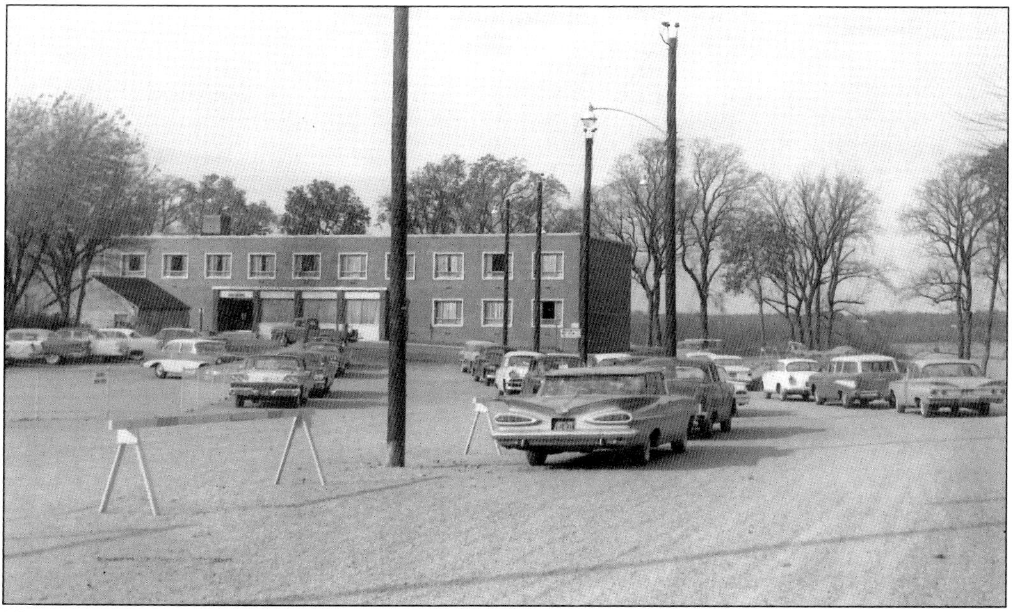

Hopewell Hospital continues its service today as it did when this photograph was taken in about 1960. Hopewell residents and industries made contributions that helped build the hospital. It was truly a community hospital. When it was eventually sold in the 1990s, the proceeds built a nonprofit foundation to carry on community wellbeing. (Photograph courtesy of Jack Daniel).

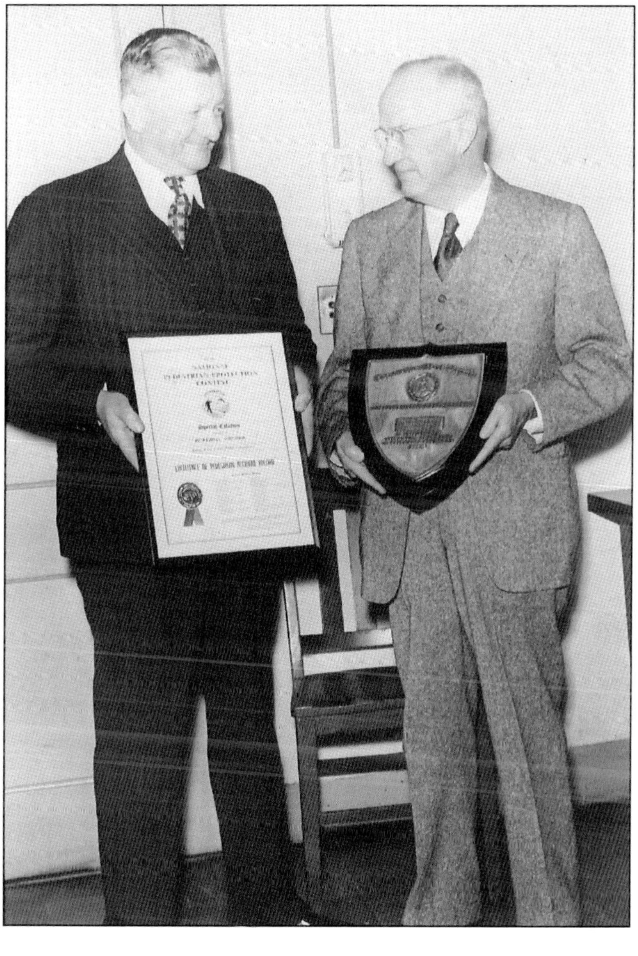

Hopewell received a safety award in 1949. Mayor D. Lane Elder (right), a prominent local physician, and Guy Ancell (left), city manager, were presented an award for Hopewell from the Commonwealth of Virginia for its safety record of pedestrians. (Photography courtesy of the *Hopewell News*; photograph courtesy of the Appomattox Regional Library.)

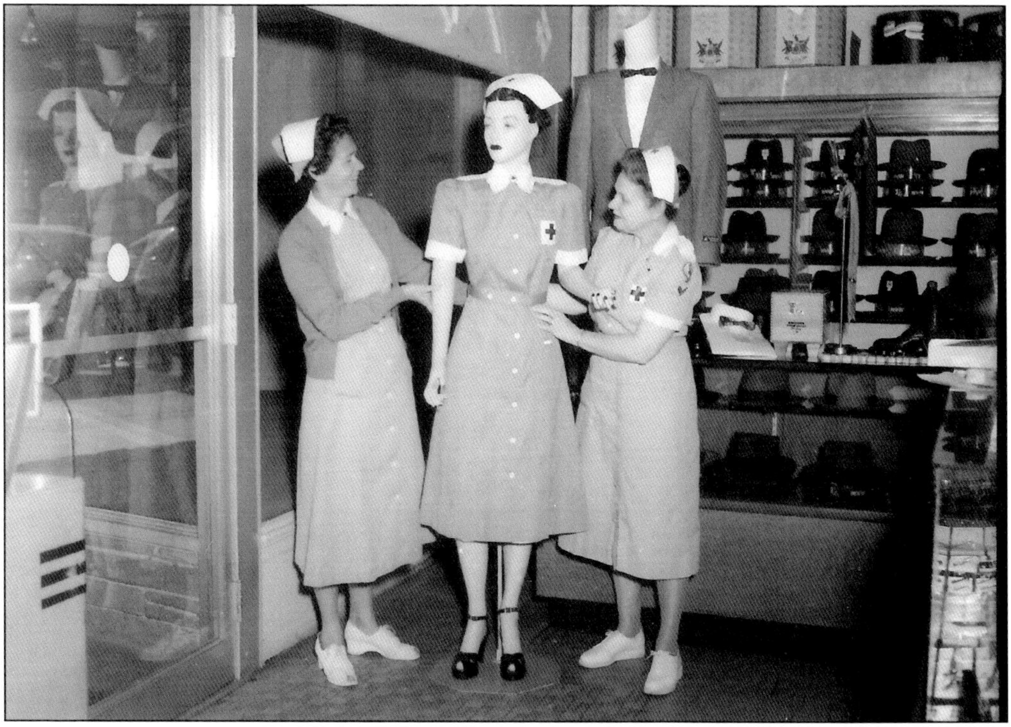

This undated photograph depicts period hospital uniforms. Hospital workers check out new uniforms in a store selling men's hats. (Photograph courtesy of Jack Daniel.)

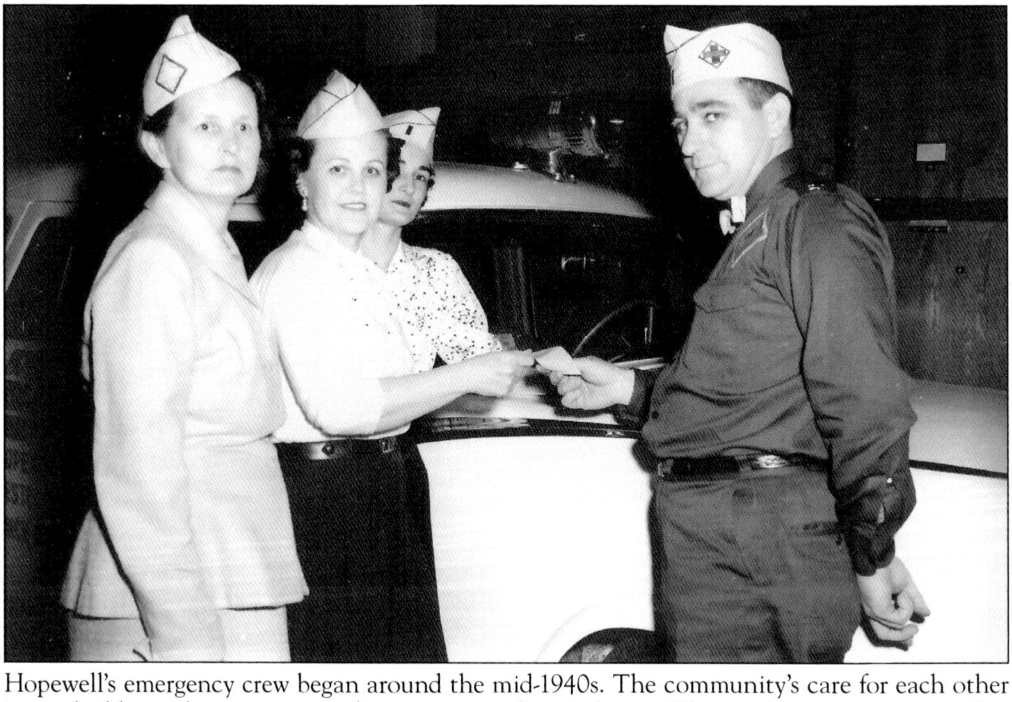

Hopewell's emergency crew began around the mid-1940s. The community's care for each other is a valuable product, just as much as any manufactured item. That tradition continues today. (Photograph courtesy of Jack Daniel.)

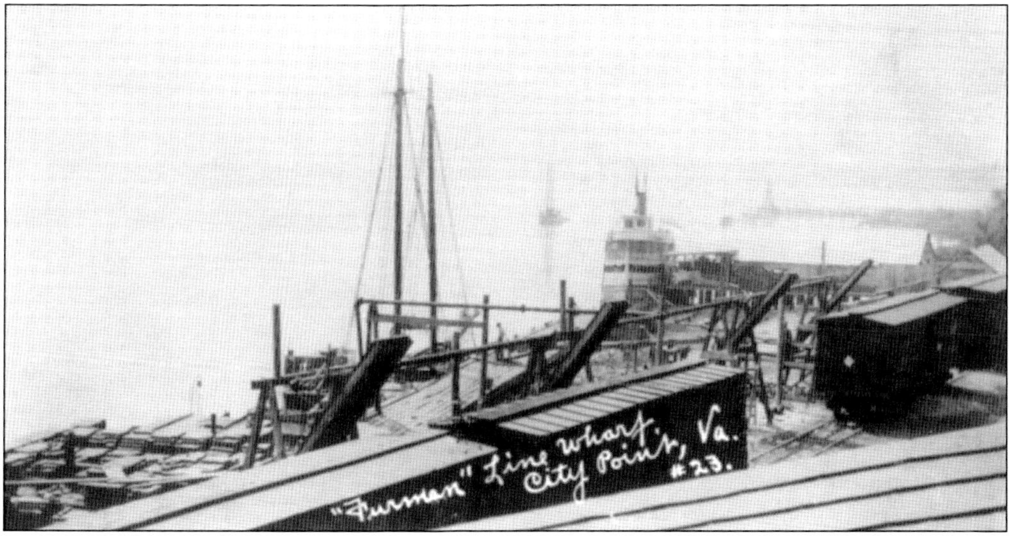

A commercial liner is docked at City Point. Written notes on this photograph, apparently from 1954, state, "Now we do not see much or many of the boats we saw back in those days. It was nice to sail down the James River to Newport News." (Photograph courtesy of the Appomattox Regional Library.)

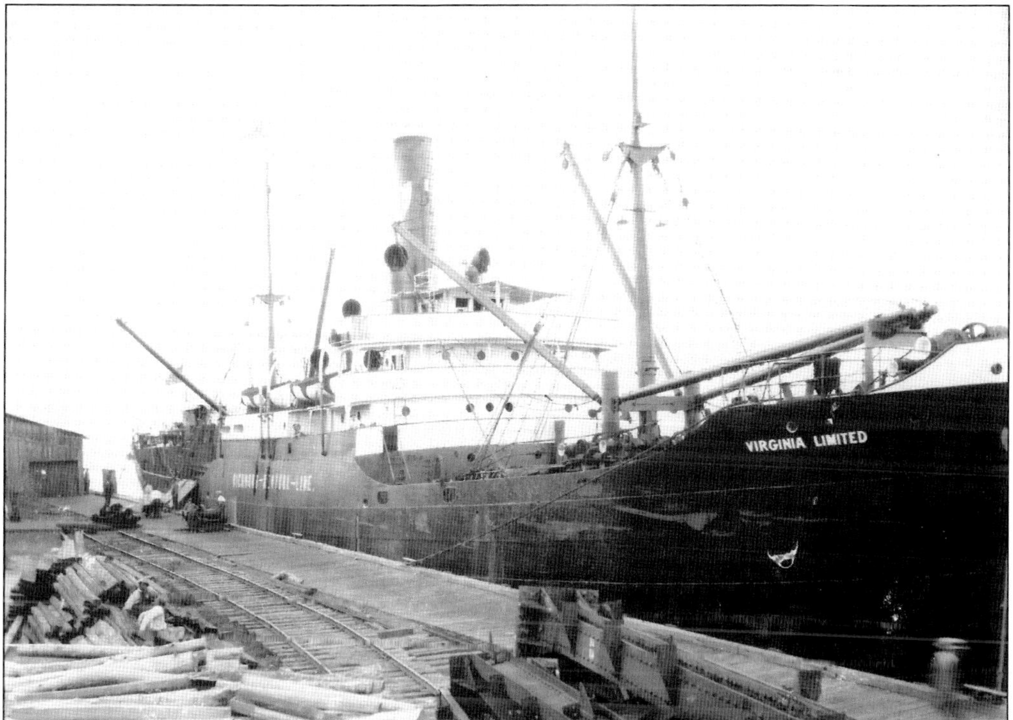

Another commercial liner stops at Hopewell's harbor. To help keep the river channel from Hopewell to Hampton Roads clear, at least in the 1950s, the federal government kept a 300-foot-wide, 26-foot-deep channel dredged. Before World War II, Hopewell ranked 23rd among US ports based on tonnage. (Photograph courtesy of Jack Daniel.)

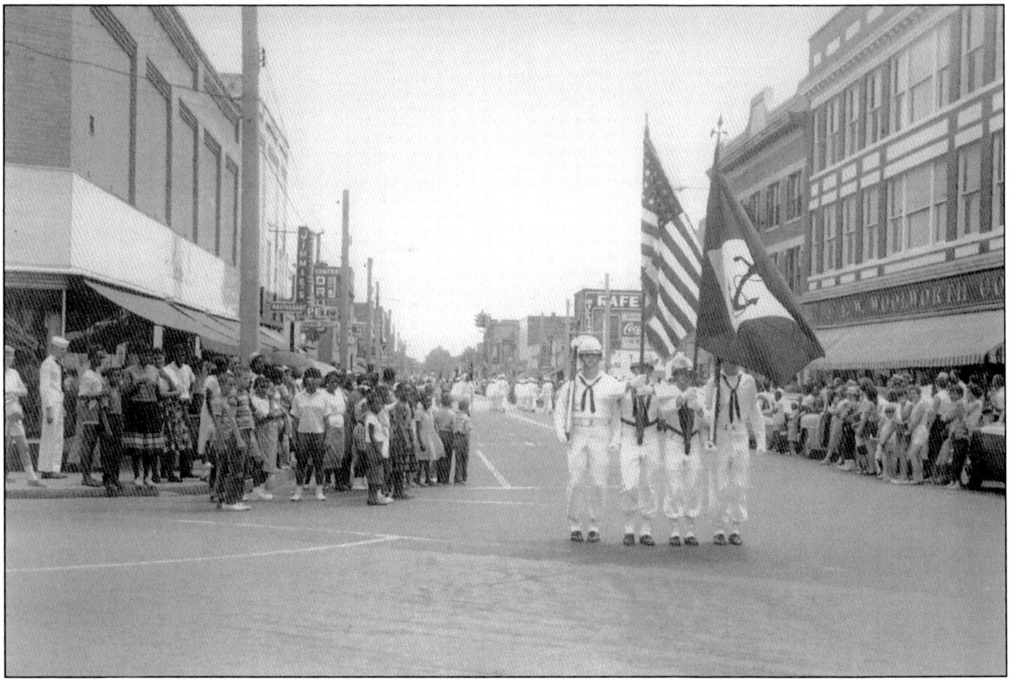

In this Memorial Day parade, sailors march toward the heart of downtown on West Broadway. The Woolworth's store on the right, no longer in existence, is now the municipal building. Stores like Central Drug and Jimmy's Restaurant can be seen in other photographs as well. (Photograph courtesy of the *Hopewell News* and Paul Karnes.)

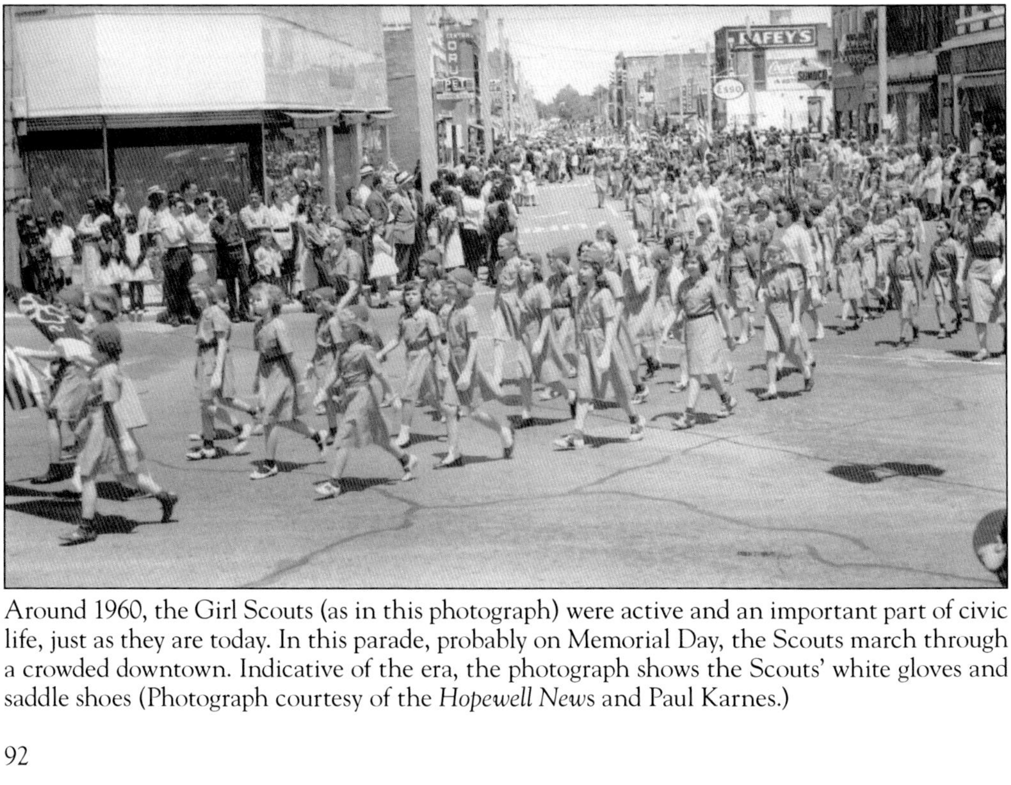

Around 1960, the Girl Scouts (as in this photograph) were active and an important part of civic life, just as they are today. In this parade, probably on Memorial Day, the Scouts march through a crowded downtown. Indicative of the era, the photograph shows the Scouts' white gloves and saddle shoes (Photograph courtesy of the *Hopewell News* and Paul Karnes.)

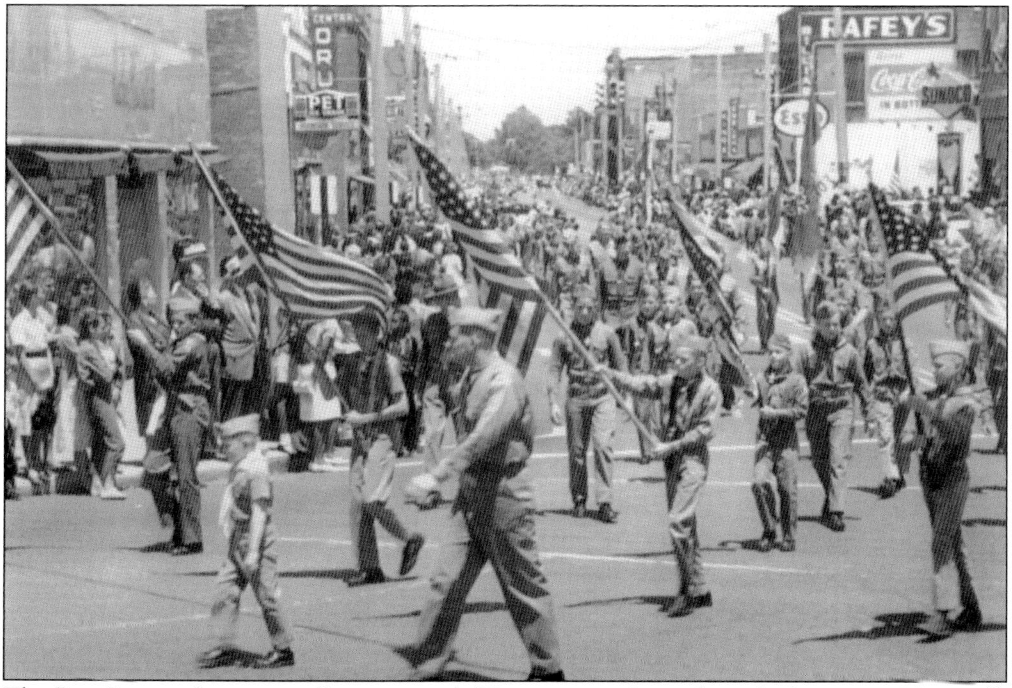

The Boy Scouts also were well represented. They are marching through downtown Hopewell. Central Drug, a longtime store in Hopewell, is seen at the center left. (Photograph courtesy of the *Hopewell News* and Paul Karnes.)

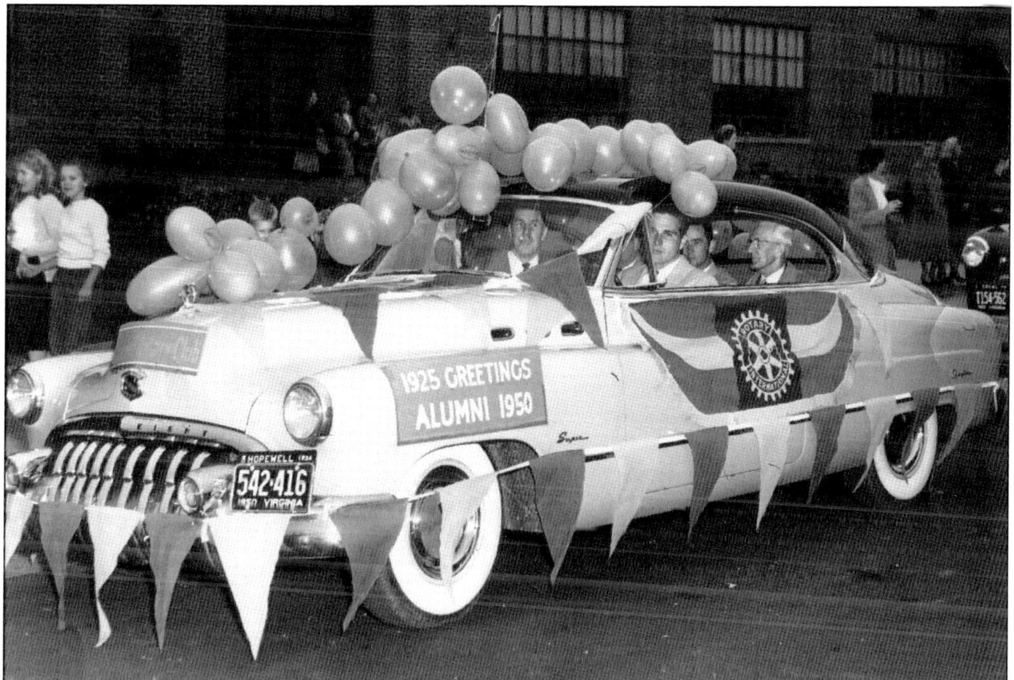

Hopewell Rotarians take quite a ride in this 1950 parade. They are riding stylishly in a 1950 Buick Super Eight. (Photograph courtesy of the *Hopewell News* and the Appomattox Regional Library.)

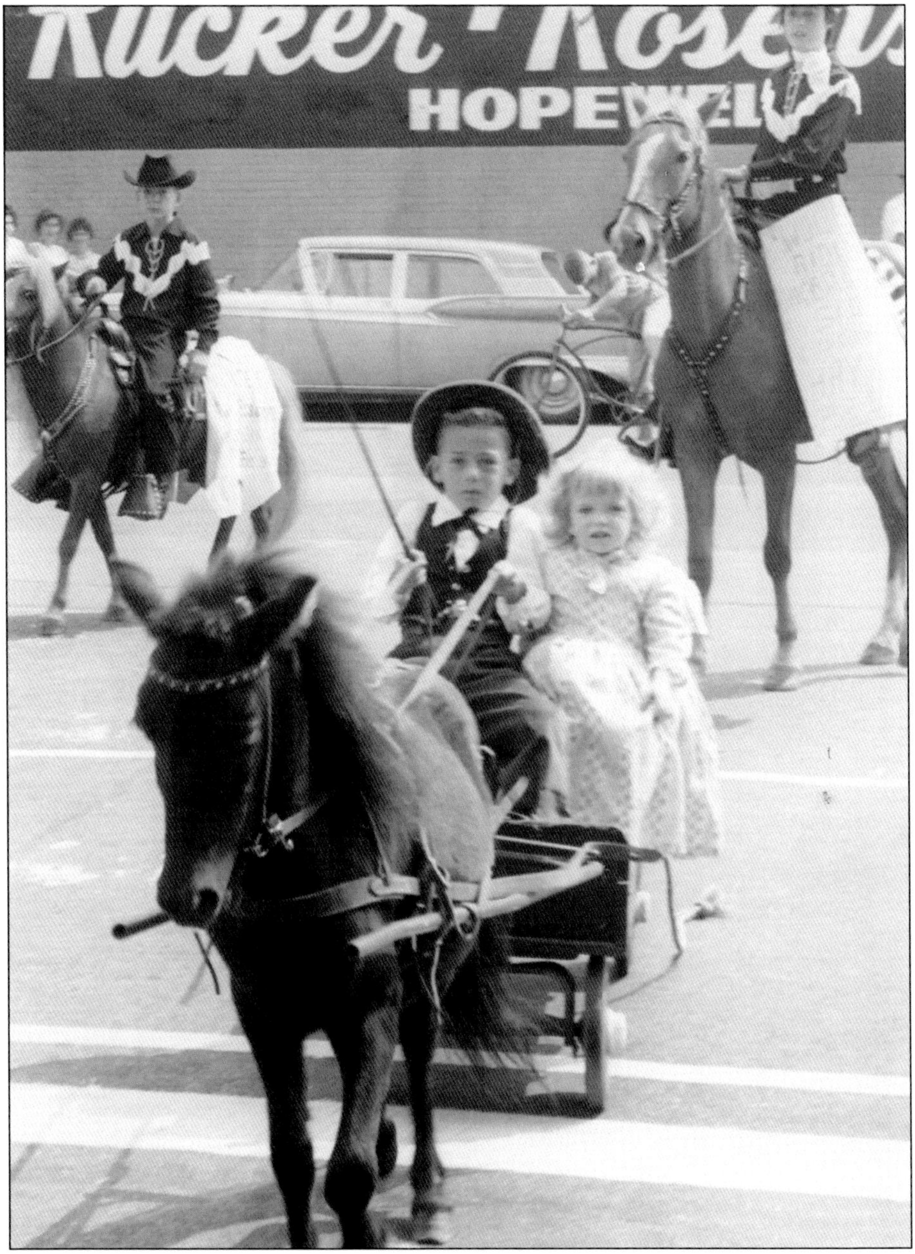

Parade pictures have so much social and cultural information. While these two young people steal the show in the foreground, some clues to Hopewell lie in the background. The mounted rider to the upper right has a sign on the horse advertising both a riding academy and hay. In the far background to the center is a Ford Thunderbird, which helps date the photograph. Finally, in the far left, is another rider with a sign on his horse. The horse drawing the two youngsters in the foreground is a miniature horse, originally used in coal mining because of their intellect and compact stature. They reputedly make wonderful pets (though many owners pad their hooves to prevent wear and tear on household furnishings). A close examination of the expression on the two youngsters' faces seems a mixture of bemusement and sheer terror. (Photography courtesy of the *Hopewell News* and the Appomattox Regional Library.)

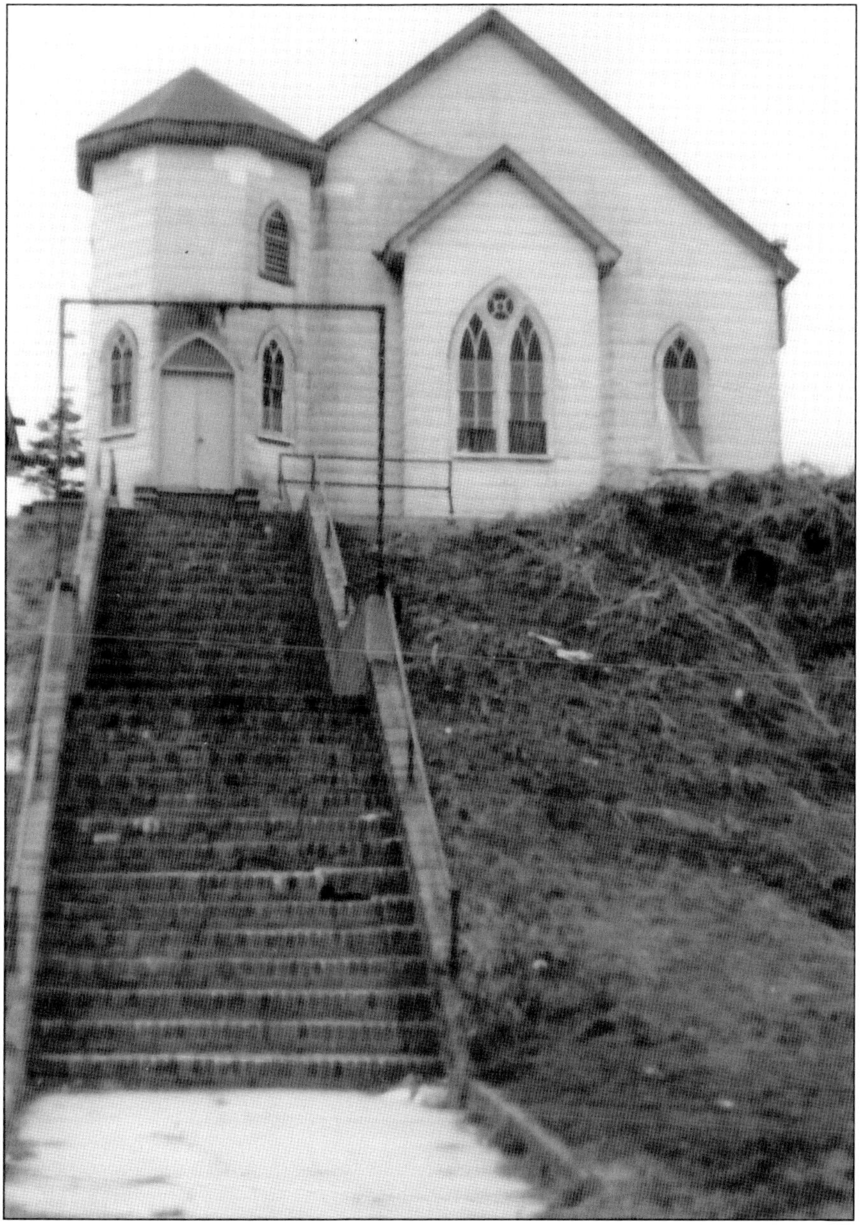

Both visitors and residents comment on the many churches in Hopewell. In 1952, Hopewell had 26 churches representing 17 different denominations. The First Baptist Church of City Point recognizes its beginnings from 1867. Begun by its mother church, the First Baptist Church of Petersburg (on Harrison Street), City Point was moved from one location to another in close proximity to its original site on Appomattox Street, near Francis Street. Locations included sites at the end of Pecan Street, downhill from the Pecan Street site, and the foot of the former Prince Henry Avenue (now Church Street). A permanent site was needed because, as its textual history notes, some of "the members became annoyed by frogs in the pond" and sought a refuge where their praises would go uninterrupted by distracting sounds. This building shows the church's Gothic windows. (Photograph courtesy of the Reverend Rudolph Dunbar.)

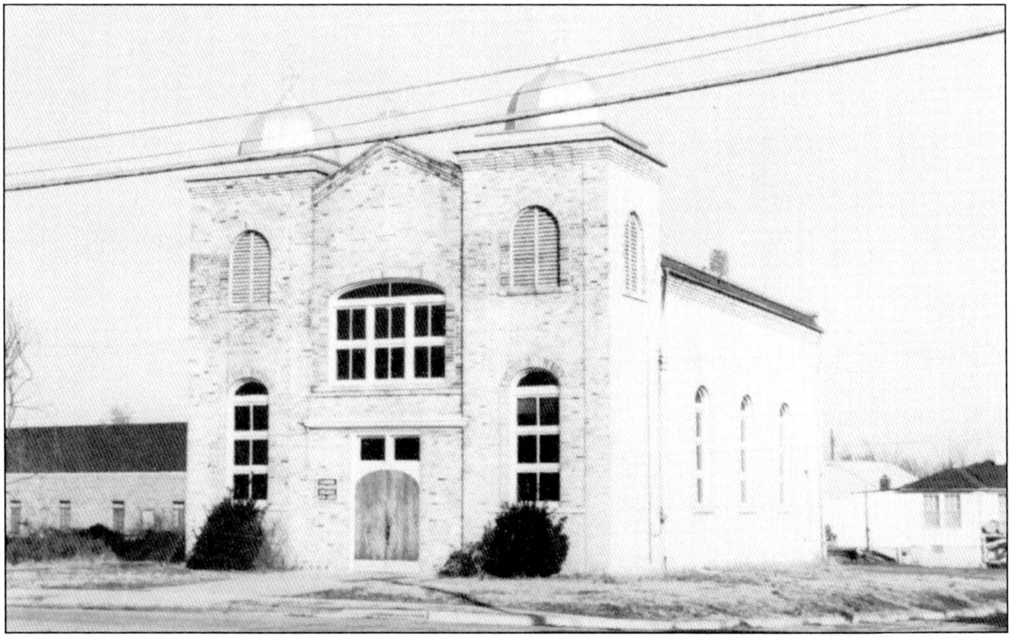

The following two photographs demonstrate both Hopewell's religious and architectural diversity. The original St. Elpis Greek Orthodox Church was built on Memorial Avenue and was consecrated in 1917. The current church is located very close by on the corner of Memorial Avenue and Poythress Street. St. Elpis (whose name means "hope" in Greek) was one of three holy martyrs in Italy during Hadrian's reign (117–138 CE). (Photograph courtesy of the Appomattox Regional Library.)

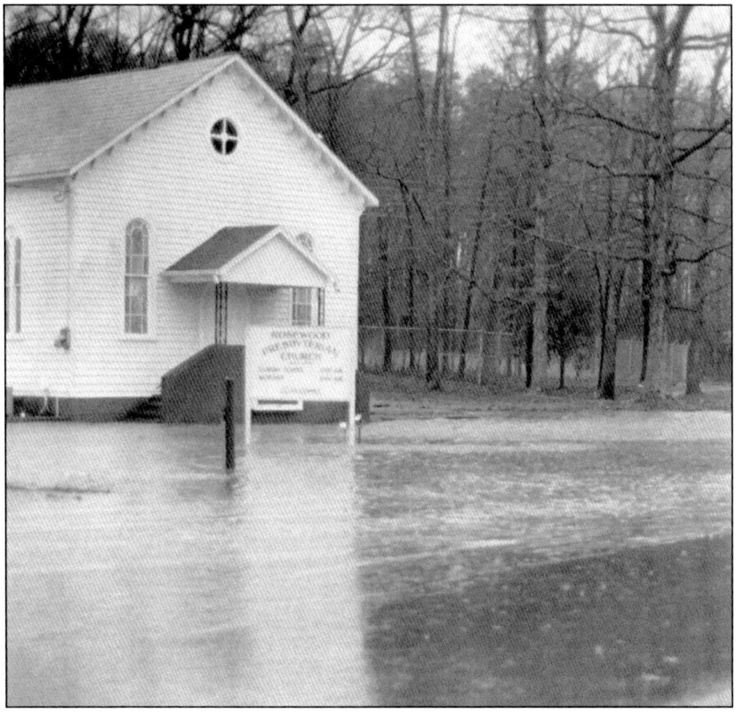

Rosewood Presbyterian Church was established in 1875, as the sign outside the church attests. This wood-frame church is located next door to the Fort Lee military base on State Route 36. (Photograph courtesy of the Appomattox Regional Library.)

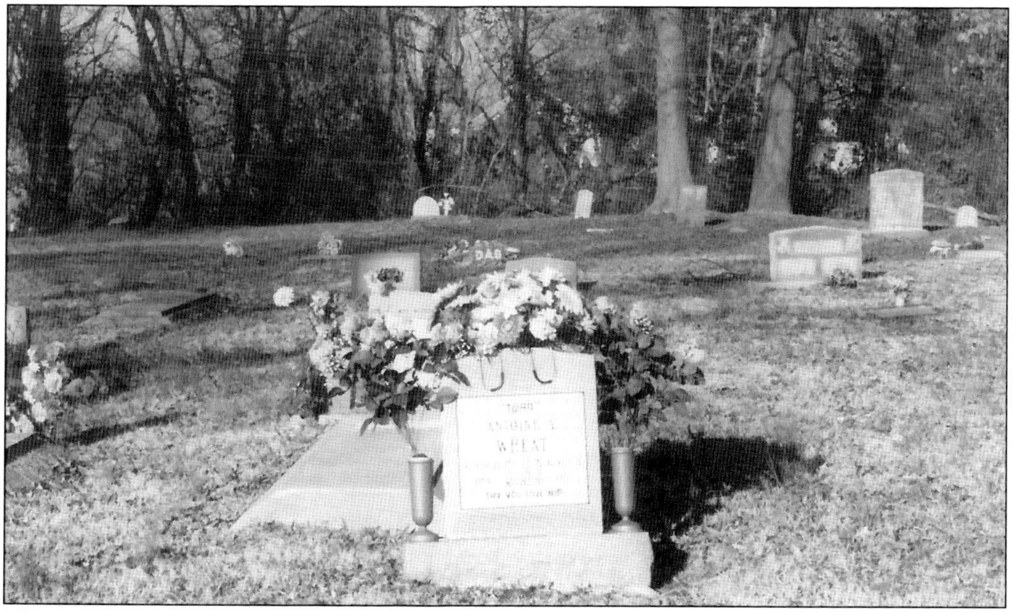

The cemetery of the First Baptist Church in City Point is recognized as having grave markers that date to the 1870s, and it is thought to have been used even before then. Located on Appomattox Street, it is still used today. (Photograph courtesy of the Reverend Rudolph Dunbar.)

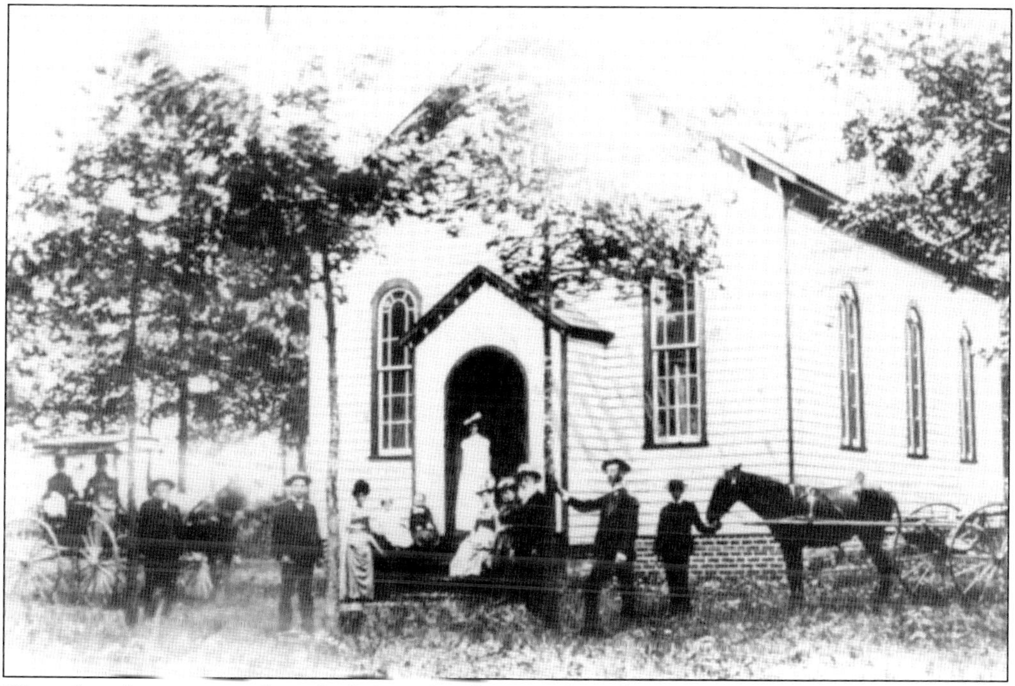

This church was not identified, but the dress and mode of transport mark it as an early religious location. (Photograph courtesy of the Appomattox Regional Library.)

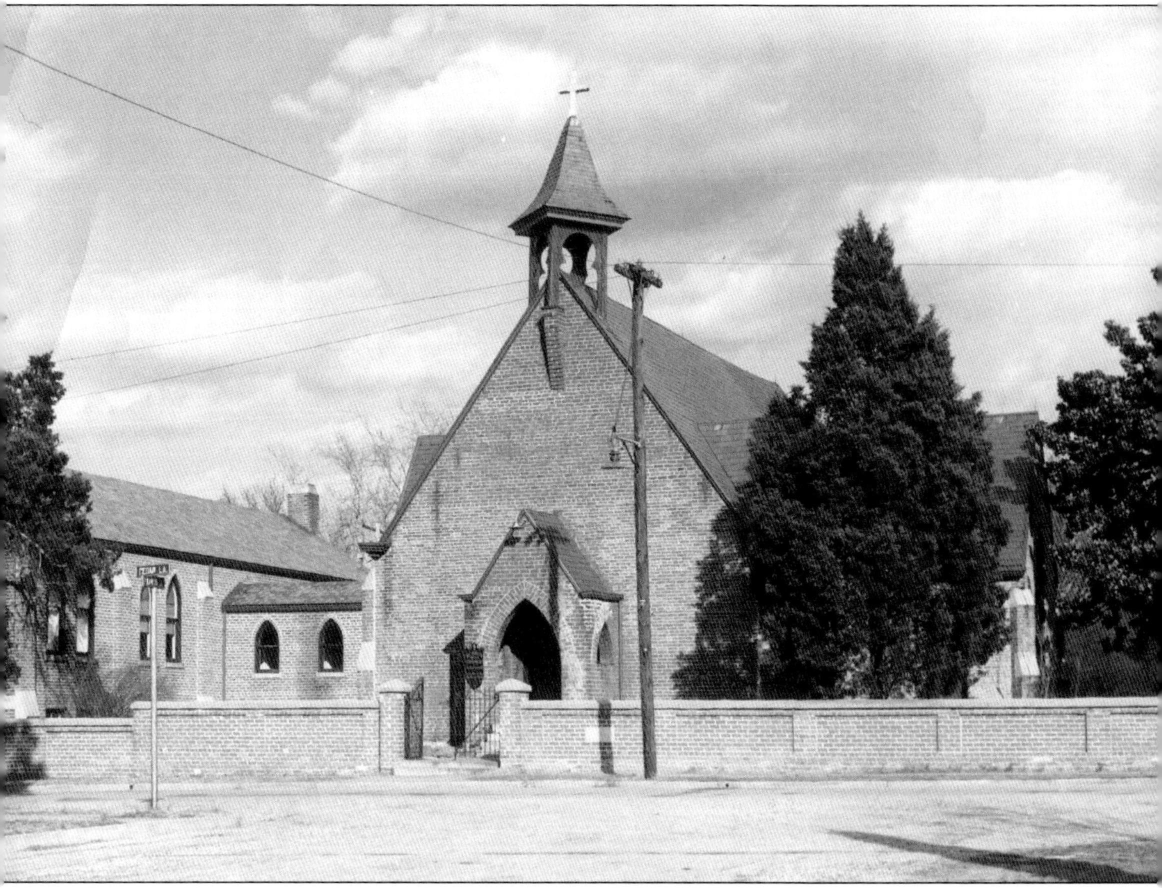

This photograph depicts St. John's Episcopal Church. Still located in Hopewell, at 505 Cedar Lane, the church's basement was a safe haven for slaves during the fight for City Point in May 1864. A history of the church (www.stjohnshopewell.org) indicates it was founded in 1840 on land donated by the Eppes family, which originally built Appomattox Manor. During the Civil War, the church was used for nonecclesiastical purposes such as a signal tower and even a dance hall. The war was hard on the building, but it was restored in 1867 and rebuilt in 1894. Restorations continued. In 1919, Tubize Artificial Silk Company donated lighting and stained glass windows were added. (Photograph courtesy of the Appomattox Regional Library.)

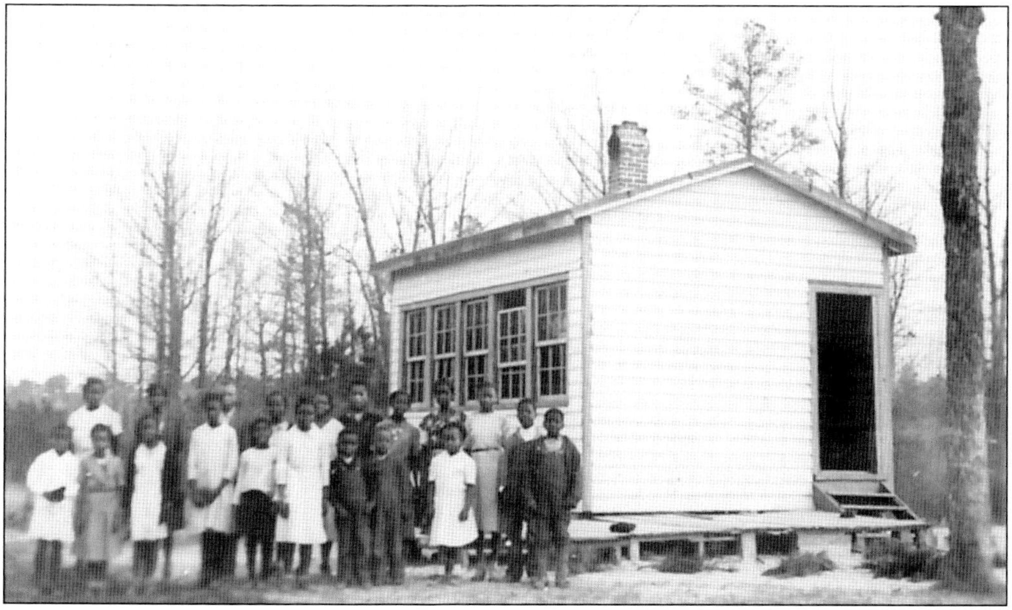

This photograph shows an unidentified African American school before the days of integration. The first African American on Hopewell's school board was Dr. Calvin Thigpen in the early 1960s. While not much is known about this particular school, formal education for African Americans around Hopewell began to 1916. DuPont wanted African Americans to be able to sign their paychecks. While informal education probably took place in homes or public buildings, later schools like Carter G. Woodson were the beneficiaries of such foundations. (Photograph courtesy of the Hopewell Public Schools.)

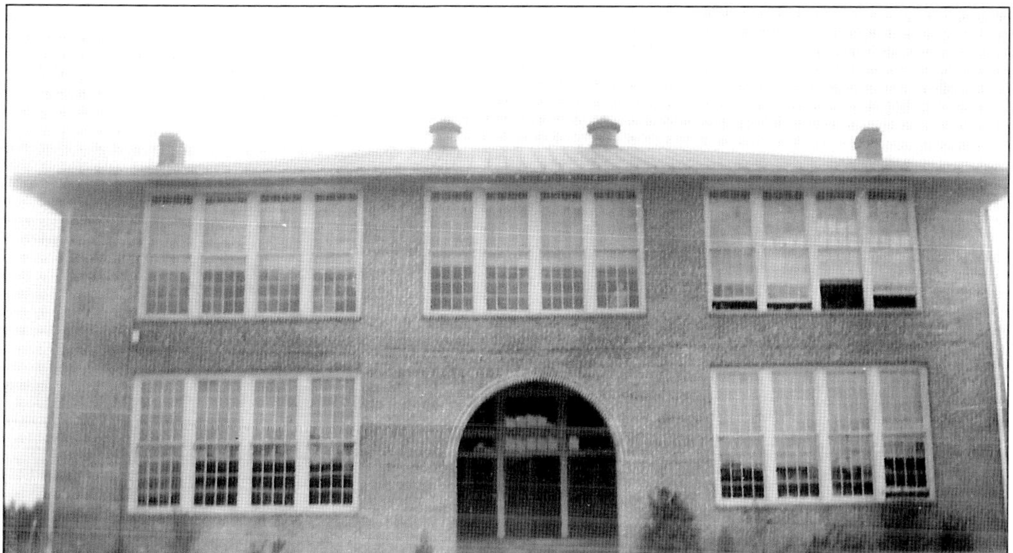

This is the Woodlawn School, built as part of Hopewell's educational system. Hopewell has a long tradition of both curricular and extracurricular activities, as many of the photographs attest. As early as 1925, the high school began its annual yearbook as the *Satellite*. A few years later, it was known as the *Kaleidoscope*. (Photograph courtesy of Paul Karnes.)

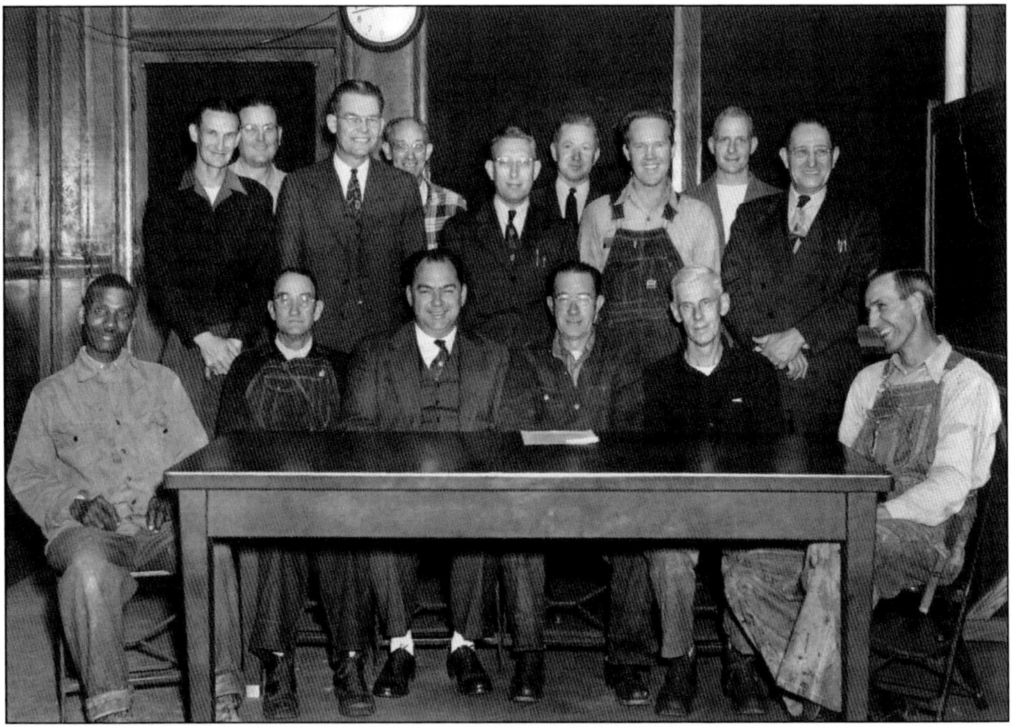

Wage negotiations were part of Hopewell's industrial life. Here, a team is negotiating a Hercules Powder Company contract in November 1950. (Photograph courtesy of the *Hopewell News* and the Appomattox Regional Library.)

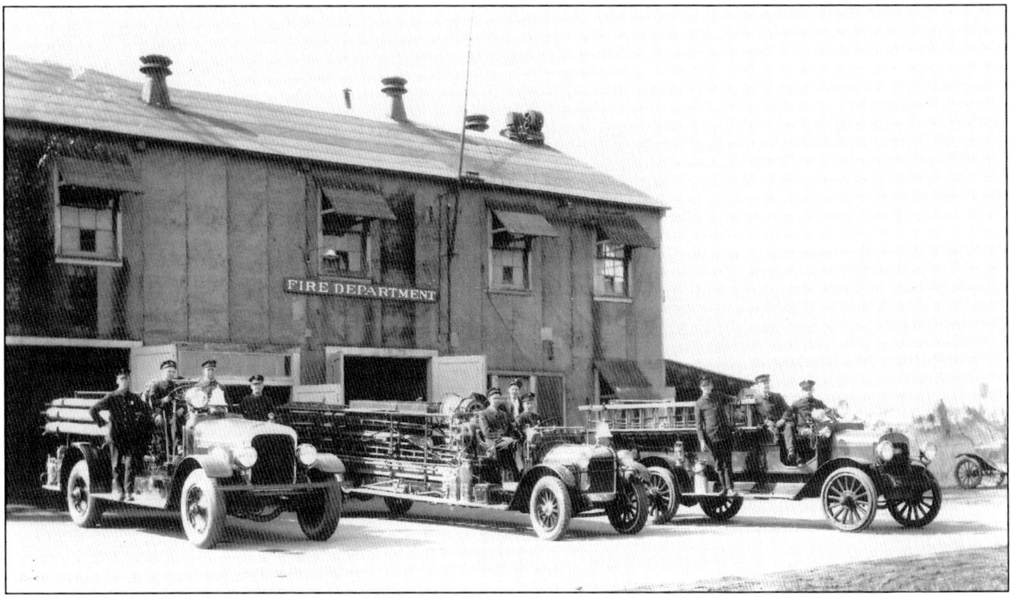

Increased industry meant greater public services. Pictured is an early fire department, probably in the 1920s. (Photograph courtesy of Jack Daniel.)

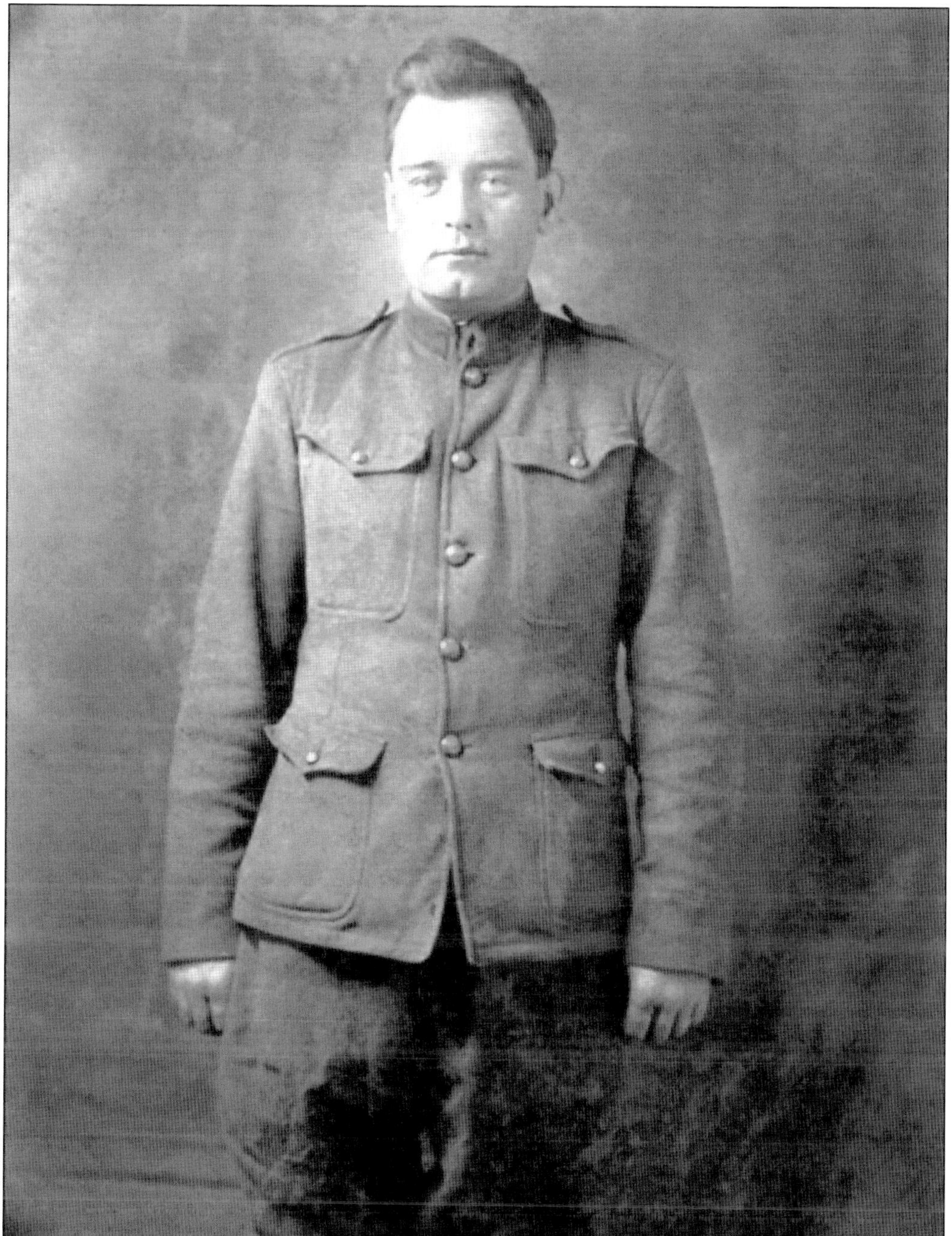

Silas Daniel, the father of Jack Daniel (who contributed many photographs to this book), stands in uniform. He was a mounted police officer for DuPont in 1916. DuPont had to be conscious of security, as it was making war material in the form of explosives prior to and during World War I. It is said, in fact, that DuPont chose Hopewell's more protected port (some 80 miles from the coast), in part, because it was safer from enemy attacks. Silas was born in Danieltown, Virginia, in 1886 and lived until 1945. (Photograph courtesy of Jack Daniel.)

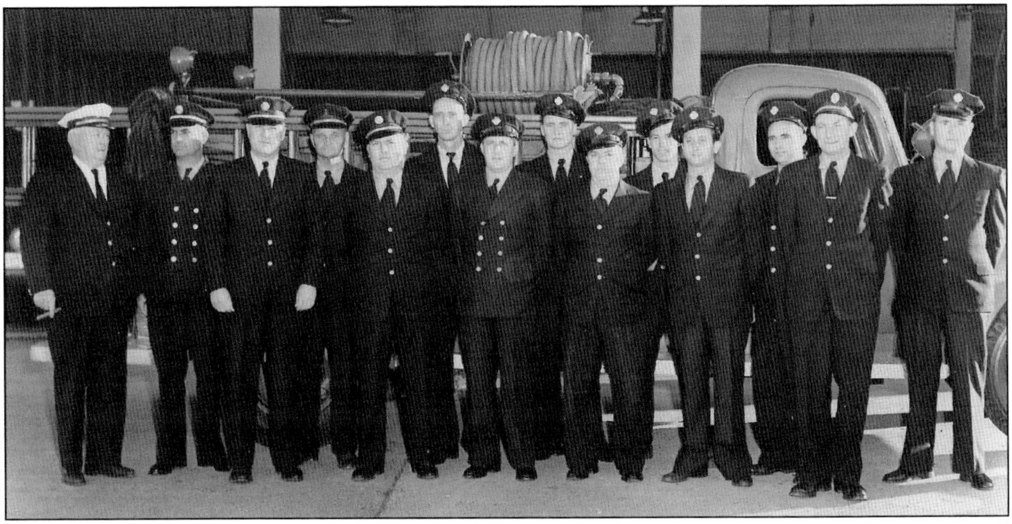

This photograph shows the uniformed Hopewell Fire Department of the 1950s. In 1951, Hopewell spent $125,000 on police and fire protection. (Photograph courtesy of the *Hopewell News* and Paul Karnes.)

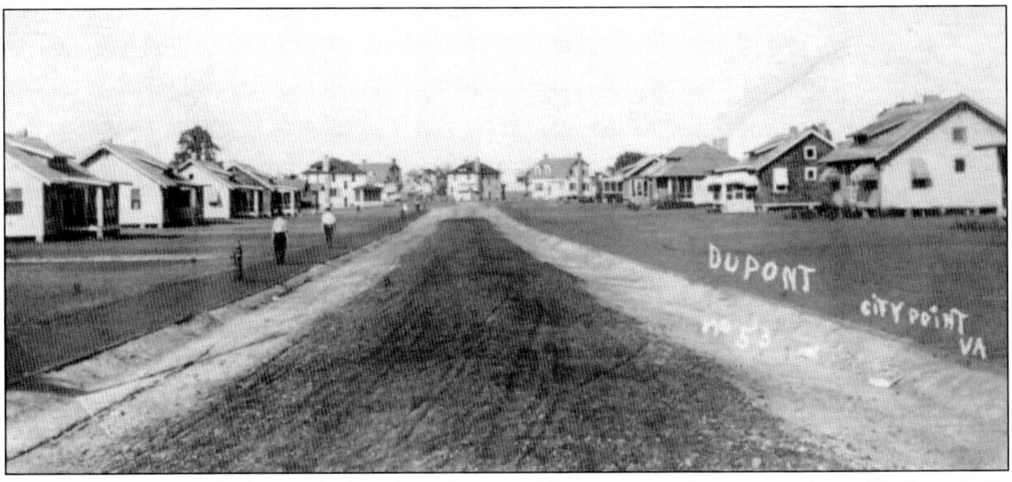

By 1952, Hopewell had paved 45 miles of streets. To accommodate its workers, DuPont built A-Village and B-Village in Hopewell on land from the Eppes estate. A-Village was located in and around the City Point area, and B-Village was located around Main Street, Sixth Street, the Appomattox, and the railroad. South B-Village was the section designed for African Americans in the pre-integration era. (Photograph courtesy of the Appomattox Regional Library.)

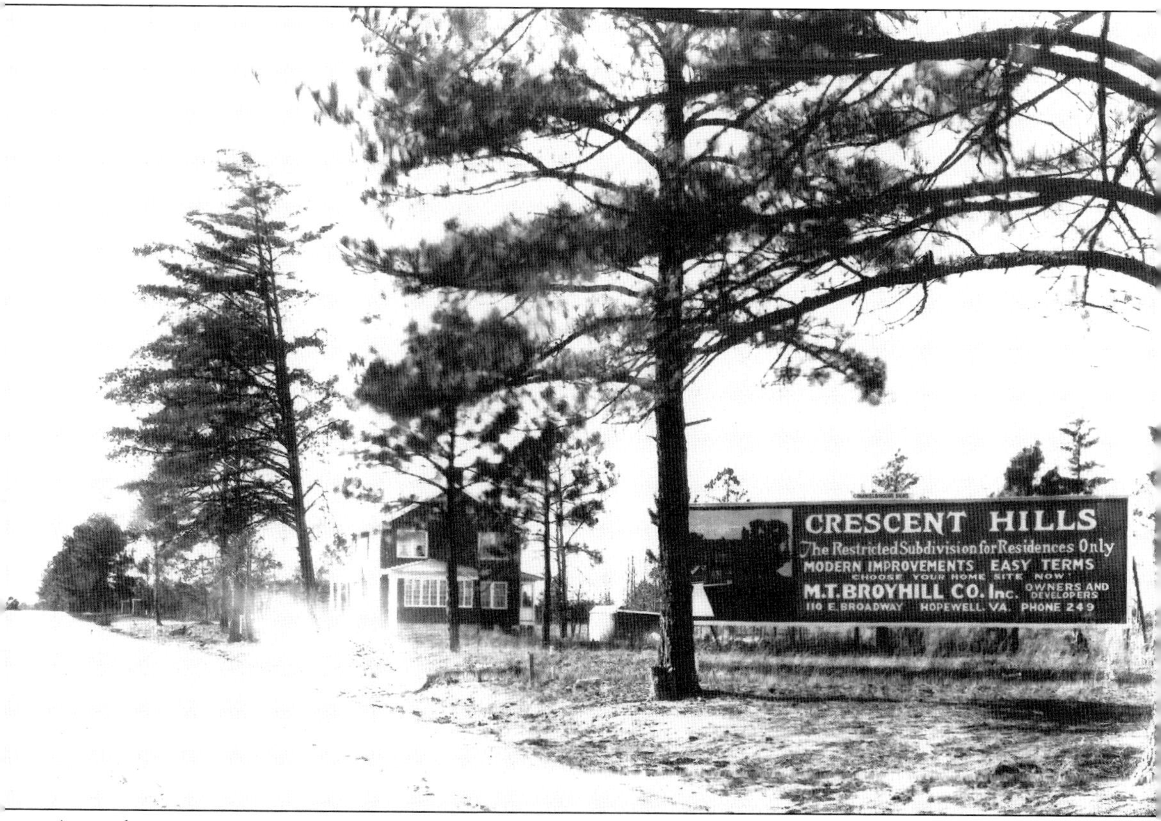

According to *Crescent Hills*, the Hopewell Visitors Center's brochure about the neighborhood, M.T. Broyhill developed Crescent Hills in the mid-1920s and into the 1930s. Customers could choose their homes out of a Sears and Roebuck catalog, and they were put together on site. Thus, parts of Hopewell were some of the first planned communities in the United States. This photograph (from about 1930) shows City Point Road heading west. The residence pictured is still standing and occupied. Originally, Hopewell was part of Prince George County. Over time, the jurisdictions separated, and around 1952, Hopewell annexed Woodlawn, Crescent Hills, Mansion Hills, Buren Gardens, Shenandoah, and Westwood Park. In 1951, Hopewell saw 35 new homes built within its environs, and the total value of building permits issued was estimated at almost $720,000. Thirty-five homes were built in 1952, valued then at $266,800. (Photograph courtesy of Jack Daniel.)

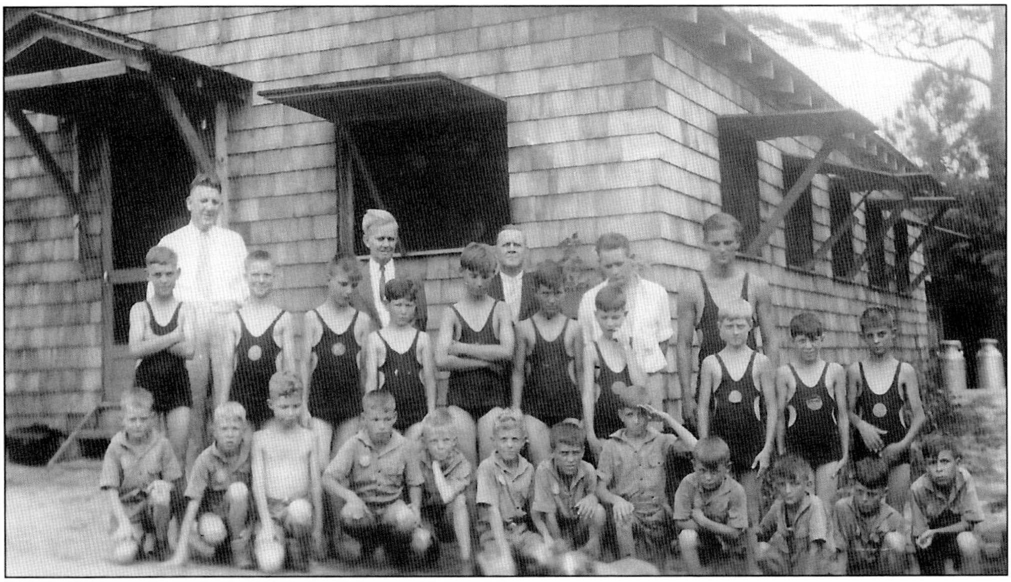

A water sports team and Scouts pose around 1930. The setting is next to a building believed to be alongside the railroad tracks on East Broadway. That building is no longer standing. (Photograph courtesy of Paul Karnes.)

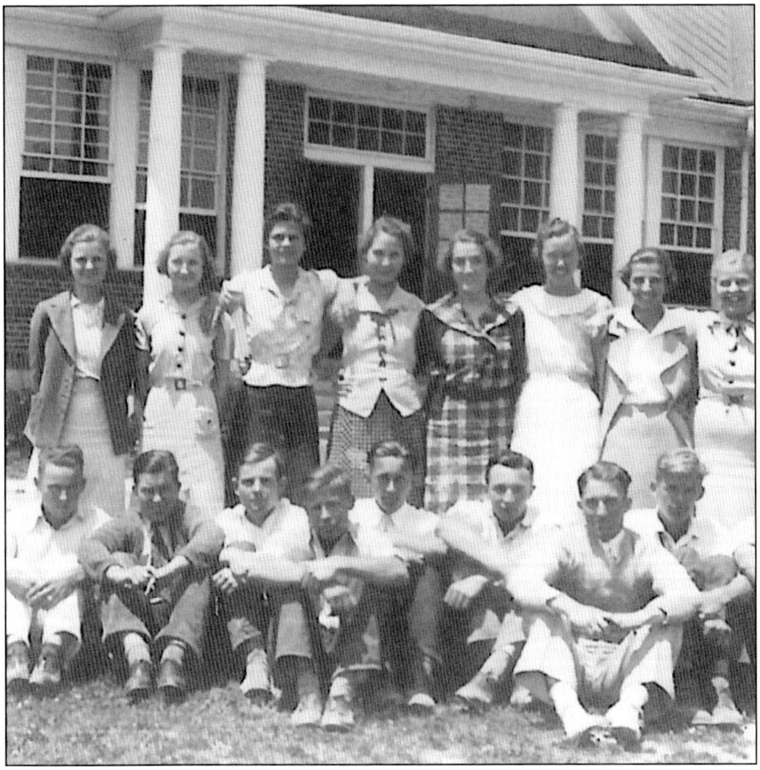

The Carson School graduated these seniors in 1936. It was located in Prince George County, adjacent to Hopewell. At that time, what are now Hopewell and Prince George schools districts were one, but they have been separate for some time. (Photograph courtesy of Hopewell Public Schools.)

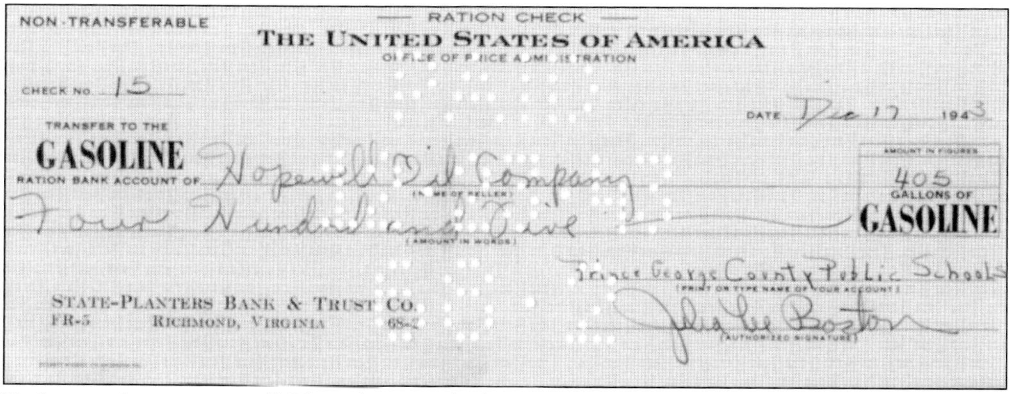
NON-TRANSFERABLE

RATION CHECK

THE UNITED STATES OF AMERICA

OFFICE OF PRICE ADMINISTRATION

CHECK NO. 15

DATE Dec 17 1943

TRANSFER TO THE GASOLINE RATION BANK ACCOUNT OF Hopewell Oil Company

(NAME OF SELLER)

Four Hundred and Five

(AMOUNT IN WORDS)

AMOUNT IN FIGURES 405 GALLONS OF GASOLINE

Prince George County Public Schools

(PRINT OR TYPE NAME OF YOUR ACCOUNT)

STATE-PLANTERS BANK & TRUST CO.

FR-5 RICHMOND, VIRGINIA 68-2

(AUTHORIZED SIGNATURE)

Fuel runs education as well. This photograph shows a ration coupon from 1943, issued for gasoline during the war years to the Hopewell and Prince George County school districts, which were the same at that time. (Document courtesy of Hopewell Public Schools.)

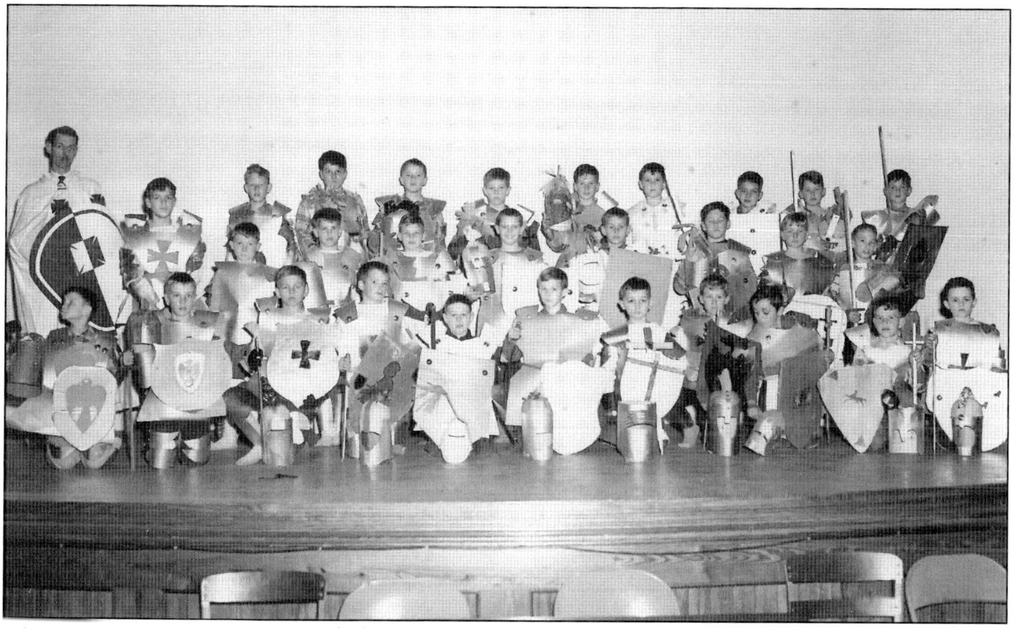

This photograph shows a school play at DuPont School in the mid-1950s. The show is *Camelot*. (Photograph courtesy of the *Hopewell News* and Paul Karnes.)

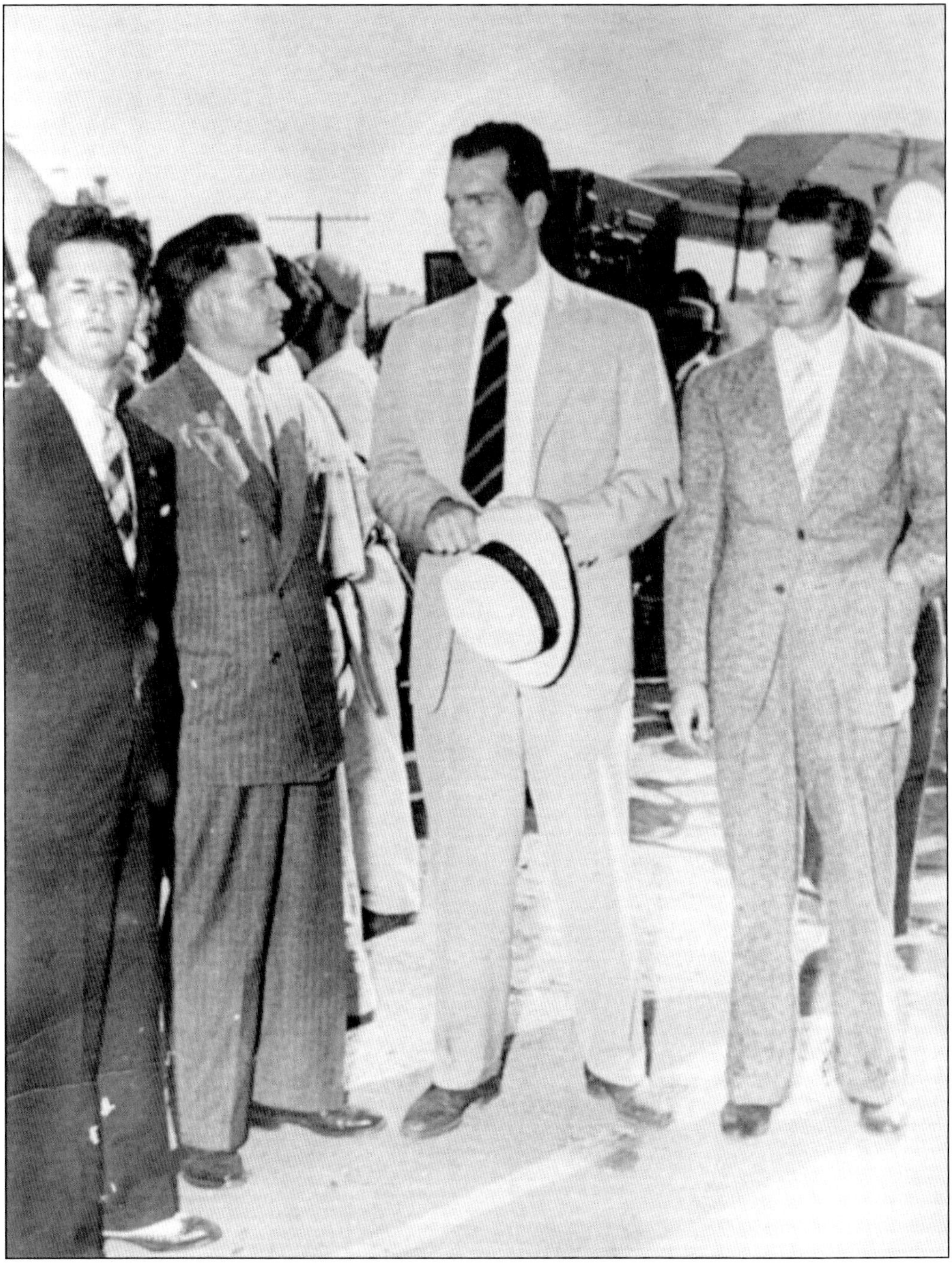

Hopewell hosted all kinds of entertainment. Fred MacMurray and costar Madeline Carroll came to Hopewell to film the 1941 movie *Virginia*. Standing by MacMurray (third from left) are James Cuddihy, Henry Blankenship, and John Aderholt. MacMurray is famous for the 1960s television comedy series *My Three Sons*, for *The Caine Mutiny* with Humphrey Bogart, and for the film noir classic *Double Indemnity* with costar Barbara Stanwyck. *Virginia*, directed by Edward H. Griffith, concerned a Southern woman (Carroll) in dire straits who had to make hard choices to live. (Photograph courtesy of the *Hopewell News* and Jack Daniel.)

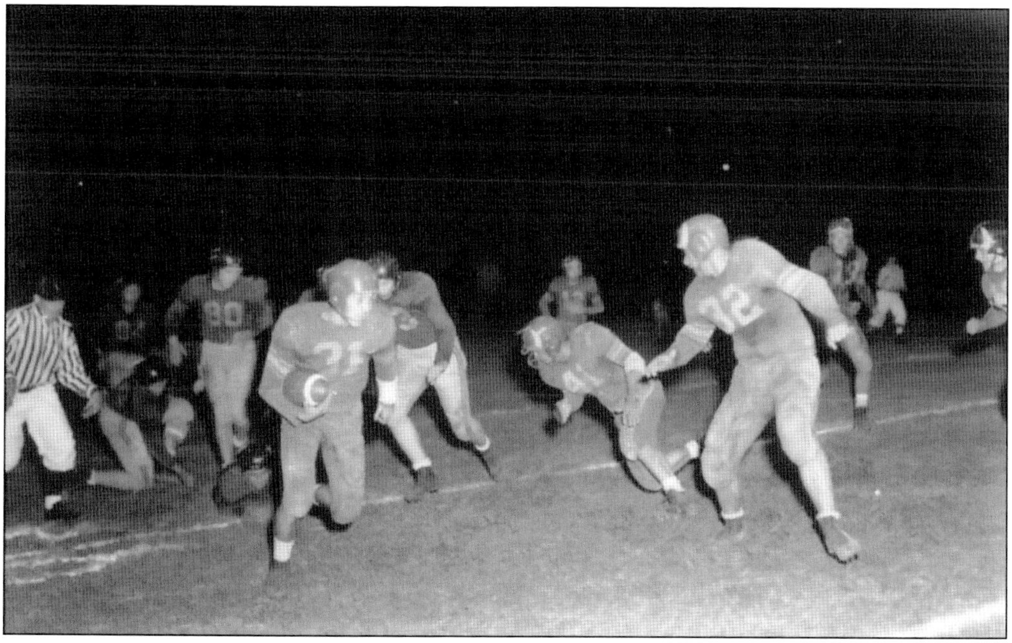

This is the Hopewell High School football team playing in 1955. This game was between Hopewell and Petersburg, longtime high school rivals. The Hopewell team won the Virginia State Championship in 1949 and tied for the state championship in 1950. It won first place again in 1951. Note that the players, although wearing helmets, have no face masks. (Photograph courtesy of the *Hopewell News* and Jack Daniel.)

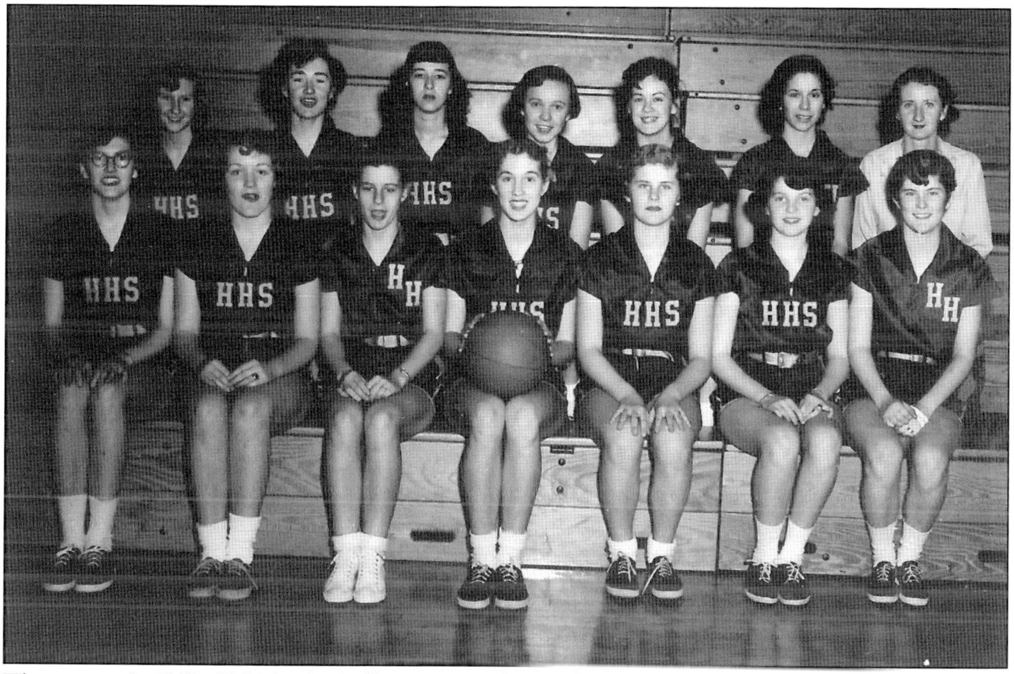

The women's 1953–1954 basketball team stands in a long tradition of women's interscholastic athletics. Hopewell fielded a women's basketball squad as early as 1923. (Photograph courtesy of the *Hopewell News* and Jack Daniel.)

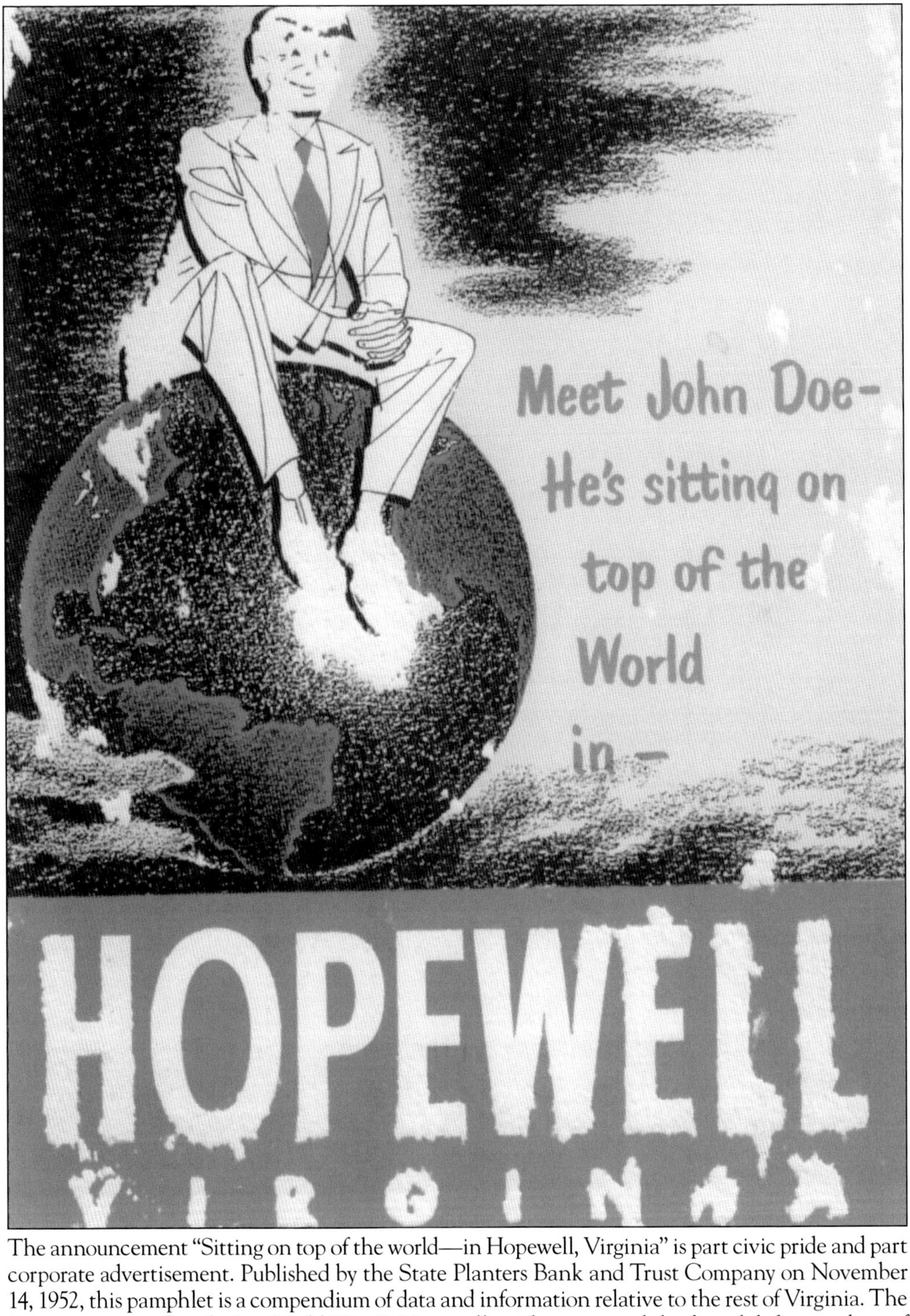

The announcement "Sitting on top of the world—in Hopewell, Virginia" is part civic pride and part corporate advertisement. Published by the State Planters Bank and Trust Company on November 14, 1952, this pamphlet is a compendium of data and information relative to the rest of Virginia. The document states that during World War II, Hopewell residents created the first club for members of the military. They raised private funds to start the club months before the beginning of the national USO. The original cover was in bold red, black, and yellow. (Brochure courtesy of Jack Daniel.)

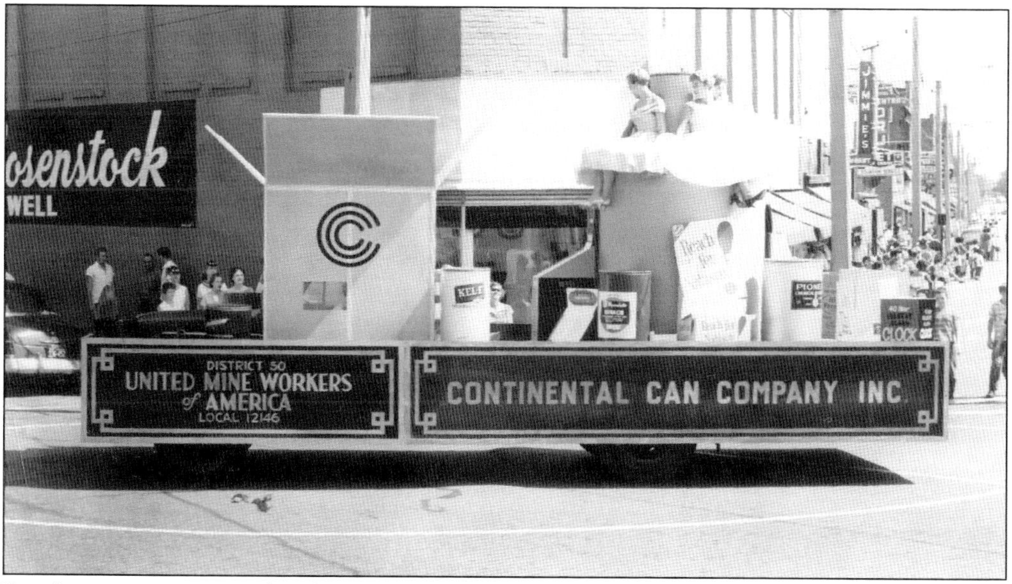

Parades sometimes are related to product. Pictured is a float decorated by Continental Can and the local chapter of the United Mine Workers. At least one product on the float is still available, but crinoline dresses seem to be in short supply. The union keeps an office in Hopewell today. (Photograph courtesy of the *Hopewell News* and the Appomattox Regional Library.)

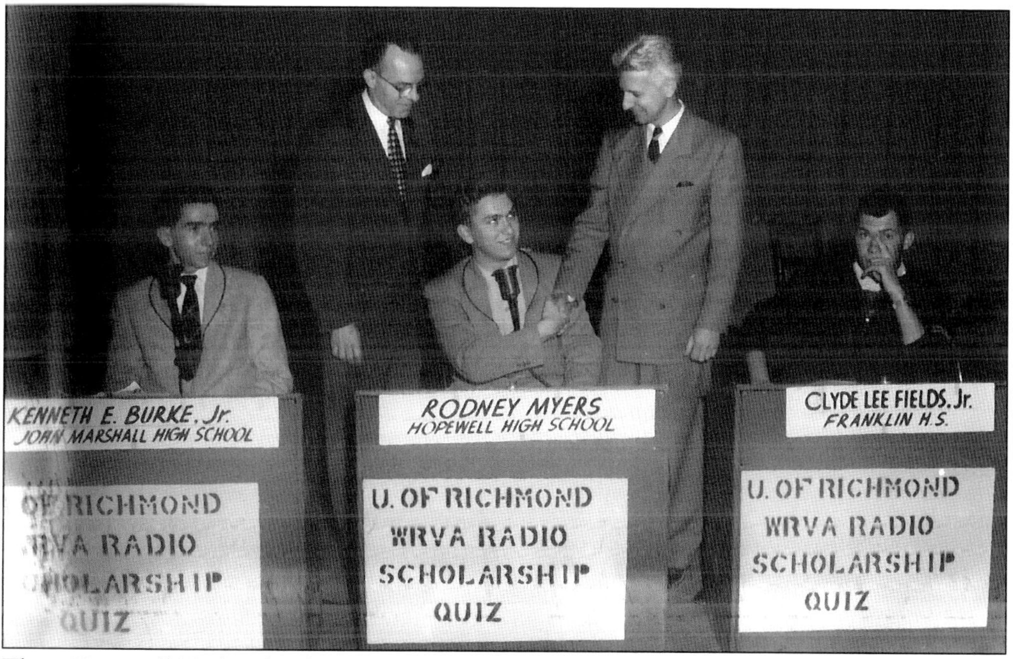

These Hopewell High School students demonstrate another kind of extracurricular competition around 1965. The Hopewell student in the center is congratulated during a quiz program sponsored by the University of Richmond and Richmond radio station WRVA. The two other schools are local as well. (Photograph courtesy of the *Hopewell News* and Jack Daniel.)

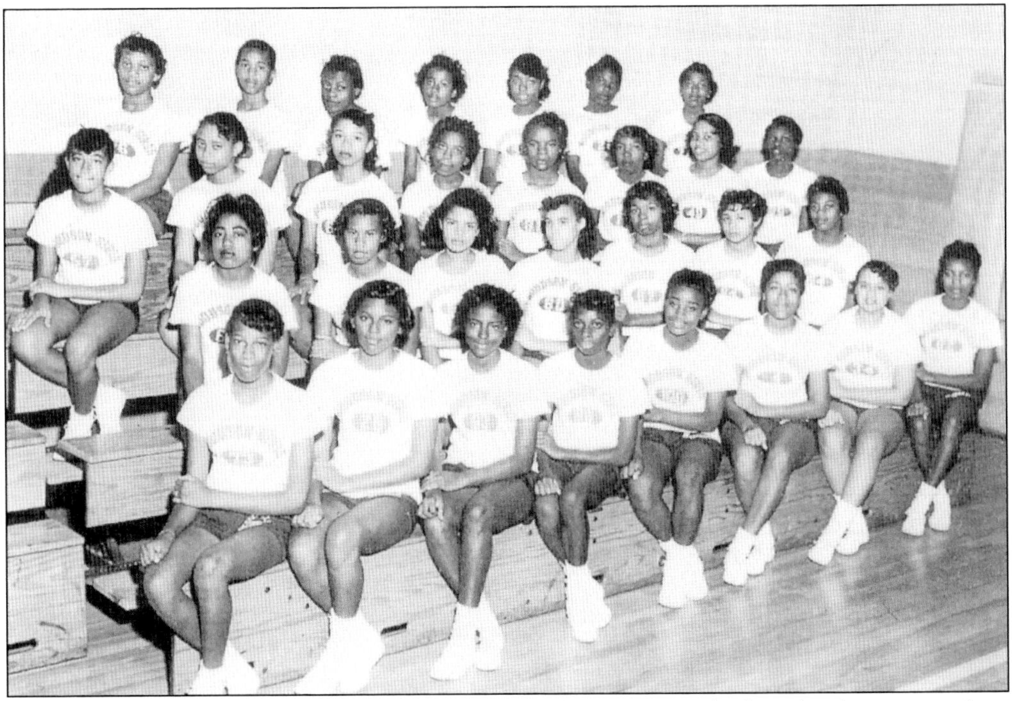

Students had intramural sports as well. Shown in about 1960 with the school name on their T-shirts, these physical education students attend Carter G. Woodson School. (Photograph courtesy of Modern Arts Studio of Norfolk, courtesy of Juanita Chambers.)

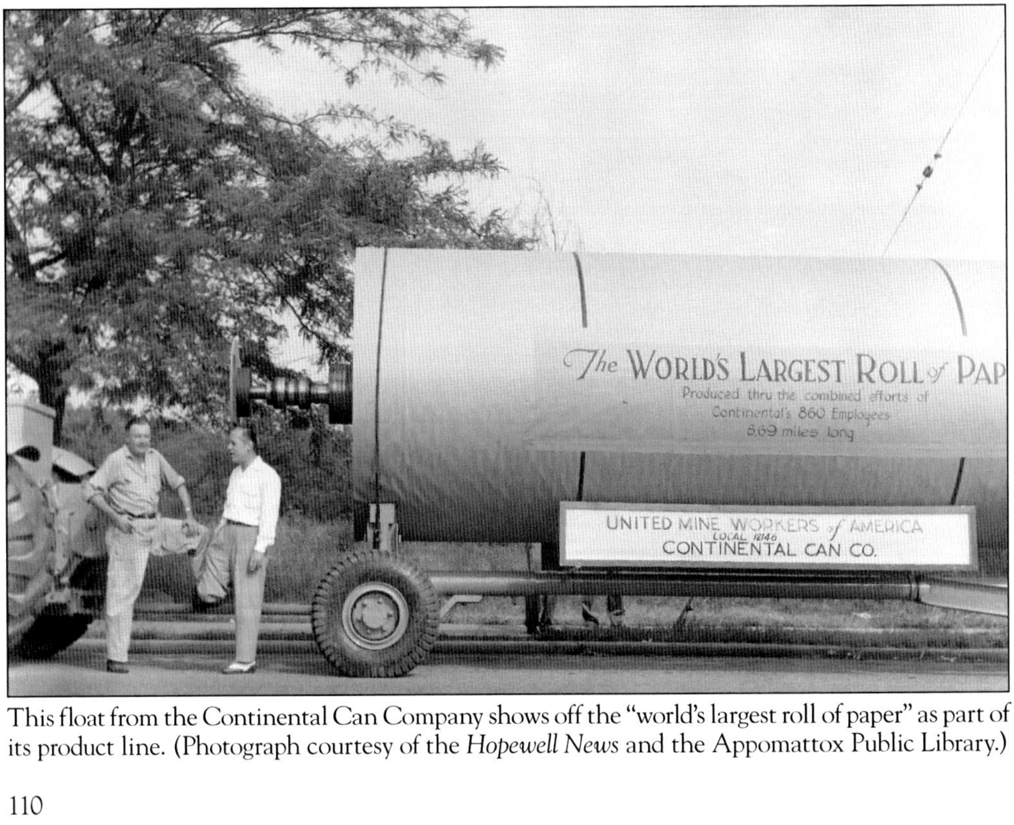

This float from the Continental Can Company shows off the "world's largest roll of paper" as part of its product line. (Photograph courtesy of the *Hopewell News* and the Appomattox Public Library.)

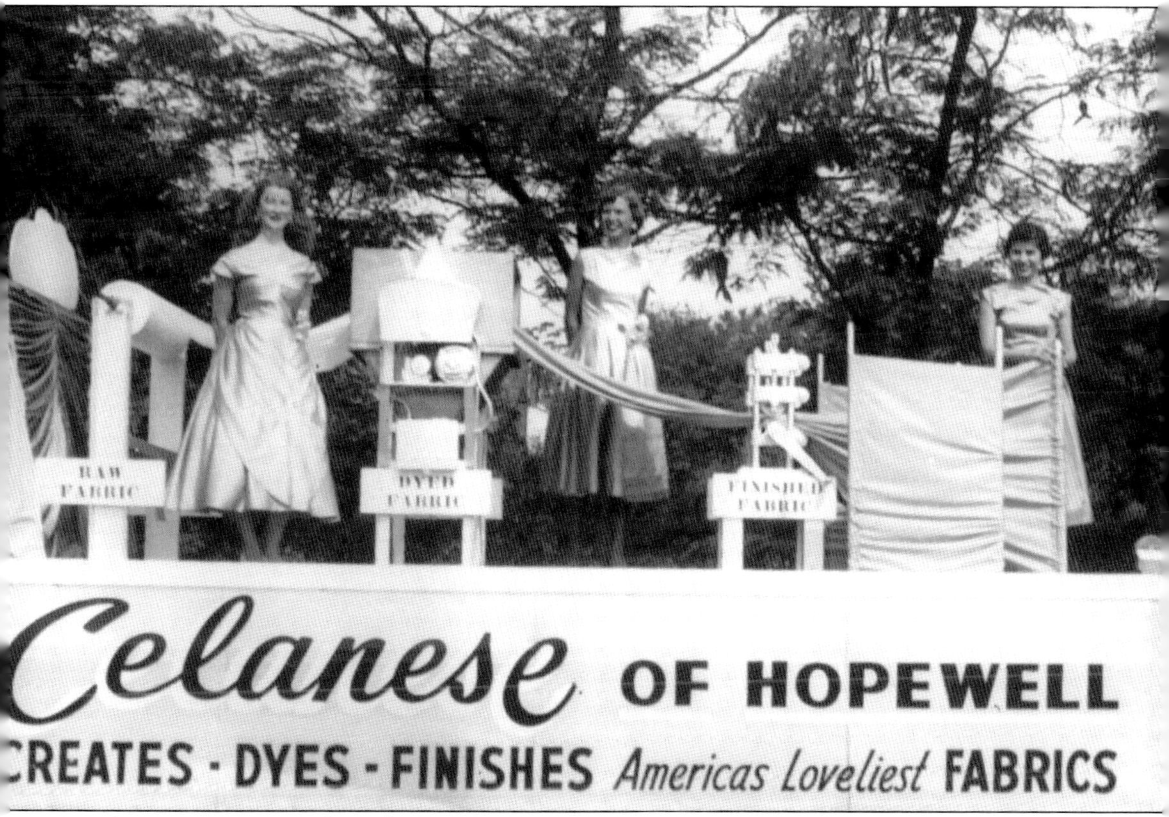

A Celanese Corporation float, shown around 1965, continues from its preceding company, Tubize Artificial Silk Company, which made artificial silk. This float shows some of Celanese's fabrics and the fashions made from them. Celanese worked with cotton linters, the silky fibers that stuck to cotton during early processing. The linters can take on different properties depending upon the type of cotton and are used to make paper and as an ingredient in cellulose, which could eventually be used in the medical and cosmetic fields. (Photograph courtesy of the *Hopewell News* and the Appomattox Regional Library.)

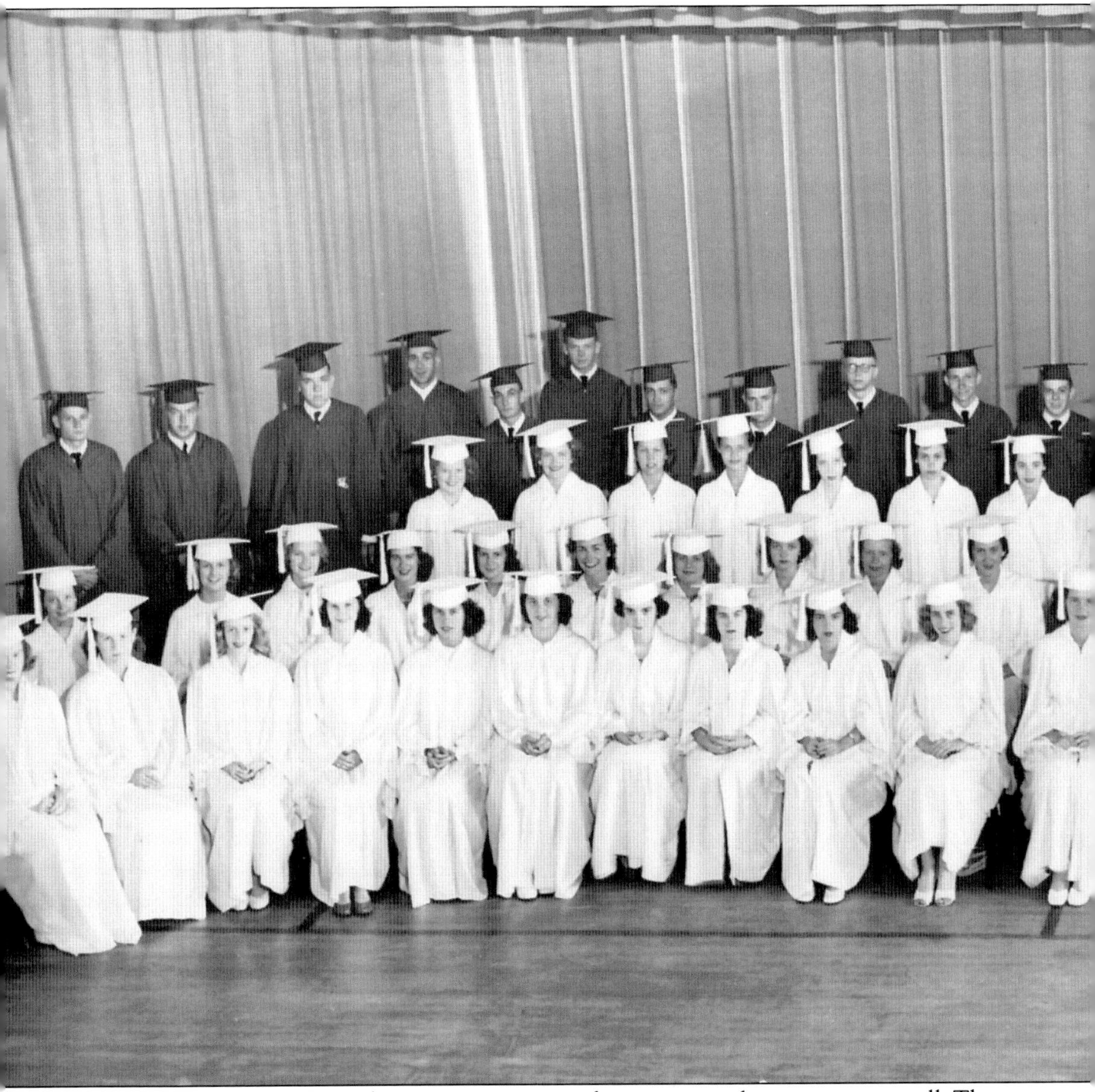

Sometimes, Hopewell's products are visions, transformations, and inspirations as well. The next pair of photographs shows the graduating class of 1953. In this class from Hopewell High School, 20 men and 81 women are pictured. This generation of graduates would see many changes in their hometown and in the world. At the end of this book are photographs of space travel, a whole new look at planet Earth, and people's roles in it. That view of the world may be old hat now, yet, to these graduates, it was a brave, new place. In Hopewell at this time, such changes were already taking place. These students' world was already expanding. The Hopewell graduating class saw other innovations and developments as well. In 1951, the number of babies born in Hopewell

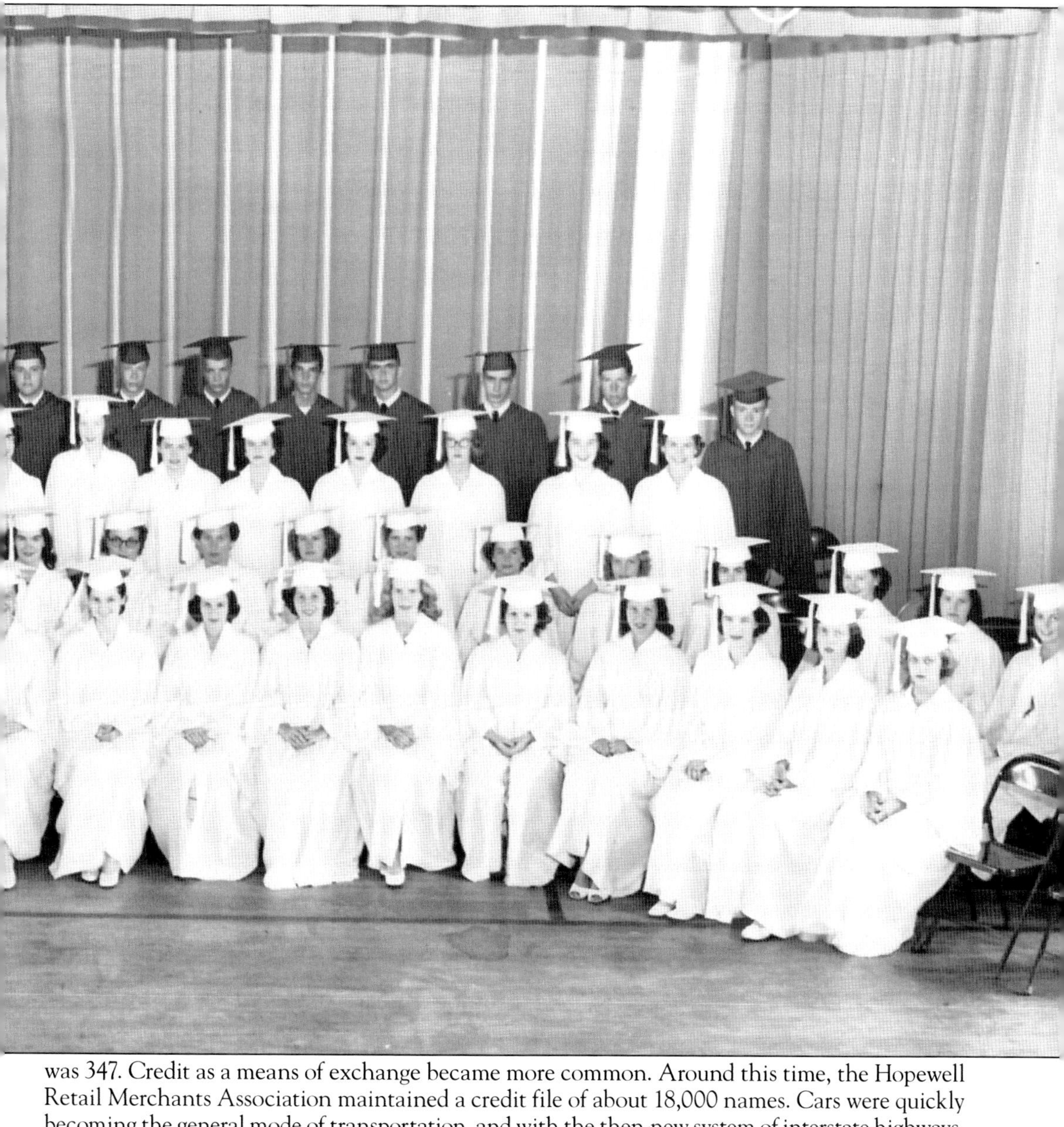

was 347. Credit as a means of exchange became more common. Around this time, the Hopewell Retail Merchants Association maintained a credit file of about 18,000 names. Cars were quickly becoming the general mode of transportation, and with the then-new system of interstate highways, cars became a symbol of personal freedom and adventure. In 1951, more than $2 million was spent in Hopewell car dealerships, and $573, 000 was spent in local gas stations. Around the time of their graduation, in a single plant in Hopewell, executives represented more than 100 colleges and universities. At that time, Hopewell Library possessed 15, 000 volumes for circulation and enjoyed an average of 40, 000 patrons. (Photograph courtesy of Hopewell Public Schools.)

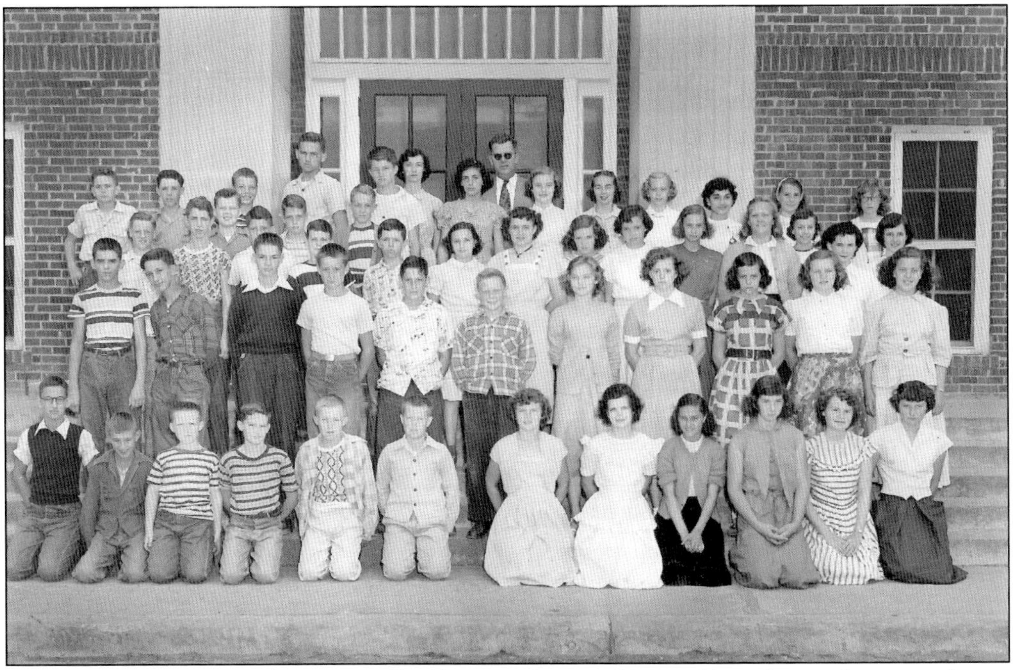

This class poses outside the Hopewell offices in about 1950. It will produce at least one future mayor of Hopewell. (Photograph courtesy of the *Hopewell News* and Paul Karnes.)

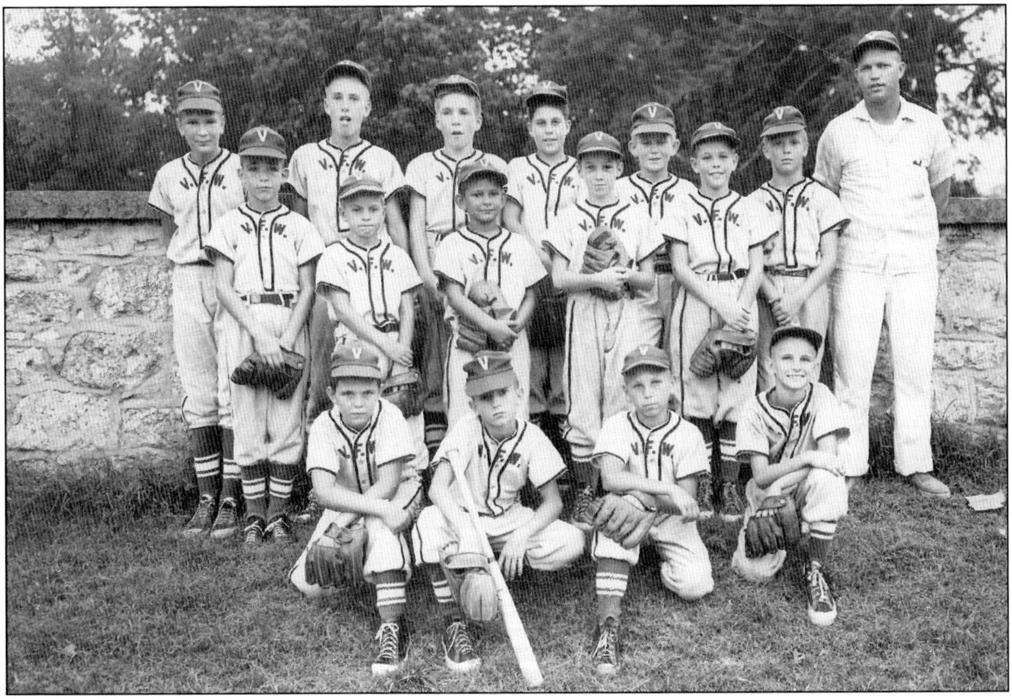

In 1955, this team was a champion in its league. As noted throughout, athletics and the ideal of an active and well-rounded mind and body has been a goal of Hopewell in both curricular and extracurricular activities. The coach is Alvin O'Berry. (Photograph by A. Ray Hash, courtesy of Paul Karnes.).

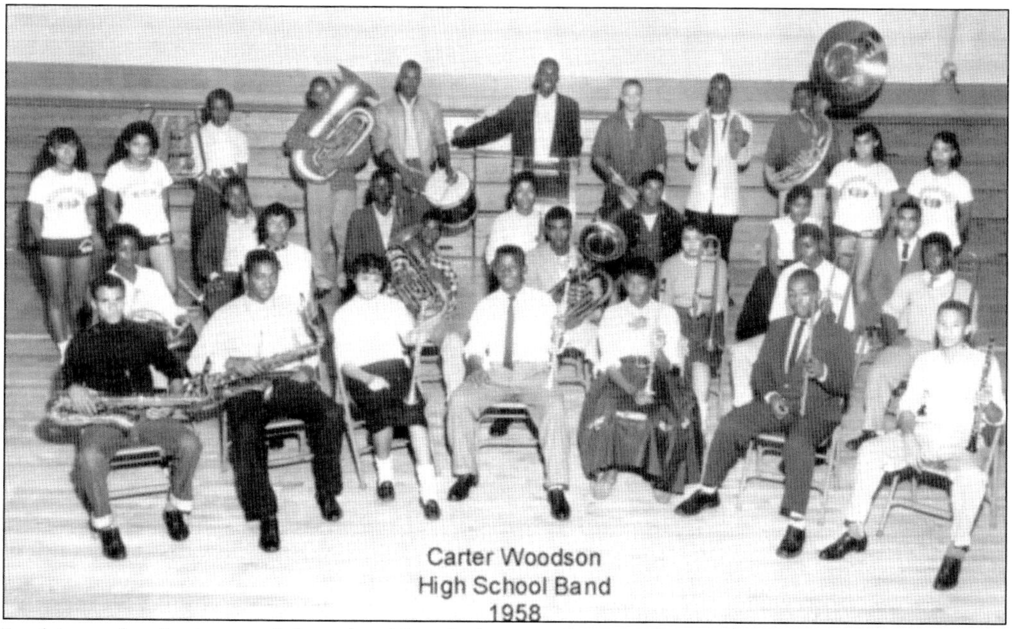

In this yearbook picture of the school band, these students gather with a variety of instruments. Some of the female students are wearing their gym outfits and may be posing for pictures immediately following gym class. (Print published by Modern Arts Studio, Norfolk, Virginia; photograph courtesy of Juanita Chambers.)

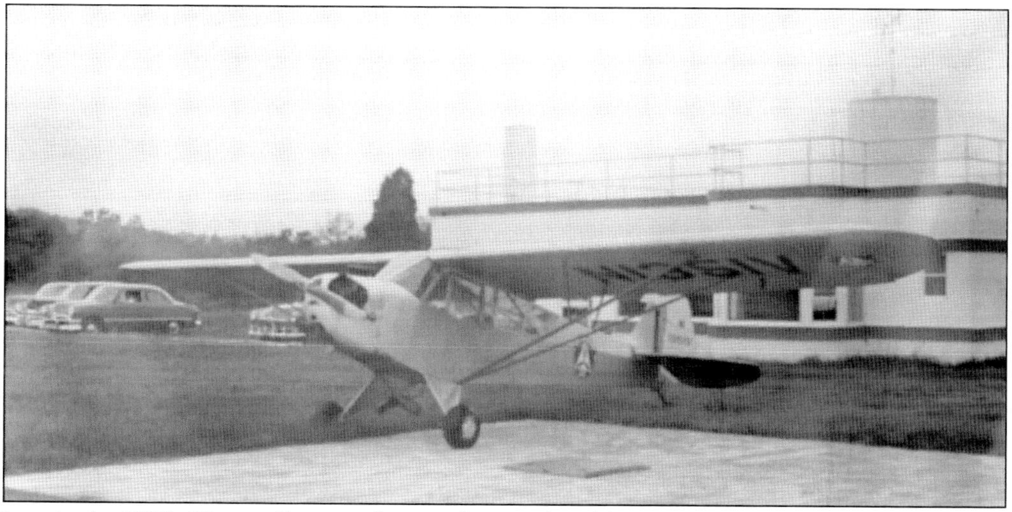

Late in the 1920s, Hopewell was preliminarily considered for a zeppelin landing field because the word was, the city never fogged in. The idea was ultimately abandoned. According to Abandoned and Little Known Airfields: Virginia (www.airfields-freeman.com) and *Virginia Airports* by Vera Rollo and Norman Crabill, the Hopewell airport applied for an operating license in April 1928 and it was granted in June 1931. In the 1934 Department of Commerce's Airfield Directory, Hopewell's airport lay on a 194-acre plot of sandy clay field on Jordan Point, slightly downriver on the James. This plane may be part of the US Air Force Auxiliary's Civil Air Patrol. Its insignia has a three-bladed prop. The Virginia Wing currently has a Southside Composite Squadron located in Chester. (Photography courtesy of the *Hopewell News*, photograph courtesy of the Appomattox Regional Library.)

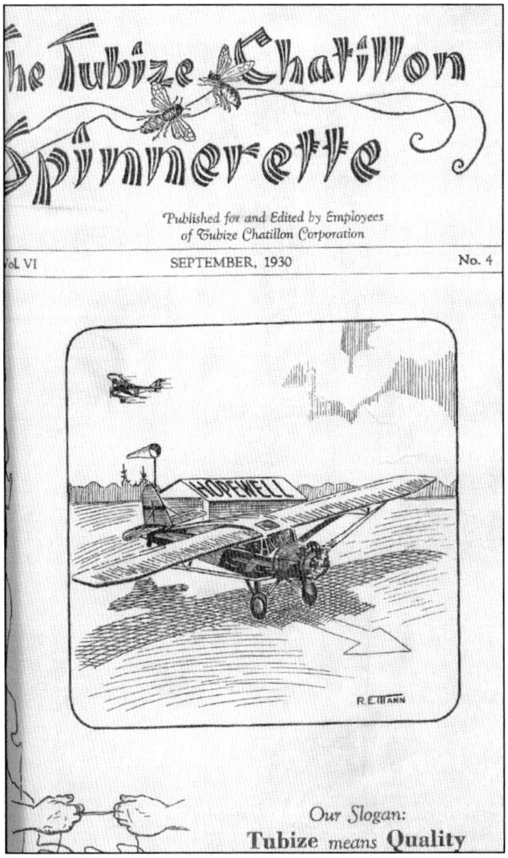
he Tubize Chatillon
Spinnerette

Published for and Edited by Employees of Tubize Chatillon Corporation

ol. VI SEPTEMBER, 1930 No. 4

Our Slogan:
Tubize *means* **Quality**

This cover of the Tubize *Spinnerette* magazine from September 1930 shows a drawing labeled as Hopewell's airfield, complete with a windsock and terminal and hanger building. (Magazine courtesy of the Appomattox Regional Library.)

According to the website Abandoned and Little-Known Airfields: Virginia, the first airmail flight from the Hopewell airport occurred on May 20, 1938, and the Army Air Field (AAF) Airfield Directory notes that Hopewell's airport had a 66-foot-by-60-foot wood and steel hangar. This photograph suggests military training flights at the airport. By 1960, the US Geological Survey shows a single east-west runway and a seaplane ramp opposite State Route 156. (Photograph courtesy of the Appomattox Regional Library.)

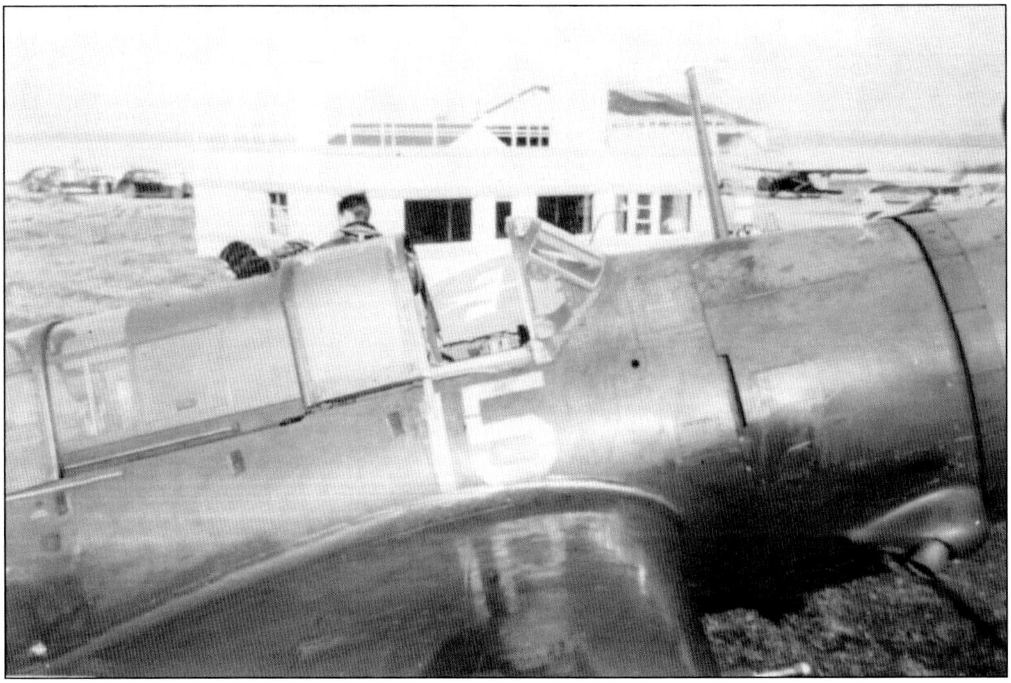

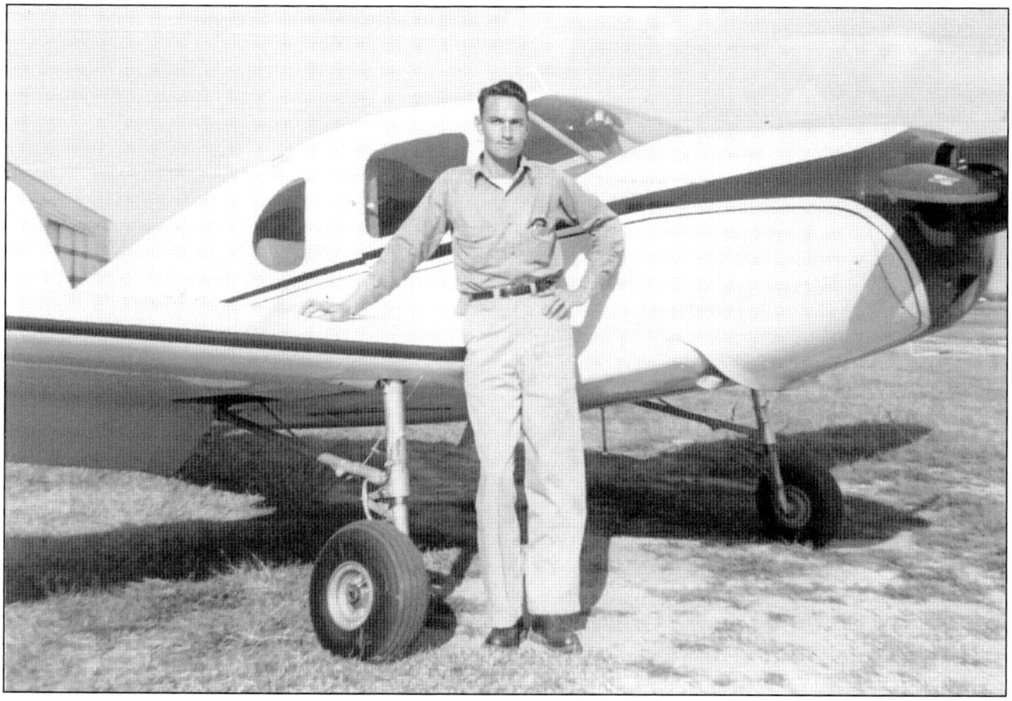

It is said that Billy Spencer, pictured in front of this plane, flied solo at age 15 and later served in the Navy during World War II. His father, Billy Spencer Sr., and Dr. D. Lane Elder were instrumental in starting the airport. Prior to World War II, the airport was used in parachute training exercises. (Photograph courtesy of the *Hopewell News* and the Appomattox Public Library.)

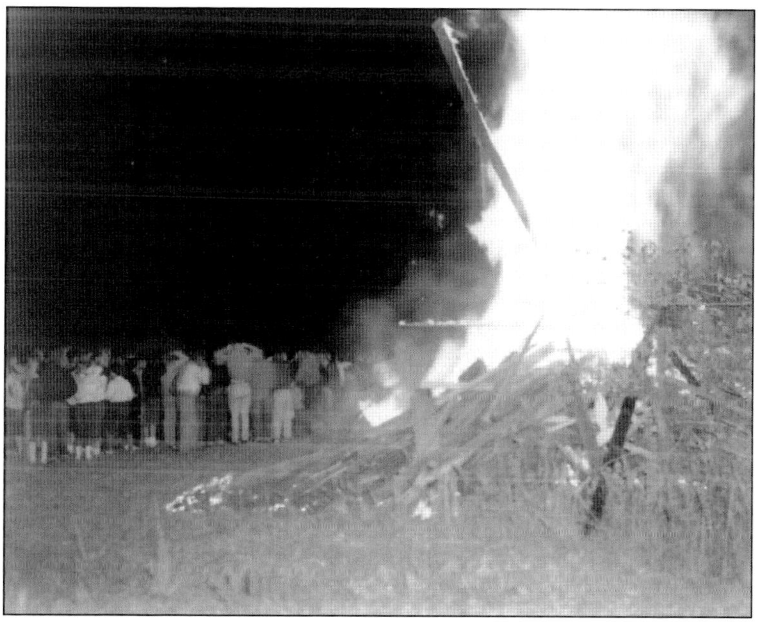

This bonfire was used at outdoor pep rallies. This rally took place in about 1955, and it looks as though the flames and sparks were getting a little too close to the students. (Photograph courtesy of the *Hopewell News* and Jack Daniel.)

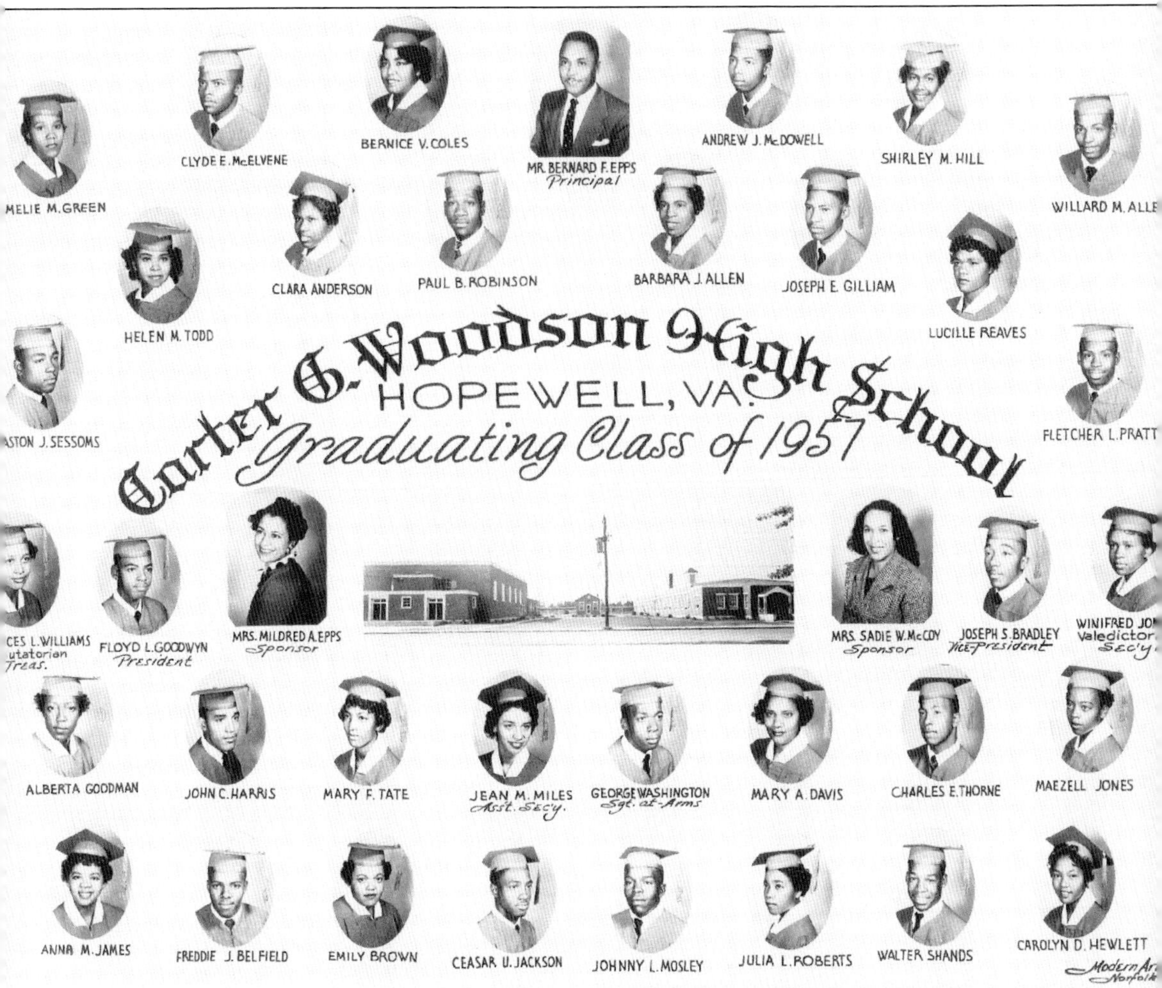

In this photograph of the Carter G. Woodson School class of 1957, Bernard Epps was the principal and Sadie McCoy and Mildred Epps served as class sponsors. The class officers are designated as Floyd Goodwyn, president; Joseph Bradley, vice president; Winifred Jordan, secretary (and valedictorian); and Francis Williams, salutatorian secretary. George Washington was sergeant-at-arms and Jean Miles served as assistant secretary. (Print published by Modern Arts Studio, Norfolk, Virginia; photograph courtesy of Juanita Chambers.)

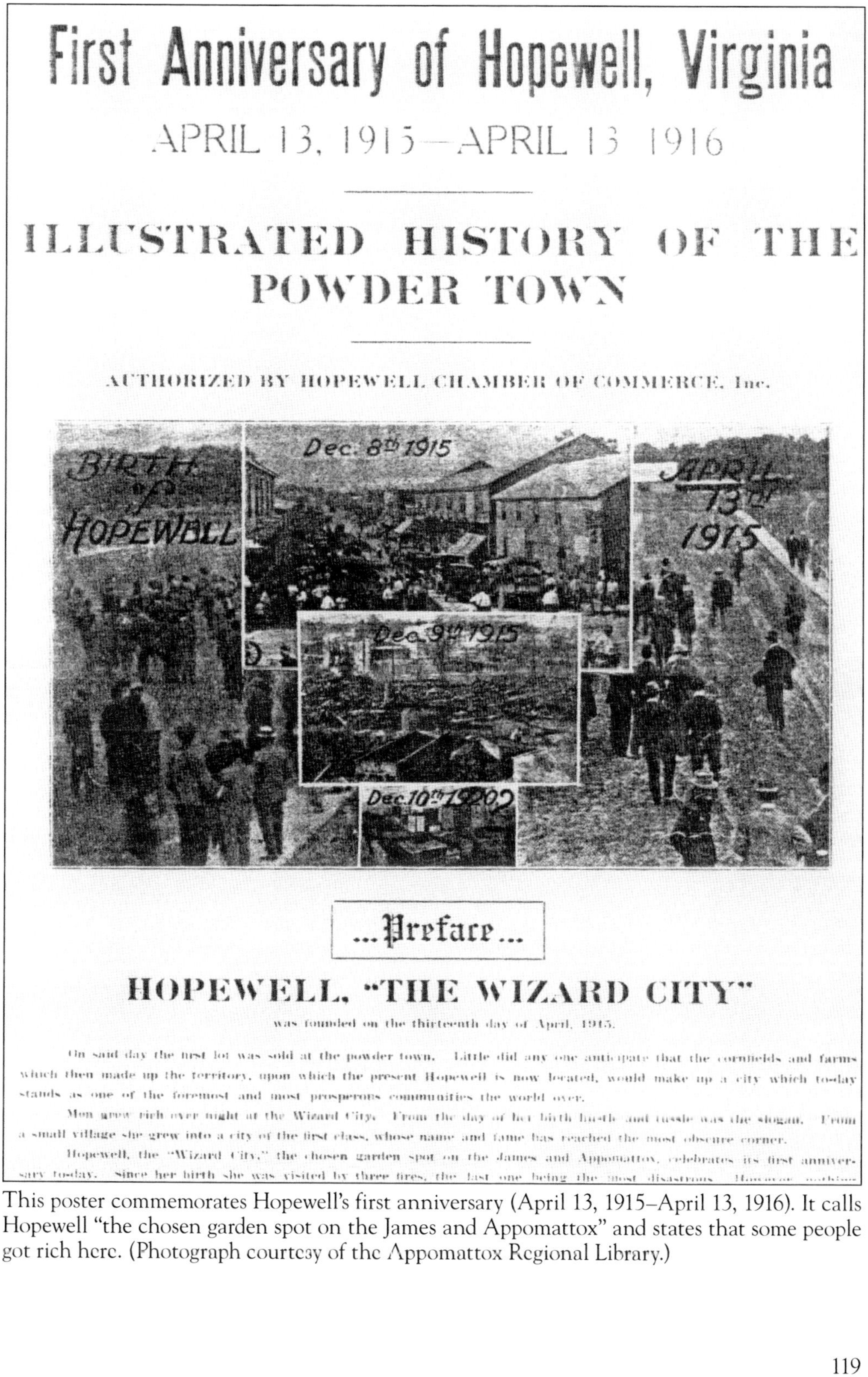

First Anniversary of Hopewell, Virginia

APRIL 13, 1915—APRIL 13 1916

ILLUSTRATED HISTORY OF THE POWDER TOWN

AUTHORIZED BY HOPEWELL CHAMBER OF COMMERCE, Inc.

...Preface...

HOPEWELL, "THE WIZARD CITY"

was founded on the thirteenth day of April, 1915.

On said day the first lot was sold at the powder town. Little did any one anticipate that the cornfields and farms which then made up the territory, upon which the present Hopewell is now located, would make up a city which to-day stands as one of the foremost and most prosperous communities the world over.

Men grew rich over night at the Wizard City. From the day of her birth hustle and tussle was the slogan. From a small village she grew into a city of the first class, whose name and fame has reached the most obscure corner.

Hopewell, the "Wizard City," the chosen garden spot on the James and Appomattox, celebrates its first anniversary today. Since her birth she was visited by three fires, the last one being the most disastrous.

This poster commemorates Hopewell's first anniversary (April 13, 1915–April 13, 1916). It calls Hopewell "the chosen garden spot on the James and Appomattox" and states that some people got rich here. (Photograph courtesy of the Appomattox Regional Library.)

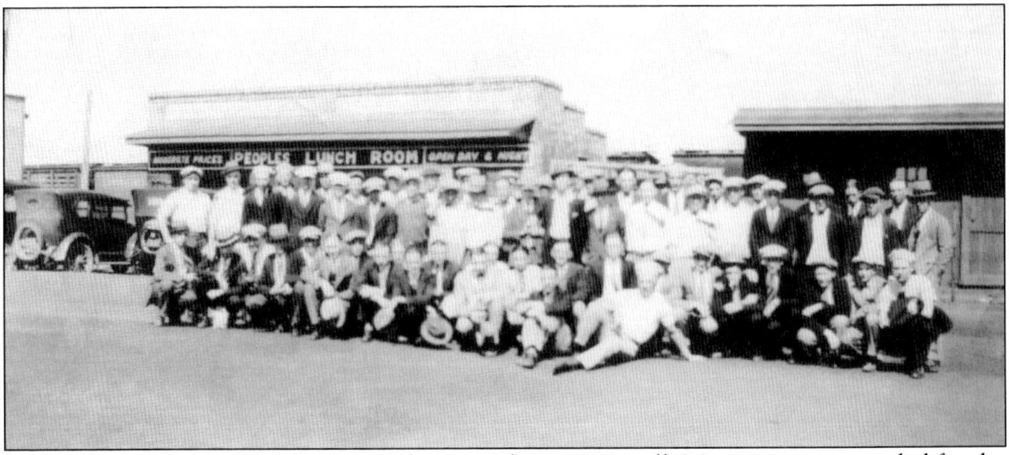

Maybe some people still seek to get rich overnight in Hopewell. Most, it seems, are glad for the chance to make a living the old-fashioned way. Sometimes a return to the past is a trip to the future. Here, employees line up outside the People's Lunch Room, no doubt before returning to their jobs. (Photograph courtesy of the Appomattox Regional Library.)

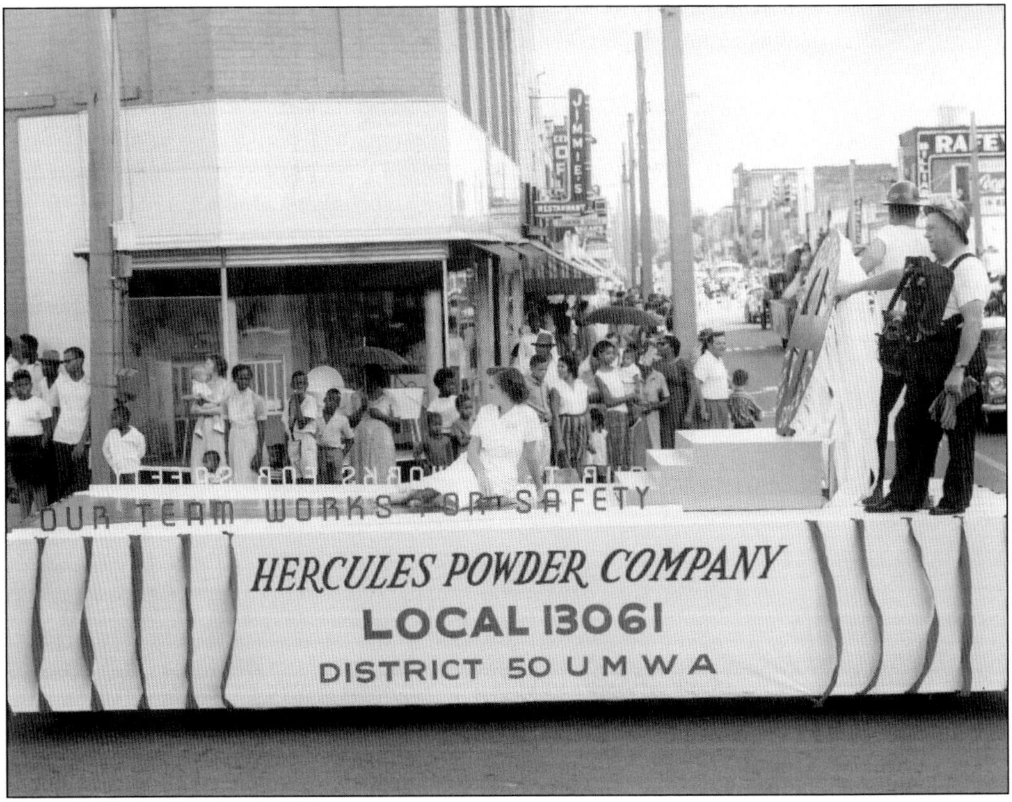

In about 1960, the Hercules Powder Company produced chemical cotton products and was the world's leader in chemical cotton cellulose. (Photography courtesy of the *Hopewell News*, photograph courtesy of the Appomattox Regional Library.)

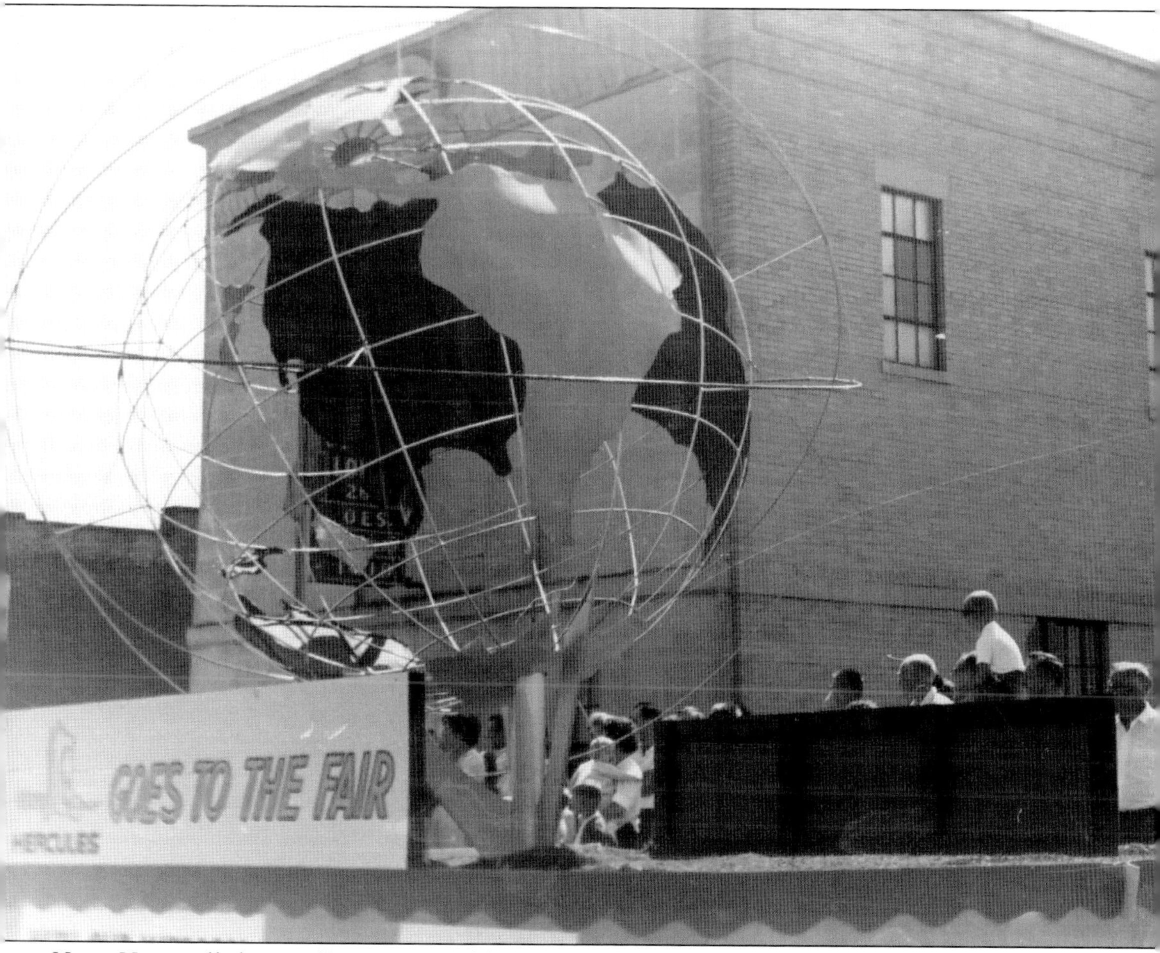

Here, Hopewell shows off its own World's Fair. The 1964–1965 World's Fair in Queens, New York, sported its iconic Unisphere, symbolizing its motto: "Man's achievement on a shrinking globe in an expanding universe." Pictured above, the Hercules Powder Company float adapts that theme. (Photography courtesy of the *Hopewell News*, photograph courtesy of the Appomattox Regional Library.)

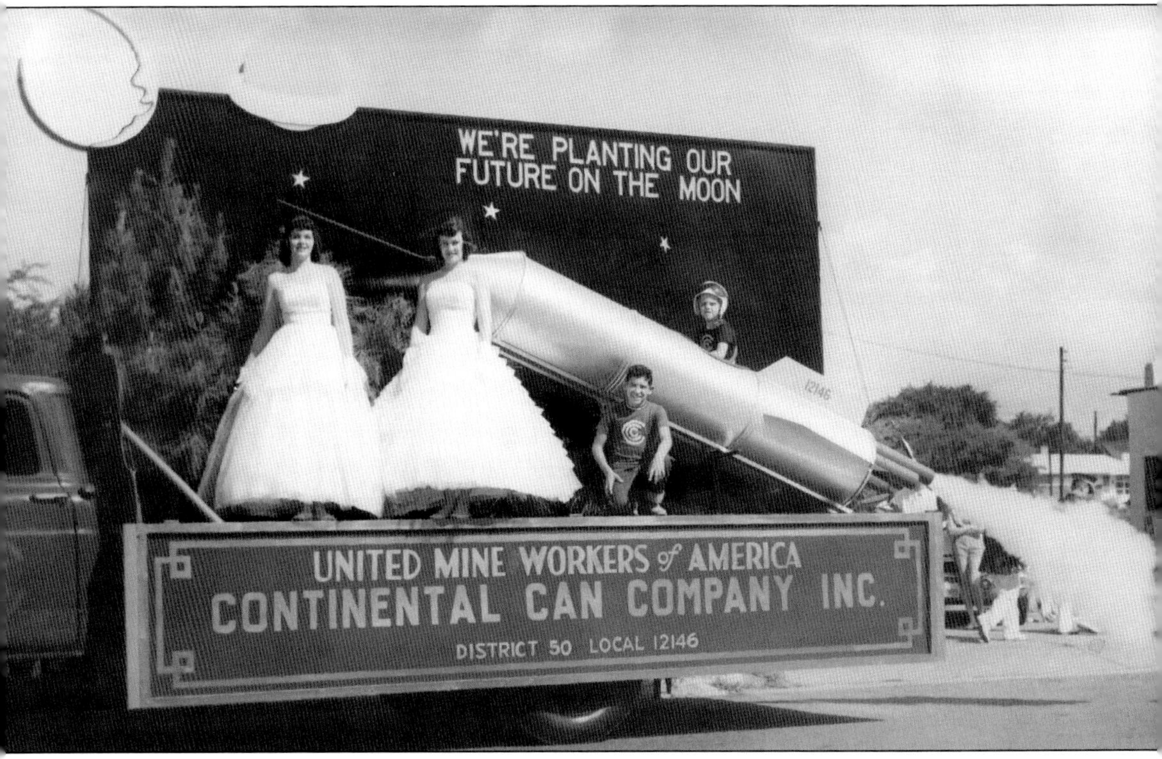

Hopewell also joined the Space Race. In a mid-1960s parade, the Continental Can Company plants its future on the moon. In this photograph, a rocket ship, complete with a trail of smoke, delights the crowd. Note the face in the moon at the upper left. (Photography courtesy of the *Hopewell News*, photograph courtesy of the Appomattox Regional Library.)

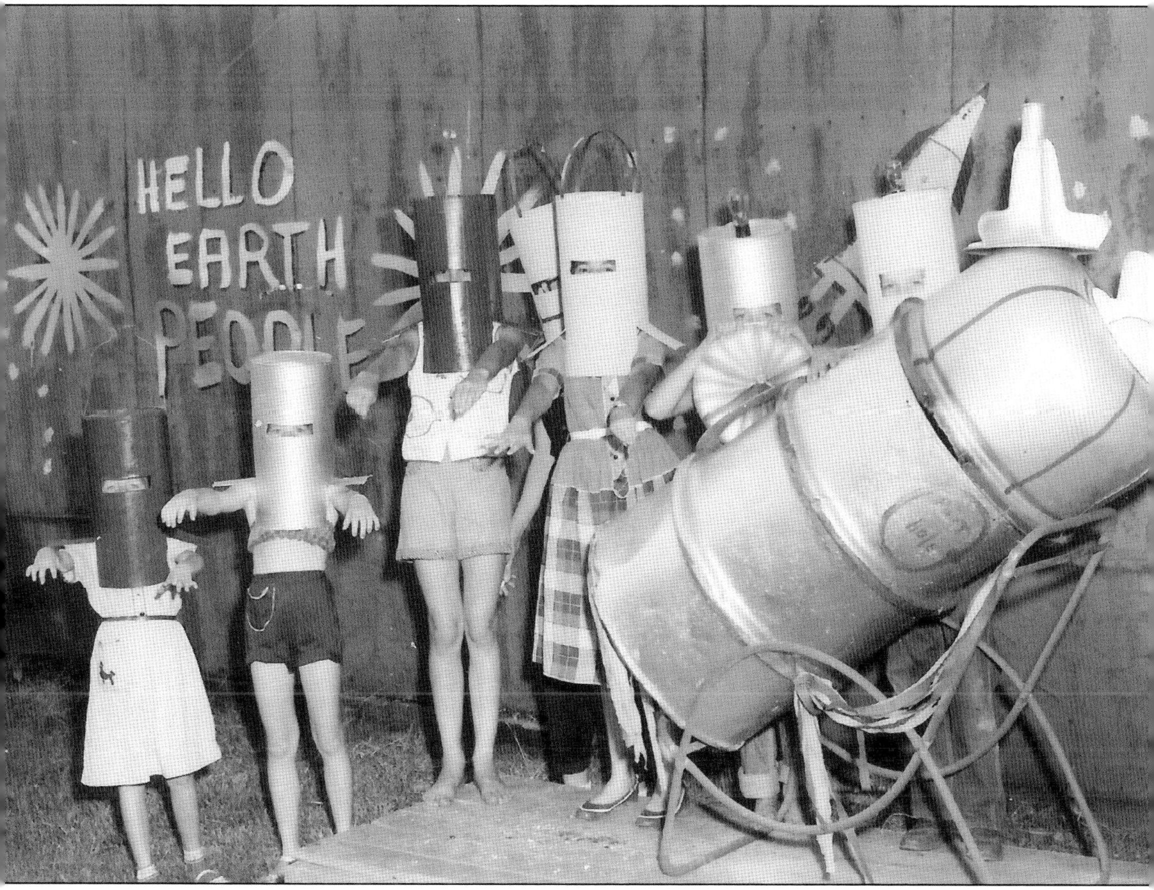

In the mid-1950s, "outer space aliens" were seen in town. Hopewell High School students made a comic nod to the science fiction craze of the 1950s. After all, this was when *The Day the Earth Stood Still* (1951) and *The War of the Worlds* (1953), both cult films depicting aliens invading the Earth, were first screened. The Soviet Union launched *Sputnik* in 1957. While no one admitted to being in this photograph during the author's research, the image represents essential character traits of Hopewell. Hopewell faces the future just how it faced the past—with a lot of grit and a fair amount of grins. To avoid confusion, the students helpfully labeled the porthole on the audience's side of the spacecraft prop. (Photography courtesy of the *Hopewell News*, photograph courtesy of the Appomattox Regional Library.)

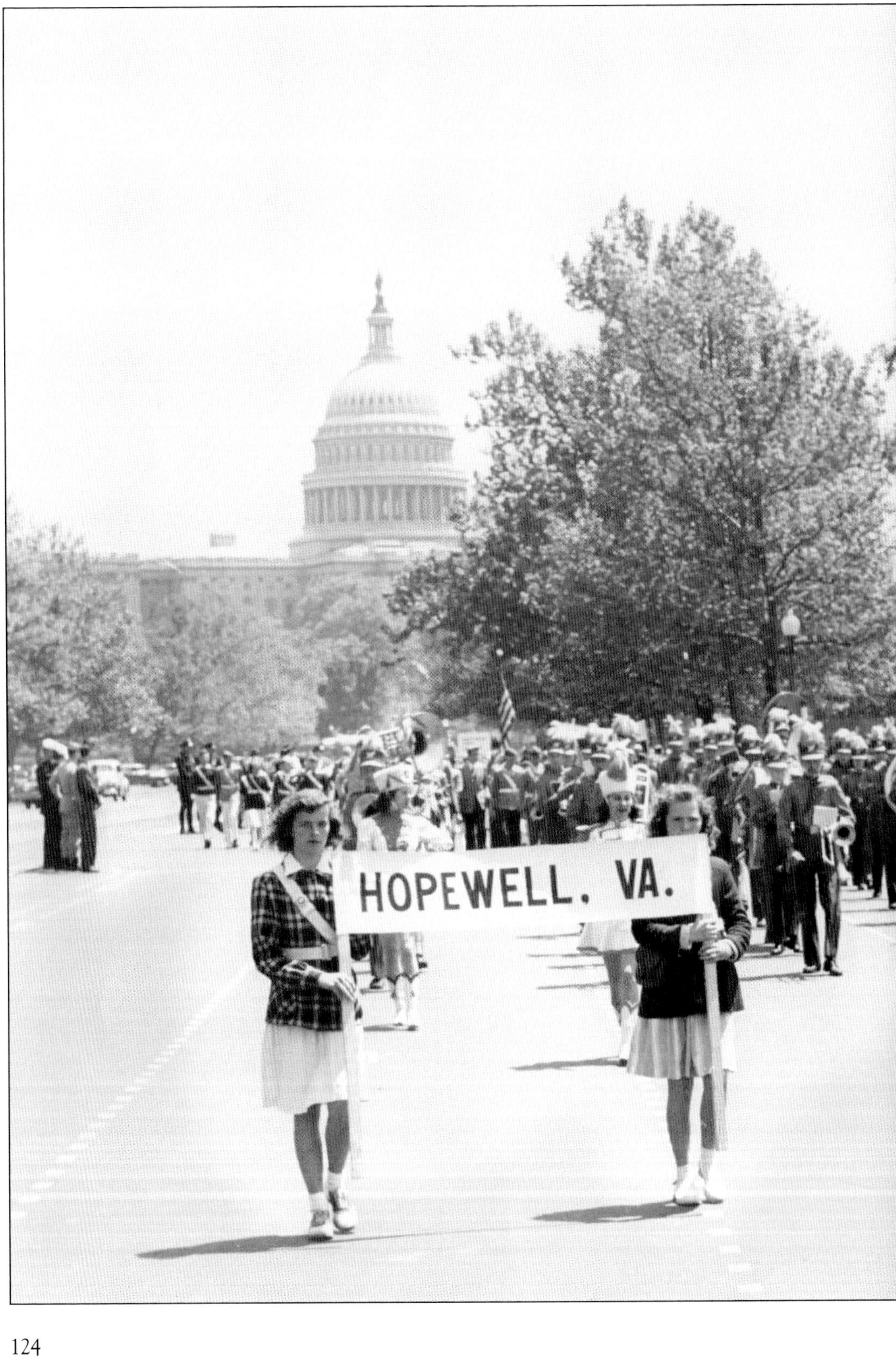
HOPEWELL, VA.

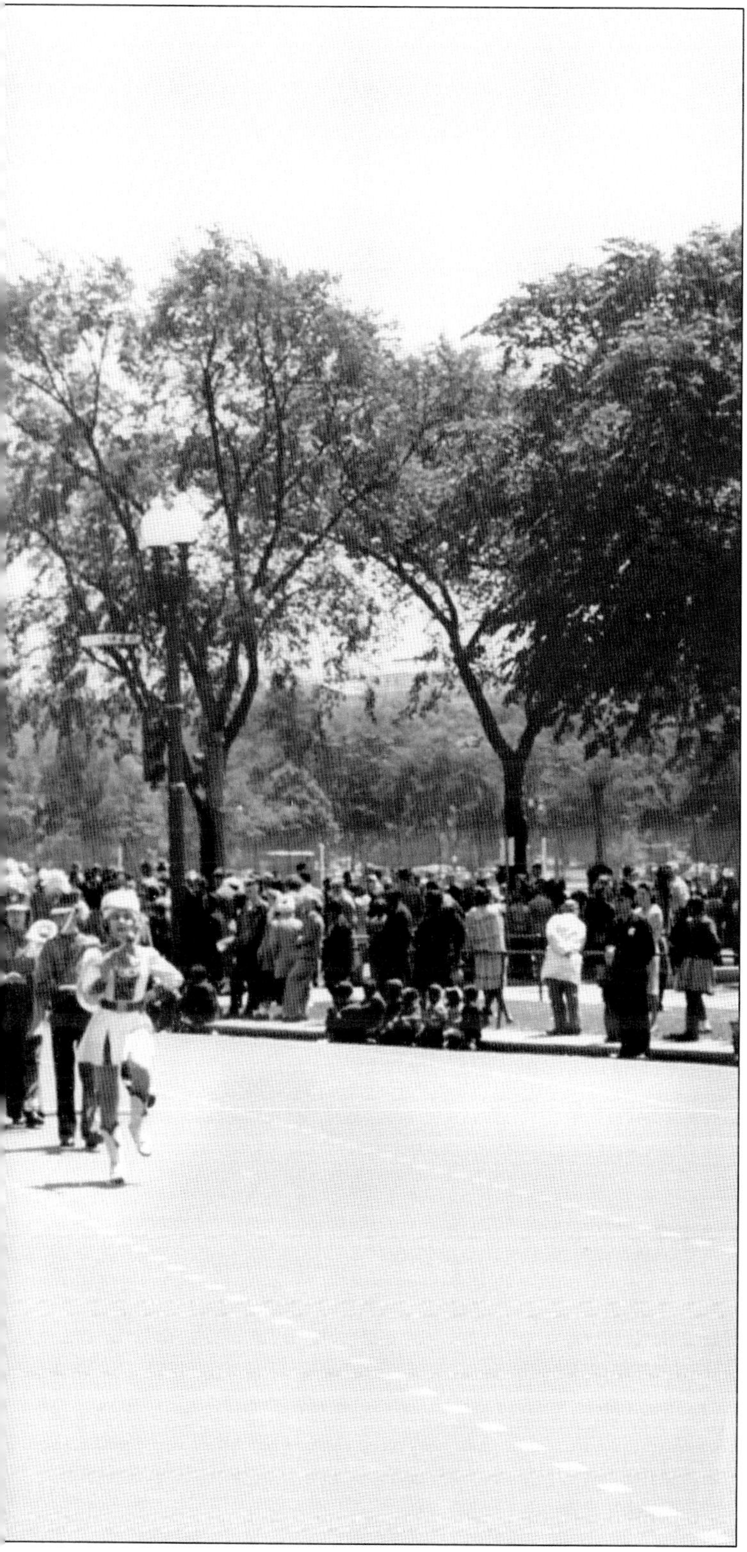

Grace is known by many names, and this photograph shows one such name. The Hopewell High School Band performs in Washington, DC. In this 1950s photograph, Pennsylvania Avenue is shut down for a parade, which included Hopewell's band. The band members seem to exemplify Hopewell's town motto, *Semper paratus*, which means, "always prepared." Hopewell has been prepared for adventure and for adventurers. The town has been home to many different people and has produced a wide and inspiring variety of products. Maybe the best product of all is a sense of honoring the past, living steadfastly in the present, and expecting confidently in the future. (Photography courtesy of the *Hopewell News*, photograph courtesy of the Appomattox Regional Library.)

References and Bibliography

Calos, Mary Mitchell, Charlotte Easterling, and Ella Sue Rayburn. *Old City Point and Hopewell: The First 370 Years.* Virginia Beach, VA: Donning Co., 1983.

Carey, Archie V. *Pictorial History of Hopewell, Virginia: Illustrating the Development of the Eighth Wonder of the World.* Hopewell, VA: 1962.

City Point Open Air Museum Walking Tour. Hopewell, VA: Hopewell Office of Tourism and Visitors Center, 2010.

"Crescent Hills." Hopewell, VA: Hopewell Office of Tourism and Visitors Center, 1999.

Fitzgerald, R.W. "The City That DuPont Built." Notes on dedication of the Hopewell Museum, Hopewell, VA, July 8, 1991.

Hopewell Public Schools Alumni Directory, 2009. Hopewell, VA: Hopewell Public Schools, 2009.

Hopewell, Virginia. Hopewell, VA: State-Planters Bank and Trust Company, 1952.

Hopewell, Virginia: A Legacy of Virginia History. Hopewell, VA: Hopewell Office of Tourism and Visitors Center, 2008.

Lee, Lauranett L. *Making the American Dream Work: A Cultural History of African Americans in Hopewell, Virginia.* New York City: Morgan James Publishing, 2008

"Visitors Guide." Petersburg, VA: Petersburg Area Regional Tourism Corporation, 2009.

Wood, Karenne, ed. *The Virginia Indian Heritage Trail.* Charlottesville, VA: Virginia Foundation for the Humanities, 2009.

About the Organizations

The Appomattox Regional Library System merits special emphasis among all of the individuals and institutions that have allowed the author to complete this project with their photographs and information. This library system has branches not only in Hopewell but also in Dinwiddie, Carson, McKenney, Rohoic, Disputanta, Burrowsville, and Prince George. The library also serves the communities with its bookmobile.

This book could not have been completed without the help of Julie Turner, circulation manager and deputy director; Jeanie LeNoir Langford, library specialist; J. Christopher Weigard Sr., librarian; and Scott Firestine, director. The facility known as the Ann and Preston Leake Local History and Genealogy Room has been invaluable. That "library within a library" has enabled the author to gain much of the information and photographs used in this book. This room is climate-controlled, has a scanner, and now houses rare books, documents, photographs, and artifacts that help preserve Hopewell's unique and significant history and culture.

That being the case, the library's work in the collection, preservation, and organization of documentary and photographic history deserves attention and recognition. Its staff members' work and the work of others like them deserve the cooperation and contributions of donors and supporters. This is a plea for preservation of images and documents for the public trust.

The Hopewell Office of Tourism and Visitors Center produces several fliers and brochures from which much of the historical data within this book is taken. Its literature is a clear and concise history of Hopewell and City Point.